'This book brilliantly captures the essence of the evolving learning mindset. With insightful examples and actionable ideas, Katja Schipperheijn shows how we can unlock the huge potential of the learning mindset to scale a more intelligent and human-led future.'
Terence Mauri, Founder of Hack Future Lab and author of *The Upside of Disruption*

'Katja Schipperheijn's *The Learning Mindset* brilliantly combines human competencies with AI to foster a thriving learning culture. An essential read for those seeking to harness the power of continuous learning and innovation. Inspiring as well as practical, this book bridges the gap between technology and human potential.'
Dr Markus Bernhardt, Chief AI Strategist and Board Advisor, Endeavour Intelligence

'Katja Schipperheijn has taken a complex topic and made it approachable and actionable. Whilst grounded in science and research, it's also full of practical ideas for both the individual to improve their own learning abilities and also for learning professionals to build and nurture effective learning cultures at work and in education. The weaving of evidence with myth-busting, real-life stories and inspiration from experts make this book engaging and fascinating. It addresses a broad scope of challenges, including the human elements of neurodiversity, stigma, imposter syndrome and more, and it also considers how technology can be used to help people and organizations thrive. Katja's own enthusiasm makes you want to keep reading, find out more and take action to learn to build a better future for ourselves and our children.'
Stella Collins, Co-founder and Chief Learning Officer Stellar Labs and author of *Neuroscience for Learning and Development*

'In *The Learning Mindset*, Katja Schipperheijn invites us into a transformative exploration of how human competencies can be harmoniously integrated with technology to foster lifelong learning and adaptability. This book serves as both a guide and an inspiration for those aiming to thrive in the rapidly changing landscape of the modern workforce. Schipperheijn masterfully

combines theoretical insights with practical strategies, encouraging readers to harness their innate curiosity and resilience. For anyone looking to elevate their learning processes or influence educational strategies within their organizations, *The Learning Mindset* offers essential wisdom and tools to transform challenges into opportunities for growth. It's a compelling read that underscores the power of learning as a pivotal force in personal and professional development.'
Dr Keith Keating, BDO's Chief Learning Officer and author of *The Trusted Learning Advisor*

'Finally, a book that bridges the gap between the human capacity to learn and the future of learning technologies. Katja Schipperheijn not only explores the added value of AI and innovation but also stresses the importance of motivating everyone to embrace a learning mindset for personal growth. In doing so, she promotes collaborative learning with the goal of building an infinite learning ecosystem where humanity flourishes. Brilliant!'
Andrew Stotter-Brooks, Chief Learner ADNOC Group and Chief Learner, Weird Human

'The importance of a learning mindset is grossly underestimated. This book shows how learning has a positive impact on well-being, engagement and the productivity of an organization. Learning is the basis of realising human potential, and when it is realised, an organization grows. This book is, therefore, a must-read for every employee who wants to achieve continuous growth and every manager who wants to become a better leader.'
Jan De Schepper, Chairman and Executive Board member

'The Learning Mindset teaches us how to integrate learning into daily life and work. Offering practical tips for adapting to digital challenges, it's an essential guide for trainers and learners eager to develop a dynamic learning environment in today's world.'
Badran Saeed Saif Al Shamsi, Assistant Deputy Commander in Chief for Academic and Training Affairs, Dubai Police

'This book can 10x your learning acceleration! Imagine recapturing the rapid learning pace you had as a toddler. Katja Schipperheijn expertly navigates the landscape of scientifically proven learning methods, combining them with practical applications you can start using today. The framework in this book empowers you to harness consilience, connecting diverse concepts and creating a ripple effect in your environment.'
John Argabright, VP Human Resources & Operational Excellence at Tetra Pak

The Learning Mindset

Combining Human Competencies with Technology to Thrive

Katja Schipperheijn

KoganPage

Publisher's note
Every possible effort has been made to ensure that the information contained in this book is accurate at the time of going to press, and the publishers and authors cannot accept responsibility for any errors or omissions, however caused. No responsibility for loss or damage occasioned to any person acting, or refraining from action, as a result of the material in this publication can be accepted by the editor, the publisher or the author.

First published in Great Britain and the United States in 2024 by Kogan Page Limited

2nd Floor, 45 Gee Street
London
EC1V 3RS
United Kingdom

8 W 38th Street, Suite 902
New York, NY 10018
USA

www.koganpage.com

Kogan Page books are printed on paper from sustainable forests.

ISBNs

Hardback	978 1 3986 1734 6
Paperback	978 1 3986 1733 9
Ebook	978 1 3986 1735 3

British Library Cataloguing-in-Publication Data

A CIP record for this book is available from the British Library.

Library of Congress Control Number

2024023311

Typeset by Integra Software Services, Pondicherry
Print production managed by Jellyfish
Printed and bound by CPI Group (UK) Ltd, Croydon CR0 4YY

CONTENTS

Foreword ix
Preface xiii
Acknowledgements xv

Introduction 1

PART ONE
Learning to thrive, not to survive

1 Understanding learning to trigger your learning mindset 5
Defining a learning mindset 6
What is learning? 9
Marcelo Alvisi De Paula, People Development Director, Saudi Arabia:
    The role of emotions and the limbic system on learning 13
Dr Anna Tarabasz, Associate Professor, College of Interdisciplinary
    Studies, Zayed University, UAE: The transformative journey:
    Learning, unlearning and relearning 24
Some myths debunked 27
Endnotes 34

2 The symbiosis of humans and machines 37
Should we be afraid of innovation? 38
Humans have created AI in their image 42
The evolution of AI 48
Some mind-blowing innovations 55
Policies and frameworks 62
Endnotes 64

PART TWO
Adopt a positive mindset to your personal learning

3 Now is your moment to embrace learning 71
The urgency of learning for the future of work 72

Negative impacts on your learning mindset 81
Helena Demuynck, Catalyst for Conscious Women's Transformation:
    Overcoming imposter syndrome 90
Endnotes 95

4 **Embrace the competencies of your inner child who loved learning** 99

Embrace competencies that are used to fuel your learning mindset 100
Stefaan van Hooydonk, Founder of Global Curiosity Institute and
    author of *The Workplace Curiosity Manifesto* 101
Consilience as a super accelerator for the learning mindset 111
Scott McArthur, The Consulting Futurist, keynote speaker, strategic
    consultant: Embracing interdisciplinary learning with
    consilience 113
Endnotes 115

PART THREE
Learning together to spark the learning mindset

5 **The ripple effect of learning influencers** 119

It starts with one spark 119
Constanza Garcia: The importance of non-verbal communication to
    amplify the ripple effect of learning influencers 125
Use your human competencies and communication skills to amplify the
    ripple effect 127
Rebels will lead the way 137
Endnotes 140

6 **Lean and social learning to maximize the group's learning mindset** 143

A lean approach to learning 143
Social learning to empower everyone in the team 151
An De Boelpaep, Founder of X-Conscious and learning innovator:
    Embrace social and lean learning 159
Don't forget to invite your artificial colleague 161
Endnotes 164

PART FOUR

The learning leader amplifies the learning mindset

7 What makes you a learning leader? 167

The learning leader adapts 168

Mossab Mahmoud: Blue Energy President and Front Office Manager
at Hilton Egypt: Challenging cross-functional teams to maximize
learning outcomes 172

The influencer becomes the learning leader 173

Monique Borst, Board Advisor, CEO Catalyst – Human WD40 180

Endnotes 182

8 An environment for the League of Extraordinary Learners 185

Recruit a diverse array of extraordinary learners 185

Psychologically safe team environments are a prerequisite for
learning 189

Cathy Hoy, CEO and Co-founder CLO100: Nurturing a culture of
psychological safety in learning environments 190

Problems are opportunities in disguise 200

Lean and Kaizen to stimulate problem-solving in the flow of work 205

Jana Gutierrez Kardum, Global Learning Experience Leader at Red
Hat: Enhancing learning within the workflow 206

Endnotes 208

PART FIVE

Learning ecosystems where the learning mindset thrives

9 Introduction to learning ecosystems 213

The learning leader becomes the LearnScaper 214

The learning maturity model 219

Endnotes 225

10 Sustainability and learning ecosystems 227

Sustainability is a global responsibility 227

Take responsibility for the future of humanity 230

Bisila Bokoko, United Nations Honoree and Executive Chair, global leadership speaker, entrepreneur, author: Use your smile to change the world, don't let the world change your smile 233
Endnotes 235

Let there be no conclusion 237

Index 241

FOREWORD

As from the beginning of 2024, we live in very turbulent times. You can even call it a perfect storm: a convergence of forces impacting us all at the same time. Most of the elements, such as geopolitics, climate crisis, energy crisis, food crisis, water crisis and so on, are interconnected. These distracted us from the underlying technological revolution that is evolving in parallel at an exponential pace, one that will have a significant impact on the way we live and organize our lives.

This has been going on for quite some time, but this exponential evolution creates so-called bifurcations, moments when the behaviour of a dynamic system changes dramatically. This has been the case with the emergence of the large language models (LLMs, such as ChatGPT) at the end of 2022. They have opened a door into a fascinating new world, even when we are still struggling to understand the potential and the repercussions. After the initial time, we need to let what we are experiencing sink in. We will take full advantage of these new capabilities that are still evolving at record speed at an ever-decreasing cost, the latter being crucial for massive adoption.

One of the areas that will benefit is learning. Until now, technology has been supplementing formal education with tablets, portables, smart screens, apps and so on. But, most of the time, these were positioned as supporting tools, changing nothing fundamental in the way we organize and approach education. In many ways, the format is still very much the same as it used to be for more than 100 years. A teacher standing in front of a large group of students, applying more or less a standard approach, is unidirectional. This is in deep conflict with the variety of approaches and styles human beings use to process information into knowledge and skills. This results in an ever-increasing effort and budget to provide additional care for those who are behind, but the more means are being poured into it, the bigger the problem seems to become. It's no wonder so many (too many) students leave the formal part of their learning experience frustrated and without any motivation to keep learning throughout their entire lives.

The ultimate dream to counter this is to provide a learning experience tailored to the needs and learning style of the individual human being, adaptable based on measured progress or the lack thereof. I do believe we are at the dawn of exactly that. The LLM allows for the development of a personal digital learning buddy that's always there, follows you as you learn and can always be consulted to explain things once more. It follows your reasoning when you are doing an exercise and points out where you made a mistake. It will provide you with as many additional examples and exercises as needed up to the point where you are confident. This digital buddy will be with you from kindergarten, all the way into your adult life, far beyond the formal education part of learning. It's never tired, never has a bad temper; it can explain things in several ways, from simple to complex, whatever you want or need. Likewise, I see possibilities for a teacher in preparing lessons, in coaching and guiding students to develop new skills and discover their talents. It will be much faster, more effective and more engaging.

You think this is far off, something for the realm of science fiction? Well, think again. Less than one year after ChatGPT came into our world, the Khan Academy, an open-source learning platform with over 140 million users worldwide, is working on exactly this. KhanMigo is an avatar that does most of the above, and it's about to go live at some point in 2024. And we are just scratching the surface of what's possible.

But let's not focus on LLMs alone. The convergence of several other technology building blocks is also important. One such evolution is the shrinking in size of the devices we use for interacting with computing, information and communication. The evolution from PCs to laptops and tablets has brought us to smartphones and smartwatches. Next on the horizon are smart pins and smart glasses, which we will simply use for communication as human beings would do, so no need for keyboards or tapping on screens. In doing so computing has almost become invisible, embedded in the very fabric of our daily lives, taking away yet another barrier to taking advantage of it. It will also make learning less abstract and more engaging, since you can always ask questions in what will become micro-learning moments. Which takes me to another important element for an engaging learning experience: curiosity.

I believe that the most important driving force for a good learning experience is curiosity. The drive to understand, to dig deep, to master something. Bill Gates calls this urge to understand and to master 'unconfuse'. Turning confusion into understanding. The capabilities described will be able to trigger exactly that. Take, for example, 'calculus' in mathematics, a much-dreaded course in secondary school for most. Suppose you can have a conversation with Leibniz or Newton, explaining why they developed the technique. (Maybe they can argue between themselves who was first.) Next, starting from simple examples, you would be taken on a tour around practical real-life applications where Leibniz maps the mathematical equations against real-life situations. Imagine the same for physics or chemistry, history and the arts. You name it! And on top of this, it's not only passive listening, but also interaction based on a human-style conversation, where you can ask 'Why?' a thousand times without someone looking at you with glazing eyeballs.

Where does that leave human interaction as part of learning? Well, I strongly believe it can be restored thanks to the deep integration of technology. Concepts like blended learning and flipped classroom will finally become achievable and restore the value of a teacher or tutor, within or outside the formal education system. It will leave more time for interaction amongst students, time to reflect on what's next with acquired knowledge and skills.

At a time where we need to unlearn in order to learn new skills and mental models to prepare and adapt for a future world, technology is coming to the rescue, once more. It made us who we are, ever since we climbed out of a tree and picked up a stick. So, the future looks bright for learning: to boldly go where no one has gone before!

Erwin Verstraelen – January 2024

PREFACE

We are building a future for the next generations, but it often seems that that future has already caught up with us. I made this observation years ago when my then ten-year-old daughter Farah said with rolling eyes that I was old and did not understand her world. According to her, I could no longer keep up with the speed of change. More so, according to her, I would never catch up if I did not step into her world soon.

Farah stressed that she needed to be on Facebook as if it was vital. But, like many parents, I thought I was doing the right thing by protecting my daughters from social media and too much digitalization. But soon Farah convinced me that I was indeed old and that I was jeopardizing her future instead of protecting her. A future where we are all connected, sharing content and learning together. When Farah said her grades would soon be worse than her friends, she had a point. After all, her friends could do their homework together, learn from each other and inspire each other, and Farah could not be part of that.

Talking to Farah made me realize that we should not hold children back from joining the new world. She was right that we need to guide them in a world that is developing faster and faster. For this, we need to encourage competencies like curiosity and imagination while enabling them to deal with this change with openness yet critically. Farah was, therefore, initially the driving force behind my first book, *Little Digital Citizens* (Dutch), and a non-profit organization through which I visit schools to talk to children about the future and emerging innovations. Today, Farah has grown up to be a professional ballerina who is also studying applied psychology. Together with her, I also started studying to learn about neuroscience and developmental psychology.

My youngest daughter, Helena, is just as much a driving force for this book. She is currently pursuing a master's degree in history and is also making connections to my research. According to her, studying history is indispensable if we as humans want to shape the future by learning from the past. Helena and Farah also inspire me not to limit learning ecosystems to enterprises but to look at the United Nations Sustainable Development Goals (SDGs). Entrepreneurship, according to them, must go hand in hand with sustainability and a better world for future generations. So, both my daughters inspired and collaborated with me on this book, which allows us to practise the super competence consilience together.

It is to these two that I dedicate this book. My daughters embrace learning and ensure I look at the past and future with an open mind. Two young ladies at the beginning of their adult lives who possess an eagerness to learn that inspires me and from whom I take an example. They and the more than 15,000 children and young people I met in my workshops have often served as inspiration for specific chapters in this book. These young people have the competencies that support a learning mindset. But these young people also struggle enormously with other challenges facing these generations: burnout, performance pressure and the many labels they are given at a young age that undermine their learning mindset.

Finally, children also inspired me to embrace human-centric technology. Still, technology is not the holy grail if we want organizations to grow through collaboration supported by innovation. People themselves must grow with it. For this, we adults can take inspiration from the younger generations, who see the ever-faster waves of change not as a threat that will engulf them, but as an exciting wave they can take to the next challenge. This mindset helps us to actively seek out new things, not to drown or survive but to be happy (to thrive).

This book was a journey for me that, like many things in my life, was unplanned and began with Farah rolling her eyes. I learnt a lot myself while researching it, and so I hope this book inspires you to embrace your learning mindset and love of learning.

ACKNOWLEDGEMENTS

I thought a fourth book would be easier because I had already developed the habit, but I was wrong. I had to go deeper than ever because I also wanted to hold the mirror up to myself and reflect on my own behaviour and topics that are often very sensitive. To do so, I also had to learn a lot that was outside my expertise, and that was not always easy. Fortunately, I had the support of my family and friends, who were willing to spar with me, challenge me and encourage me at times when I wanted to give up.

Above all, my thanks go to those who were closest to me. My daughters Farah and Helena, who noticed my fear of failure on several occasions and repeatedly said they believed in me and were proud of me. My father, George Schipperheijn, and Christiene Verhasselt, who were the first to proofread all the chapters and challenged me to rethink some parts. My dear friends An de Boelpaep and Jana Gutierrez Kardum, who discussed the overall concepts with me and made inspiring contributions to this book. Of course, I also thank all others who shared their experience and expertise, such as Dr Anna Tarabasz, whose contribution underlines the need for learning, re-learning and unlearning. Stefaan Van Hooydonk, according to whom the power of curiosity cannot be repeated enough. Scott McArthur never ceases to amaze me with his insane insights, embodying consilience. Mossab Mahmoud, with whom I can talk for hours about learning teams and his vision of leadership. Monique Borst, with whom I share the conviction that leadership must evolve with the rapidly changing world. Marcello Avisi De Paula calls attention to emotions and well-being. Constanza Garcia, who for me is a learning influencer par excellence and knows the power of non-verbal communication like no other. Helena Demuynck, who calls attention to stigmas and imposter syndrome that undermine our learning mindset and, of course, Cathy Hoy, for whom a safe emotional work environment is essential.

Finally, I would like to thank Bisila Bokoko, who, as United Nations Honoree and Executive Chair, is an inspiration when it comes to a learning mindset, leadership and the importance of an infinite learning ecosystem that builds a better future for all.

Introduction

Anyone who still believes that the impact of technological innovations will not dramatically affect our world is living under a rock! Only people with a learning mindset will survive and thrive in this ever-faster-changing world.

Artificial intelligence (AI) already surpasses humans in many ways and those who do not learn to deal with it will soon put their own future, and by extension that of society, at risk. This need to learn and adapt to new circumstances is a challenge not only for you but also for companies and governments. This prompted a controversial statement by a Belgian Professor of Labour Market: 'If necessary, we must force people to keep learning.'[1] However, the controversy is not about recognizing the need for lifelong learning, but about the assumption implying that people do not want to learn and should be forced.

Forcing someone to learn who thinks they have no capacity to do so will be counterproductive. It undermines well-being and fuels fear of falling further and further behind until the gap can no longer be closed. Fear of learning is often justified, but know that everyone can learn once we set aside preconceptions and create the right framework. With this book, I want to convey an infectious love of learning by encouraging you to embrace your learning mindset. Learning thus becomes a passionate pursuit of knowledge. A continuous journey towards self-improvement from competencies we embraced as children but seem to have forgotten during our school years. Because learning is not about textbooks and classrooms; it is about the excitement of discovering something new every day. It is about pushing boundaries and venturing into the unknown. In this exciting world, a setback, obstacle or criticism is not a threat but an opportunity to grow.

This book is structured in several parts that all contribute to building a learning mindset that contributes to personal growth, social and collaborative learning as a team, leadership in a learning environment and, ultimately, creating an infinite ecosystem. To this end, it is structured into four parts that build a learning ecosystem one step at a time, with your learning mindset as the foundation.

Part One: Learning to thrive, not to survive. These chapters give insights into learning from the approach of the human and artificial brain. The concepts from neuroscience and computer science form the basis for the following chapters, as well as the concepts explaining what learning is and what it is not. Above all, this part will show you that you no longer have any excuses not to embrace learning.

Part Two: Adopt a positive mindset to your personal learning and reject anything that prevents you from learning. Forget that school-based approach to learning and embrace learning for the future of work and to support your well-being. The emotions we have built up and the labels we were given during our younger years will no longer determine this. Instead, it will be the human competencies you deploy to grow nimble.

Part Three: Learning together to spark the learning mindset. When you can learn together with others, you create a ripple effect. Dare to take an exemplary role yourself as a learning influencer who knows the power of connecting communication to stimulate learning. Within learning teams, however, the individual is still central; therefore, it is important that you understand the drivers of social and lean learning.

Part Four: The learning leader amplifies the learning mindset. If you are a learning influencer yourself, the next step is to inspire extraordinary teams as a learning leader in the future of work. To do this, embrace (neuro)diversity in your team and initiate challenges that turn obstacles into innovation and continuous improvement.

Part Five: Learning ecosystems where the learning mindset thrives. Learning leaders who want to go one step further not only inspire their team but also challenge the organization's status quo. They bet on people-centred innovations, accelerating lean learning in the learning ecosystem. In doing so, they do not let the boundaries of their organization hold them back, but look for sustainable solutions that also have a ripple effect far beyond their influence.

In this book, international learning influencers share their experiences and try to inspire you with stories. They offer insights and real-life examples that will support you on your learning journey. But more than that, they show you that you are not alone in facing challenges and that others have walked the same path.

Love learning and be bold to create a better future for all!

Endnote

1 Professor Stijn Baert (2021) https://zigzaghr.be/we-moeten-mensen-desnoods-dwingen-om-te-blijven-leren/ (archived at https://perma.cc/V8W2-TD63)

Learning to thrive,
not to survive

1

Understanding learning to trigger your learning mindset

The opportunity to learn is the greatest gift you were given at birth. Yet you, like many, may have a love–hate relationship with it. Because learning often also goes hand in hand with negative memories, anxiety and emotions. It may feel like an obligation or a lifelong punishment, like a Tantalus torment where you keep thinking that the end is in sight and then you realize that you have to start again.

In this first part, I want to share with you the complexity and versatility of learning. Learning is so much more than the memory of school, mandatory training on the job or wading through boring books. Learning supported by a learning mindset is an adventurous journey that you do not take alone. It opens up a life of wonder where obstacles are transformed into opportunities for improvement. To feed this learning mindset, I first explain what it is and how a growth mindset can transform it into a *superpower*.

Learning is more than the narrow school concept we have of it. It is an often unconscious and complex interplay of personal, cultural, social and experiential factors that we can take control of. Therefore, understanding some basic concepts from neuroscience is a trigger to look for the stimuli that support your well-being and happiness by embracing learning like the young child in you did.

Understanding the complexity of learning is the basis for further developing your learning mindset. For this, it is important to open up and recognize that learning often happens unconsciously and that if you consciously open up to it, you can unlock its joy. To this end, I will debunk some myths, after which, in the following chapters, you can build a learning mindset to not only survive but also thrive in times of increasingly rapid innovation.

Defining a learning mindset

A learning mindset is an indispensable mindset in today's rapidly changing world. It is like a superpower that helps you face challenges and obstacles by embracing them as learning opportunities. From your learning mindset, you actively seek learning gains and opportunities for continuous improvement. For this, you are not only open to new experiences, but you also seek them as learning adventures full of new opportunities to discover knowledge and skills in different areas.

You may have heard of the growth mindset, which Professor Carol Dweck discusses in detail in her book *Mindset: The New Psychology of Success*.[1] A learning mindset is closely linked to a growth mindset, and without this growth mindset there can be no learning mindset. It can be confusing, I know. Therefore, I will explain both with some examples.

A learning mindset fuelled by a growth mindset

A growth mindset is the belief that one's abilities and intelligence can be developed and improved over time through effort, practice and learning. Consequently, individuals with a growth mindset embrace challenges, overcome obstacles and see failures as opportunities for personal development. Moreover, they turn obstacles into opportunities for continuous improvement. Organizations committed to a growth mindset subscribe to the idea that employees' skills and abilities are not innate traits, but are nurtured through effort and a corporate culture that embodies this mindset.

In contrast to the growth mindset is a fixed mindset. With a fixed mindset, you believe intelligence, talent and other qualities are innate and immutable. If you are not good at something, you usually believe you will never become good at it. Both are a vision or state you adopt for yourself or others around you. A fixed mindset profoundly affects how you live your life and see others, based on that deep-seated belief that you are pre-programmed and that there is a limit to your ability.

To my enormous frustration, I have discovered through my work with schools that a fixed mindset can be passed on to children at a very young age through their environment and social background. For example, during my group sessions with high school students, where I imagined the future with them, I noticed it was tough to motivate young people in certain schools to think outside the box about their future. For them, it was often impossible to imagine a future beyond the beliefs and expectations imposed on them by their parents and teachers. During the process, I also noticed that students in these groups reinforced each other's beliefs that certain dreams seemed unattainable to them. To my regret, young people who did have dreams did not dare to express them because they did not find support in their environment.

Fortunately, I noticed even then that one person can sometimes offer that glimmer of hope that can inspire an entire community like wildfire.

Just one person or one incident can bring about a change among their friends, sometimes creating a ripple effect throughout the school and even the community. Encouraging one person to break free from the fixed mindset that seems to be especially prevalent and contagious among vulnerable youth is therefore often my ambition. I saw an example of this first-hand with a boy I later took with me on my tour of schools to inspire others. His early years were overshadowed by alcohol, drugs and violence, which landed him on the streets at the age of 10, after first caring for his mother for several years until she was hospitalized. Without any support, this young hero managed to find a shelter family for himself as he drew strength from his dreams. These dreams would help him become a playwright and teacher. Now, just short of 20, he travels through graduate schools himself to continue his positive work as a teacher.

Believing is not the same as doing

The learning mindset and growth mindset both have at their core the belief that you control your own future. You learn from failures and see every obstacle as an opportunity for improvement. This is in contrast to the belief that what you can do is fixed by your abilities, environment and background.

- **A growth mindset** is the belief that one's abilities and intelligence can be developed and improved over time through effort, practice and learning. Consequently, individuals with a growth mindset embrace challenges, overcome obstacles and see failures as opportunities for personal development. Moreover, they turn obstacles into opportunities for continuous improvement. Organizations committed to a growth mindset also subscribe to the idea that employees' skills and abilities are not innate traits, but they can be nurtured through effort and a corporate culture that embodies this mindset.

- **A learning mindset** emphasizes the importance of actively seeking new knowledge and skills. It requires openness to new experiences, curiosity and a constant drive to increase understanding in different areas. A learning mindset focuses on the process of acquiring knowledge and understanding; it encourages adaptability and a willingness to learn from both successes and failures. Therefore, the organization's growth mindset complements the learning mindset by encouraging the sharing of both successes and failures in order to learn.

So, it is not because you know you can grow from experiences and learn from these that you actively commit to acquiring knowledge and skills. A learning mindset suggests that you consciously learn and also encourage others to acquire knowledge with you. It means actively looking for opportunities, involving others to come up with innovative ways to shape the future together. With a learning mindset, continuous improvement is an active experience as you focus on building learning ecosystems of which you are an essential part.

When you embrace your learning mindset, you can break free from your previous experiences, interpretations, environment and emotions that influenced your learning outcomes (see Figure 1.1). In doing so, you can strengthen your learning mindset by nurturing those competencies that make you human, as I describe in Part Two. Competencies like curiosity and imagination support your intrinsic motivation to learn, like a sponge soaking up water. Like a newborn baby who is super curious about the world around them and looks around with big eyes full of wonder. Like the toddler in whom curiosity sometimes gets almost out of control and where parents and teachers often try to temper it out of good intentions. Unfortunately, they do this not only to protect the toddler, but also because schools and parents start conditioning at an early age. But a child does not want to sit still; they do not want to be restricted. A child wants to learn and especially if others learn something, as with cycling, even if it involves endless trial and error.

This intrinsic ability to want to learn, as Swiss development psychologist Jean Piaget describes, we all developed as children.[2] It is our environment and background that should feed this flame, yet who can also extinguish this flame? Parents and teachers try to constrain the natural desire to learn to what they think is relevant or appropriate by forcing children to conform to set learning methods, pinning labels on them and presenting them with uniform tests.

These conditions can extinguish the spirit of the learner, and it can be difficult to rekindle this flame on your own. That is why I want to encourage you to rekindle the flame of the learning mindset together. You will find that a positive learning mindset can be contagious. It can spread like an Olympic fire to others in your teams and hopefully further into the learning ecosystem.

FIGURE 1.1 Drivers of a learning mindset

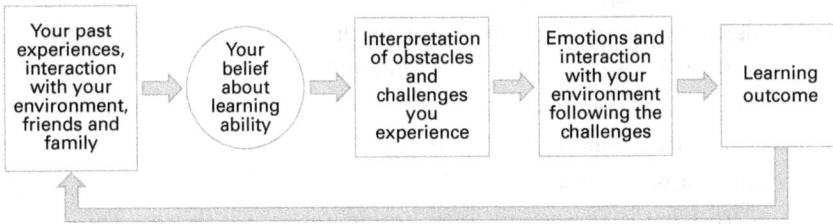

| Your past experiences, interaction with your environment, friends and family | Your belief about learning ability | Interpretation of obstacles and challenges you experience | Emotions and interaction with your environment following the challenges | Learning outcome |

Emotional impact on the learning mindset

It is not only schooling but also your background and upbringing that can extinguish that fervent desire to learn. It can be the emotions you have while learning that determine whether you keep the flame burning. Therefore, it is important to surround yourself with others who have a positive influence on your emotions, such as alleviating anxiety or even depression. We already see this in the younger generations, who seem to experience more stress from their environment. Young people are influenced by a fear of the future due to global causes such as wars or pandemics that have left a mark. Further in this book, I discuss not only how to nurture your own learning mindset, but also why it is important to surround yourself with people who support you in your mental well-being.

The impact of emotions you have picked up while learning, the stigma you have internalized and the self-confidence you have gained all help determine your attitude towards learning. In Part One, I will focus on how to turn negative experiences into benefits. In Part Two, I will explain how (neuro)diversity in itself can add value to a team. This requires everyone to work together to create a safe psychological environment in which everyone can thrive. Throughout this book, emotions will be a common thread and the various learning influencers who share their stories and experiences will often return to this with telling examples.

What is learning?

Learning is a complex concept[3] and depending on who you ask, you will often hear a different definition. Personally, however, I find the following definition most appropriate in relation to this book and my views on learning: 'Learning is a process that leads to change, which occurs as a result of experience and increases the potential for improved performance and future learning."[4] The change we are trying to achieve may occur at the level of knowledge, attitude or behaviour. As a result of learning, learners begin to see concepts, ideas and/or the world differently.

This description goes beyond the cognitive aspect of what happens in our brains and talks about your attitude towards learning and adjusting your behaviour as a result of learning. Therefore, I have chosen to give an introduction to what happens in our brains when we learn. This basic understanding of neuroscience will hopefully inspire you to activate your learning mindset as much as possible.

The neuroscience of learning

It is not my intention to write an academic book, nor am I a neuroscientist like Stella Collins, who inspired me with her book *Neuroscience for Learning and Development* to learn more about the complex and fascinating process of learning that has intrigued scientists, teachers and learners for centuries.[5]

Without going into too much detail, I want to inspire you and show you that happiness and learning can go hand in hand based on the scientific knowledge we have from neuroscience. With this knowledge you can experience more effective, efficient and fun learning. Embracing this will give you a lifelong adventure full of knowledge and personal satisfaction. Because, even though you might often associate learning with frustration, anxiety and other negative emotions, learning can also give you that feeling of happiness that comes with learning something new. Actively seeking out this feeling of happiness is what a learning mindset entails and what gives us waves of positive emotions.

You have probably experienced that euphoric rush of happiness and satisfaction when you have successfully learnt something new. Whether it is mastering a musical instrument, solving a challenging puzzle or understanding a complex concept, the feeling of satisfaction is universal. This phenomenon of feeling happy when we learn something is closely linked to our brain's chemical messengers, neurotransmitters, and the interplay of emotions. In this section, I want to convey how the feeling of happiness that accompanies learning something new is an interplay of neurochemicals, emotions and cognitive processes.

NEUROCHEMICALS: OUR HOMEMADE HAPPY PILLS
In Part Two of this book, I will talk about labels and pathologies that often leave a stigma on our learning mindset and how to turn them into

superpowers. Not with medication, but with our own happy pills that we can summon when we embrace our learning mindset.

- **Dopamine** is our 'feel good' neurotransmitter in the brain and plays an important role in the feeling of pleasure and reward. When you learn something new and experience success, your brain releases dopamine, which makes you want to re-experience that feel-good moment. Think of it as your brain's reward mechanism for when you set a goal, learn something new and eventually achieve it. Recalling these feel-good moments regularly can be done by setting achievable goals and celebrating small victories that enable you to keep getting your dose of self-made happy pills.

  Learning innovations that use games or immersive experiences can provide extra stimulation in this respect, but do know that too much is never good. Taking in too much dopamine will even be negative if stimulated externally and not from your own goals. That this can also be addictive, as I probably don't need to explain. The triggers built into these experiences can hamper and disrupt your natural reward system. So, as with many fun things, it is important to not overdo it and seek the right balance.

- **Serotonin** plays an important role in regulating mood, emotions and overall well-being. While dopamine mainly affects motivation and reward, serotonin is associated with feelings of satisfaction and happiness. You may remember those moments when you learned or achieved something new, and you felt that incredible sense of pleasure and happiness. You radiated it and took others along with you in that blissful feeling. This is because serotonin levels rise in your brain. Regularly releasing serotonin also helps stabilize your mood and promotes a sense of contentment. In Part Three, I discuss the ripple effect of learning that makes social learning and collaboration an even more enjoyable experience. Learning together and achieving successes together, and of course celebrating this, is the trigger for the learning ecosystems of which you are at the heart.

- **Noradrenaline** may not have as direct a link to happiness as dopamine and serotonin, but it contributes to the emotional aspect of learning. This neurotransmitter plays a crucial role in excitement, alertness and the body's response to stress. When actively engaged in the learning process, your brain releases noradrenaline (also known as norepinephrine). This neurotransmitter helps you focus, stay alert and retain information better. The heightened state of awareness and focus can contribute to the feeling of achievement and happiness when you successfully learn something new. It is important to know that optimal levels of noradrenaline are necessary for learning, as too little or too much can negatively affect cognitive performance and emotions.

As a mother of two studying daughters, I know that staying actively involved in the learning process is often the hardest thing about learning. So, I try to convince them to choose a strategy where they have regular *Aha!* moments that fire up their neurons, releasing the aforementioned neurotransmitters. We also actively share fun new things we have learnt that encourage and inspire each other. Sharing these positive waves also distinguishes the successful learning teams I describe in Part Three.

EMOTIONS AND THEIR INFLUENCE ON LEARNING AND YOUR STRESS HORMONE

As described above, emotions are inseparable from the learning process and play a crucial role in determining the quality of your learning experiences. Positive emotions, such as curiosity, excitement and joy, can enhance learning by improving focus, motivation and information retention. If you approach learning with enthusiasm and a positive attitude, you are more likely to be able to give your all, which in turn leads to better understanding.

Conversely, negative emotions such as stress, anxiety and frustration can hinder your learning. This is because high stress levels lead to the release of cortisol, a stress hormone that can impair memory and cognitive functions. It is therefore important to control negative emotions. With the above insights from neuroscience, I want to encourage you to pay more conscious attention to how positive and negative emotions affect learning and wellbeing in general. For this, I want to inspire you with the connection there is between active learning and developing a lifelong love of learning for a constant source of joy.

Emotions have a great impact on your learning mindset, which is also recognized by my good friend Marcelo Alvisi De Paula. According to him, more attention should be placed on learning to deal with this better and developing emotional intelligence.

MARCELO ALVISI DE PAULA, PEOPLE DEVELOPMENT DIRECTOR, SAUDI ARABIA: THE ROLE OF EMOTIONS AND THE LIMBIC SYSTEM ON LEARNING

With 30 years of experience in training, I started a new job in Saudi Arabia and decided to take a different approach. I delved into the complicated world of learning and development, and embarked on a quest. My mission was to revamp and modernize the learning strategy within my organization. It was clear that corporate learning had reached a crossroads and needed transformation to match the rapidly evolving landscape of the modern era. I was therefore inspired by the book *Learning Ecosystems* by Katja Schipperheijn, which fits enormously with my vision of approaching learning from a holistic and connecting strategy. I am also convinced that we should look for innovative ideas that challenge conventional wisdom and provide a fresh perspective on learning in the corporate sphere.

Through my own learning experience and 10 years of research on emotional intelligence, I have come to realize how much our feelings play a role in how we learn. It is something I am passionate about exploring and sharing. Think about it: when we learn something new, it's not just about the facts and figures. How we feel in that moment can make a huge difference. When we are excited or curious, it is as if our brain is ready to absorb every bit of information. But when we are stressed or just don't feel like it, it is much harder to remember anything.

In my time working with emotional intelligence, I have found that people who understand their emotions and understand the feelings of others can really play the game differently when learning. They know how to keep their cool and can work well with others, making the whole learning process much more enjoyable and effective. I am not just saying this. Science confirms it. Our brains have an area called the limbic system that deals with emotions, and it is super connected to the parts that deal with learning and memory. So, our emotions and learning are pretty much neighbours in our heads!

So, what I want to say is this: when we teach or learn, we need to pay attention to those feelings. They are powerful things. By making learning something that feels good, we all get much more out of it. And that is what I am all about – making sure that when we learn it is not only effective but also feels good.

The limbic system plays a big role in learning. Take the amygdala, for example. It's like the doorman at the club of your memories, deciding whether an experience is cool or problematic. This 'emotional validation' is super important for remembering things. The hippocampus, which befriends the amygdala, helps turn those experiences into memories that stick around for a long time.

There are studies that have shown that the amygdala sometimes flips under stress, which can interfere with learning. However, when we feel good, the amygdala and hippocampus can work together to help us remember things better.

So, how do we make learning fun? Add some stories, link what you are learning to real life or use examples that make people feel something. This can help make learning stick, just as Immordino-Yang and Damasio said in 2007 – we are feeling creatures who also think.[6]

Make sure the learning space feels safe. When people are relaxed and not stressed, their brains can learn more easily. Give compliments when people do something well. It's like giving the brain a high-five with dopamine, the feel-good juice that makes those memories stick.

Make people think about what they felt while they were learning. Goleman said in 1995 that being aware of our own emotions is the key to emotional growth and better learning. Buddy-up learning with others can be much more fun. Because our limbic system is all about social feelings, learning together can be a party and work really well.

The limbic system plays a big role in learning. If we are smart about emotions and use them to our advantage, we can make learning not just something we have to do, but something we enjoy doing. As we continue to figure out how our brains deal with emotions and learning, we can find new ways to teach that really connect with people, making learning a journey we all want to take.

Unravelling the confusion between training vs learning

In the ever-evolving landscape of personal and professional development, the words 'training' and 'learning' are often mixed up. But make no mistake; they do have a different meaning and interpretation in relation to how we learn. I want to clarify the fundamental differences between training and learning, because, in my opinion, you can learn some things and you should train others. This will also be relevant later when I discuss lean learning or learning on the moment of the moment, which is not training on the moment of the moment. The easiest way to explain this without too much boring theory is with a story, which will hopefully stay with you longer.

Many children get curious at some point about what their parents do all day, and I was no different. At that time, my father was a trainer, and I had no idea what to make of that. Especially since we also got a puppy during that period and we had to take her to dog training. I did not understand: did my father make people do tricks all the time until they mastered them and then give them a treat? No, he was a sales trainer, but my father explained to me that the difference was not that great, because the same principles applied in his approach to training.

So, what is the analogy between training a dog and sales training? In both cases, it is about developing a new behaviour or skill through conditioning. Sales training, my father taught me, is about how we behave in a conversation with a potential customer, and you can practise that. To get good at sales communication, he also taught me tricks, namely systematic FAB-ing: naming features, advantages and benefits of what I was trying to sell. For this, he had me practise on the most random things, like a pen, for example. I then had to talk not only about the features of that pen – that it writes – but also, which was more important, about the advantages, for example that a pen is useful for taking notes during a lesson. However, that is not yet the benefit for the user of the pen, which is that you can read things later and don't have to remember everything. The latter was the main selling point. Features, benefits and advantages, the whole time he had me repeating this. Not just with a pen but with all kinds of objects, until I did it automatically in all my practices. He conditioned my observable behaviour and the reward was there when I got better and better at it and could convince people to follow me in what I presented and not only in sales conversations.

This equation of observable behaviour being conditioned with a reward also applies to successful salespeople who are rewarded with commissions or bonuses. Indeed, operant conditioning, as described by American psychologist Burrhus Skinner,[7] is what many sales trainers and sales managers apply. But not only trainers use this method to teach or unlearn behaviour. Marketers too are often masters in changing learnt behaviour by provoking positive emotions, as I describe further in the unlearning section on page 24.

So, we now know what training is, but how does it relate to learning and how do both go hand in hand? Think of it like this: training is like a guided path, where learning is more of a journey across an unknown terrain.

TRAINING

In training, the road is clearly laid out, with signposts leading you along a predetermined route. It is structured, goal-oriented and often carried out within a specific time frame. Think of it as a GPS for acquiring skills, where the following elements are essential to make a difference to learning.

- **Structured curriculum:** Training programmes usually follow a predetermined learning plan. Whether you are in a classroom, attending a workshop or taking an online course, the content is carefully designed to meet specific objectives tailored to the target audience.

- **Instructor-led:** Training often involves an instructor or facilitator who imparts knowledge and guides participants through the material. A good trainer knows how to effectively apply the added value of operant conditioning with positive rewards. This training method is particularly useful in formal education and corporate training aimed at mastering basic skills. Or, as described by Bob Mosher and Conrad Gottfredson in their method, which focuses on the 5 Moments of Need for Learning, to seek depth in the skills we have already mastered.[8]

- **Goal-oriented:** Training is aimed at achieving specific goals. It aims to teach a set of behaviours, skills or knowledge within a certain range. This can be anything from learning a programming language to, as described earlier, mastering a particular sales technique.

- **Evaluation and assessment:** Learners are often subjected to assessments and evaluations to measure whether they understand and remember the material. The reward when we have done well then takes the form of grades, certificates and qualifications that take us a step further in our goal of gaining expertise.

LEARNING

Learning, however, is more like an adventure expedition. It is a dynamic, continuous process that does not necessarily follow a set route or timeline. It is driven by curiosity and other competences that I will describe in Part Two. Some defining characteristics that differentiate it from training are the following:

- **Self-directed:** Learning is, first and foremost, self-driven. It is driven by an individual's desire to acquire knowledge or skills. In this case, you are your navigator, deciding what to explore and when. It's that young child still inside you when it goes on a journey of discovery and perseveres through trial and error.

- **Informal and diverse:** Learning is not limited to the classroom or training space. It happens everywhere. Whether you are reading this book, watching a documentary or trying out a new hobby, you are learning.

- **Continuous and lifelong:** Learning knows no boundaries. It is a lifelong endeavour. From childhood to old age, you are constantly picking up new things, adapting to changing circumstances and developing.

- **Adaptive and flexible:** Learning is versatile. It can be adapted to the individual's pace and preferences. There are no rigid schedules or predetermined outcomes; instead, it is about personal growth and self-improvement.

- **Often unconscious:** Unconscious learning, also known as implicit learning or incidental learning, is when you acquire new knowledge, skills or attitudes without being aware of them. It is the innate way people and animals develop naturally, without realizing it is happening. I talk more about unconscious learning and how to use it consciously further in this chapter.

While training, on the one hand, is a valuable tool for teaching specific skills or knowledge within a structured framework, it is often limited to what is explicitly taught. Learning, on the other hand, enables individuals to go beyond the confines of training. It encourages creativity, innovation and the ability to synthesize information from different sources. Understanding the difference between training and learning is vital for your personal development and for organizations that want to support their employees with new knowledge and skills. Recognizing this distinction can, therefore, be a game-changer. In short, training and learning are two sides of the same coin. While training provides you with the necessary skills and knowledge to perform specific tasks, learning equips you with the skills and competences to thrive in a rapidly changing world. Embracing both can lead to a harmonious and successful personal and professional development journey. So, whether you follow a clearly defined path or venture into unknown territory, remember that every step you take is an opportunity to grow, evolve and make the most of your incredible ability to learn.

The hidden power of making unconscious learning conscious

Have you ever wondered if learning could take place unnoticed, outside the confines of your consciousness? I was fascinated by this idea as a child when I hid my textbooks under my pillow, believing it would help me learn even while I slept. Recognizable? The concept of unconscious or implicit learning has made me, and perhaps you, curious. Researchers and academics have long been fascinated by it as well. It challenges our traditional conception of how knowledge is acquired, and that naturally draws scepticism from the scientific and academic world about the inherent difficulty of scientifically investigating a process that takes place beneath the surface of our consciousness.

So, let's be clear right away: we are not here to debate the extent to which unconscious learning can be substantiated. Instead, we are embarking on a journey to explore this enigmatic area of learning without placing it among the myths I describe later in this chapter. What I do want to accomplish with this section is to make you aware of what you are not aware of and to allow it to play a more active role in your learning and life.

You may have experienced unconscious learning yourself and not thought about it. Suppose you were at a party with a catchy tune playing in the background. Days later, you notice yourself humming that tune, even though you didn't consciously try to remember it. How did this happen? It's the magic of unconscious learning, an incredible and often overlooked aspect of how our brains function.

More theoretically, what I just described is a process by which your brain absorbs information and knowledge without being aware. This kind of learning can occur in various ways, such as exposure to irrelevant information while swiping on your cell phone. Or experiences that affect you emotionally but that you don't store as a learning moment at the time. But not everything is equally inexplicable, as children who learn a language from their parents at a very young age also do so unconsciously. Although you may not be actively trying to learn, your brain quietly and effectively absorbs data, makes connections and adapting to the environment.

From various studies that are also often opposed to each other, I want to give some examples showing how unconscious learning can occur. Some may be recognizable, so I want to share them to get you thinking about unconscious learning, after which you can make it happen more consciously.

- **Emotions,** as previously cited, have a great impact on your learning ability. They can block you, but they can also be powerful teachers, especially if the emotions are very pronounced, as in the case of fear or sadness. The emotions you have unconsciously picked up make you modify certain things or behaviours in the future. Perhaps this has happened to you – that you feel anxious about certain people or situations without knowing the exact cause? This is because your subconscious mind learns from past experiences that often go back to your childhood. This unconsciously learnt information is often retained longer because it becomes deeply embedded in your neural pathways. As a result, in a similar situation, these emotions and feelings can suddenly resurface. Coming back to music that you have not consciously stored, for example, for a long time I did not know that my father always put on Vivaldi's 'Four Seasons' when I was very small to calm me down. When I hear it again now, feeling those emotions of peace and security reminds me what I need to do to calm down.

- One of the most basic forms of learning is **habituation** or habit formation, a form of conditioning. This can come about in several ways. For example, on the one hand there is getting used to certain stimuli so that they are pushed into the background, after which you do nothing more with them. You can compare this to a clock ticking in the background: although it bothered you enormously initially when you wanted to concentrate, you no longer hear after a while. On the other hand, when you perform certain behaviours repeatedly, your brain forms neural pathways that make these actions more automatic and effortless. This explains how you can tie your laces or ride a bike without consciously thinking about the steps involved. Becoming aware of unconscious stimuli and the feeling, or emotions, aroused thereby is why Vivaldi, even though I am sometimes unaware that it is on, always helps me focus.

- **Priming**, like habituation, is a form of unconscious learning or conditioning where you are unaware of its often-negative effect on you. This effect, whereby you store past perceptions, was discovered through studies of memory in persons with dementia. But it is just as relevant to people whose brains are working normally. When we refer to priming, you are not aware of things from the past, just like people with dementia. Yet these may have left traces that can be seen in your behaviour in certain situations. This effect, which the American social psychologist Robert Zajonc[9] calls the mere exposure effect, I explain further in Part Two. In that part, I want to make you aware of the influences that undermine your learning mindset through biases about your ability to learn that have subconsciously shaped you.

- In times when artificial intelligence (AI) seems to defeat us on every level, **pattern recognition** is perhaps one of those *superpowers* we use too unconsciously. By understanding what it is and how we can use it to our advantage, we can try to use it more consciously for active learning. Even though we will no longer beat AI at pattern recognition and making connections, your brain still excels at this. With this ability, you absorb recurring issues, habits and trends in your environment without being aware of them. For example, you subconsciously know the fastest route to work, depending on the day of the week. This is because you have memorized this without knowing it. You subconsciously know that more and more people are working hybrid, and therefore Tuesdays and Thursdays are the busiest days on the road. You also know not to take roads near schools when the children are just out at the end of the day, but that these roads are much faster during holidays. Pattern recognition is often reinforced with emotional learning. Sometimes you can't explain why you know someone is being unfair to you. However, it is the unconscious, subtle stimuli of past experiences that we recognize and that alert us.

- A final form of unconscious learning happens through **observation**. This means that you learn unconsciously by observing the behaviour and actions of others. This is how children acquire language and cultural norms and how we acquire new skills and knowledge without formal instruction. Making observations conscious is relatively easy if you take the time to think about them. It is also the fastest way to learn from your unconscious, strengthen your neural pathways and activate the neurons that support your well-being. Moreover, in Part Three, I will explain the added value of mirror neurons and collaborative learning.

When you become aware of what you know unconsciously, you can work with this. You can discover what drives your emotions, how patterns develop and how habits are formed. If you recognize this, you can learn to deal better with negative stimuli or unlearn certain habits.

By systematically giving your observations more attention, you strengthen your neural pathways. This allows you to make choices and decisions more efficiently, based on what you have stored. An added benefit is that you activate your innovative mindset by being extra aware of everything around you. In fact, many groundbreaking ideas and innovations have their origins in the subconscious mind. Actively paying attention to the subconscious opens the door to creativity and new solutions.

To activate this superpower more, quietly observe or reflect on what you have unconsciously stored earlier in the day. Reflect on what that did to you and how you can learn from it. That is why I write down what I have learned every day just before I go to sleep. I find that taking time to do this very consciously helps organize my thoughts and I sleep better. Sometimes I can do this really fast, but there are days when I have to take my time and dig deep to remember everything. However, by doing this consistently, it becomes a habit and then it becomes easier. What is more, during the day you will store things consciously, making it easier to find them in the evening.

So, unconscious learning is often an underused superpower of your brain. It is a continuous process always at work in the background, shaping your thoughts, behaviours and perceptions. Understanding and actively using this powerful mechanism can increase your adaptability, resilience, creativity and overall learning mindset.

The power of retrieval practice

As mentioned, making what you store unconsciously more conscious is important, but there is more. When you think of learning, you probably think of memorizing things. For example, good students in school were those students who only had to take a quick look at their notes just before the test and still scored the best marks in the class. But, make no mistake, that is not learning; that is memorization. And even though short-term memorization may be useful for long-term testing, short-term memorization does not help strengthen the neural pathways we need to support learning in all its aspects.

To benefit from learning in the long run, and to enjoy it more, you need to adopt retrieval practice. This is a strategy in which learning is enhanced by recalling knowledge to your consciousness. Deliberately recalling information forces you to retrieve knowledge from your memory. By doing this regularly, you strengthen the pathways to what you already know. Recalling consciously stimulates the firing of neurons, releasing rewards such as dopamine and serotonin. Those rewards, in turn, will incentivize you to learn more.

Thinking in the evening about what you learned that day, whether uncon-sciously or not, makes you go back to your memories. To make this easier, you can use retrieval clues, such as, 'Where was I when I did that, and how did I feel then?' These steps or clues help you link the memory back to what you learnt that day.

The practice of reinforcing learning is recognized in many scientific stud-ies as one of the most efficient modes of learning. Unsurprisingly, I will come back to this a few more times, both at the individual level and in the context of social and collaborative learning.

Introduction to lean learning

Lean learning is a concept I first described in 2014 for developing learning from an employer's perspective. I use 'lean' here in the sense of transferring knowledge without all the unnecessary extras or waste that do not add value to the learner – relevant knowledge in the moment of need in the most appropriate way for the learner to use it. In the following paragraphs, lean learning will often be mentioned. I will discuss it as an added value for team learning and for shaping learning ecosystems from the intelligent symbiosis between humans and machines. In this section, however, I want to outline in advance the added value for you to consciously deploy lean learning to support the learner mindset. But, first, let me clarify what lean stands for.

Lean in relation to learning, contrary to what many (unconsciously) think, is not related to cost savings. However, the misunderstanding is understandable because of the association made with lean production, where cost-cutting is indeed one of the central tenets. Lean learning, as I developed it with Christine Verhasselt in 2014, indeed finds its basis in the pioneering concept of efficient production/operations that emerged from the Toyota Production System in the mid-20th century. However, from the perception of the learner, it is more analogous with lean thinking and lean start-ups, where the method of eliminating waste has even less to do with cost reduction.

Underlying this is the philosophy that value must be defined from the end customer's point of view. This value can only be created by eliminating waste through continuous improvement. In this, lean focuses on maintain-ing value through efficiency improvements and eliminating anything that does not contribute to the value for the end customer. This waste is not primarily related to cost efficiency but to creating added value by enabling each employee to reach their full potential and thus make the greatest possible contribution for the end customer.

Let me explain how we came to lean in relation to learning. Originally, lean was a systematic approach developed by Toyota. Since the publication of the groundbreaking book *The Machine that Changed the World: The story of lean production – Toyota's secret weapon in the global car wars that is now revolutionizing world industry*,[10] we have seen more and more organizations adopting lean. This has led to a debate in both the practitioner and academic communities about the applicability of the lean approach outside manufacturing environments. A debate in which I actively participated, this time by questioning its applicability to learning organizations.

As I said, you can approach lean learning from multiple perspectives, from the learner to the ecosystem. In the ecosystem approach, you see most associations with manufacturing environments. For the ecosystem, it is important that performance can be measured lean. That mistakes due to insufficient knowledge and skills are prevented to contribute to the ultimate goal, which is a satisfied customer. But you can also turn the whole philosophy around with lean learning. That is, the employee should be able to achieve this end value by being informed and having relevant knowledge available at all times.

The common ground with thinking and lean startups is the underlying philosophy of value creation through the consistent application of practices and principles to help practitioners of lean improve efficiency and quality. By applying lean thinking, everyone is encouraged to participate in this philosophy, which ultimately benefits society as a whole. Based on the lean startup approach, I am particularly inspired by daring to take risks with a goal in mind. Risks that are manageable because, from the continuous improvement approach, you can quickly discover mistakes and learn from these failures. In the lean startup approach, making the journey together and complementing each other is also essential. I therefore discuss this approach as adding value to exceptional teams in which roles are often flexible and everyone complements each other, learns from each other and therefore strengthens each other.

Lean is thus one of the central starting points to support your learning mindset. It starts with yourself in relation to your personal learning mindset, where you actively seek out relevant knowledge when you need it. Lean learning also strengthens collaboration between team members and the learning leader should help facilitate this. Ultimately, lean learning comes together in the ecosystem approach where lean principles lead to value creation for everyone in that ecosystem.

Unlearning is also learning

In the age of accelerated innovation, unlearning is not a choice but a necessity. To adapt, grow and thrive, we must be willing to let go of old knowledge, habits and biases that no longer serve us. While unlearning can be more challenging than learning something new, it is an attitude we can develop and improve with time and effort.

In Part Four of this book, we return to the need for the learning leader to embrace unlearning and to be a role model in doing so. When we all embrace unlearning, it becomes a habit that supports learning and relearning.

Reiterating the importance of the transformative journey in terms of learning, unlearning and relearning is one of the many things I have in common with Dr Anna Tarabasz. My dear friend always inspires me with her unquenchable hunger for knowledge. I am therefore happy to share her contribution to encourage you to embrace the art of unlearning. If we all do so consciously and consistently, we will open the door to a world of endless possibilities and growth in this age of accelerated innovation.

DR ANNA TARABASZ, ASSOCIATE PROFESSOR, COLLEGE OF INTERDISCIPLINARY STUDIES, ZAYED UNIVERSITY, UAE: THE TRANSFORMATIVE JOURNEY: LEARNING, UNLEARNING AND RELEARNING

In the relentless march of time, the quest for knowledge, skills and competences reaches beyond static accumulation of facts and experience. It is re-wired into a pursuit: a dynamic, continuous and cyclical process in the ever-evolving landscape. This approach to personal and professional evolution goes beyond the linear, one-way path and reflects the transformative journey of learning, unlearning and relearning. All this dictated by the need for adaptability to change and resilience in the face of the unknown. Each phase becomes, therefore, a doorway into self-discovery and growth. Moreover, such a tri-step approach helps to foster a learning mindset – receptive and flexible enough to shed the obsolete and embrace the novel.

Learning: The foundation of growth

At the core of human development lies the innate capacity to learn. In all of its forms, learning permeates the very essence of our existence. Formal education provides the cornerstone, bringing the required toolset – essential knowledge and skills. However, learning extends beyond classrooms and textbooks. It is a process, a lifelong pursuit that encompasses both formal and informal experiences.

The core of learning is not just the acquisition of facts but also a step in perfecting critical thinking, problem-solving and creative abilities. It is a process that opens minds to new perspectives, ideas and cultures, enriching our understanding of the world. From the first steps in a child's educational journey to the mastery of complex skills in adulthood, the continuum of learning equips individuals with the mental agility required to navigate the complexities of a constantly evolving society. However, I believe that learning is only the first step in the loop of continuous improvement.

Unlearning: The art of letting go

As indispensable as learning is, it lays the groundwork for a paradox – what was once foundational can become a hurdle. Here enters the challenging and often underestimated phase of unlearning. Unlearning is not merely the absence of knowledge but is also an active process of shedding outdated beliefs, habits and perspectives that may have once served a purpose but now hinder progress.

In an age of accelerated innovation and swiftly evolving societal norms, unlearning is not a luxury but a survival skill. It demands the courage to question the status quo, the humility to admit that what was once true may no longer be applicable, and the fortitude to break down mental barriers. It resembles a psychological and intellectual housecleaning – a process of decluttering the mind to make space for new and more relevant information.

Unlearning is a journey that challenges the very fabric of our comfort zones. It compels us to confront cognitive dissonance, reconcile conflicting ideas and dismantle the mental scaffolding that might have provided stability in the past but now restricts our view of the future. The ability to unlearn is, in essence, a skill that can be cultivated, refined and improved over time. It is an indispensable tool for those navigating an ever-changing landscape.

Relearning: The evolutionary leap

This transformative journey does not end with unlearning. It simply morphs later into the subsequent phase. Relearning allows for staying relevant in the evolving world. It is the conscious and proactive acquisition of new knowledge and skills that align with current needs and realities. It is the embodiment of adaptability – a deliberate response stays agile in the face of technological advancements, societal shifts and global challenges.

Relearning is not about a passive acceptance of new information, but an active engagement with emerging trends, technologies and paradigms. It requires a commitment to continuous skills development and a readiness to embrace innovation. Through relearning, individuals not only stay relevant in their professional pursuits but also contribute to the societal tapestry by addressing contemporary challenges with fresh perspectives.

In the same way that learning broadens horizons and unlearning clears the path, relearning is the visionary leap forward. It is the process of not just keeping pace with change but actively staying ahead of it. The ability to relearn is a testament to an individual's resilience, foresight and commitment to personal and professional growth. All three, interconnected, represent what every marketer knows well from practice: transcend or perish, urging the loop of iteration and the need for continuous improvement.

The interconnected cycle: Navigating the learning landscape

The transformative journey of learning, unlearning and relearning is not a linear progression but a continuous, interconnected cycle. It is a dynamic process that shapes not only individual trajectories but also the collective evolution of societies. The ability to navigate this cycle is not just a skill but a mindset – one that embraces curiosity, adaptability and a relentless pursuit of excellence.

In a world where the only constant is change, those who embark on this transformative journey emerge not just as learners but as architects of positive change. The interconnected nature of these three phases creates a synergy that propels individuals and societies toward a future where innovation, adaptability and continuous growth are not just survival strategies but also the foundations of a thriving, dynamic existence.

In conclusion, the transformative journey of learning, unlearning and relearning is an odyssey that defines the human experience. It is a commitment to intellectual curiosity, adaptability and growth – an acknowledgement that the journey itself is as valuable as the destination. In an era where the pace of change is unprecedented, those who embrace this cycle not only stay relevant but also become trailblazers in an ever-evolving landscape of knowledge and possibilities.

Some myths debunked

There are quite a few myths around learning and teaching. And, I agree, they sometimes seem recognizable and applicable, especially as excuses for why you shouldn't be able to learn. Yet, they are just myths and sometimes real falsehoods. You will discover why I find myth debunking extra fun when I discuss misfits and rebels challenging the status quo in the next part. However, it is not just because I am a rebel that I want to debunk myths. Sticking to or believing in these myths undermines your learning mindset.

The examples below are not the only myths – I could write a whole book about them – but they are relevant to get you thinking about what keeps you from learning. This first chapter is a plea to you to embrace again the love of learning you had as a child, and no falsehood should inhibit you in that.

Learning and age will not be an excuse anymore

One such hype that unfortunately has a huge impact on our learning mindset is the widespread belief that our ability to learn quietly declines after age 25. And, even though this research can be traced back to American psychologist Edward L. Thorndike in 1927,[11] we know from many scientific studies since then that this is an error.

What is more, according to much more recent research by Kegan and Lahey and others, the opposite is possible. Indeed, this longitudinal research that plots the complexity of learning against the age of test subjects strongly revealed two other findings.[12]

On the one hand, it showed that learning ability and mental complexity, or how you deal with problems and challenges, increases with age. On the other hand, the study showed that within each age group there are significant differences. For example, you may have reached a much higher level of mental complexity at 30 than someone else at 40. Several factors come into play here, including the intrinsic motivation to learn and the learning mindset you have developed.

According to this research, our ability to learn is influenced not only by innate abilities, but mainly by how we think about learning and solving complex problems. In other words, our mindset is a much more important factor, along with the knowledge that we can maintain our neural pathways and connections by using them often, just like muscles that you can grow and maintain even in old age.

We see that our environment and our interactions with others also affect our mental complexity and ability to learn new things. These are often linked to age, because we often link certain life phases to age. You probably won't become a learning leader on the first day at work, but may do after several years of experience. Yet this is not true for everyone. So, depending on how we go through these phases and how our careers develop, different individuals develop different capabilities at different ages.

I will try to explain the above with a simple comparison. In the first stage, where you are still inexperienced in a team with more experienced colleagues, you often need direction. You therefore work with others and learn from them. In the second phase, you take the lead in specific projects by partly relying on your own compass and experience. This is the second level of mental complexity. As you learn from these experiences and gain more and more confidence in your own ability, you start to push boundaries. By doing so you become more mindful of all aspects of complex problems. You learn to deal with contradictions, you see coherence and you learn to take charge of others. In the process, you will help others take their mental complexity to the next level.

This is also the premise of this book: the learning mindset starts with yourself. So, as you read this book, regardless of your age or stage of mental development, there is always the opportunity to learn, grow and continuously improve. So, leave this myth aside and embrace all experiences and interactions with others to thrive by recognizing lifelong learning as your greatest gift.

Unboxing learning styles, preferences and the learning pyramid

Of the many myths out there related to learning styles, two stand out because they are widely accepted as truth by educators in education and corporate settings. They are the basis of many academic studies; therefore I can say with certainty today that they are false. Moreover, many studies indicate that they can be dangerous because they stigmatize people from an early age and thereby undermine the learning mindset.

LABELS AND LEARNING STYLES

No myth is talked about as much as the one about learning styles. This myth claims that people process information in their own, specific way depending on how their brain functions and that this is fixed at birth. I have found at least 71 different mentions since French philosopher and educator Jean-Jacques Rousseau first mentioned it in his book *Emile*. This probably made him one of the most influential people in education of modern times.[13] His view was that learning should start from the child's point of view. However, it is noteworthy that he lived between 1712 and 1778 and did not explicitly emphasize learning styles as they are described today. What is also notable is that learning styles only became popular and spread as truth in the 1970s. That this idea was suddenly widely adopted so much later may be due to the urge at the time to categorize everything. Unfortunately, that was also the beginning of the pigeonholing that apparently so many people still seem to crave.

The VAK theory (visual-auditory-kinetic), for example, which is definitely a myth, states that some learn better through images, others through sound and the rest through movement.[14] Kolb's Learning Style Inventory, in turn, claims that we differ in learning style as doers, thinkers, watchers and feelers.[15] Image-thinking, on the other hand, is a myth that has gained support mainly in the Netherlands and Flanders,[16] and so on. And I understand you if you're now thinking, 'I'd rather read a book than listen to a podcast so it might work for me.' However, do not make the mistake of presuming that learning styles are the same as learning preferences. For instance, I definitely prefer reading to watching YouTube or TikTok videos, while my daughters find videos a more convenient way of learning. Does that mean I learn better from books? No, preference does not always yield the best learning gains, as I will try to explain below with a perhaps recognizable example.

For years I tried my grandmother's recipe to make a thick apple pie, yet the more I studied everything in her old cookbook, the less I understood what I was doing wrong. However, when I recently found a video by a well-known chef, I suddenly managed to make a pie that didn't collapse after I took it out of the oven. Unfortunately, it was not yet the perfection I knew from my grandmother – not perfect but already much better.

What I had not understood was the complexity of adapting to the type of apples you can buy in the supermarket these days, which are different from the apples she used. Letting the dough rise with yeast from a packet also turned out to be different from the fresh yeast that my grandmother used. This all ended up affecting the cake. The chef's explanation of the type of apples and their firmness, the difference between yeasts and even the room's temperature made everything so much clearer. As a result, I can now make my own recipe based on my ingredients and environment. In other words, he made something very abstract very simple by using examples. As a result, I think I can now experiment with other more complex cakes myself, based on the right knowledge of the basic rules. So, my preference for books turned out to have no added value for the outcome of my cake. On the contrary, it caused me to fail time and again without understanding why and thus not learning from it and getting more and more frustrated.

The above indicates the absurdity of learning styles. I understood the influence of other products and the environment in which I made the pie by following instructions in a different way. This had nothing to do with my abstraction ability being innate and fixed, as is claimed by those who believe the alleged learning styles. Nor did I benefit much from my label as being a 'thinker' according to Kolb's theory. The only relevant thing to learning is keeping an open mind and finding what is the most relevant method for you to learn something at any given time. Because of this, I look at learning from a lean perspective, where you consider what has value to you at the moment of need.

The false belief in these theories is increasingly the subject of new academic studies on labels or stigma undermining a learning mindset. As early as kindergarten, teachers and parents, with the best intentions, try to label a child's learning style to help them. As a result, the child is often presented with a one-sided menu of learning that makes them miss out on learning opportunities. What is more, the child does not get the chance to discover the joy of learning by experimenting with other methods as well. It should also be noted that if the material is not suitable for a particular way of studying, the learner is at a disadvantage, because the learning process is not maximized by using the strategy that best suits the material. But, worst of all, it instils a fixed mindset on how to learn and therefore the rest of your life is already partly determined for you.

I hope you can keep an open mind about different learning styles and stop making excuses that you cannot learn something because it is not your learning style. Now that you know they have been leading you astray since childhood, you can take control of your life and experiment with other ways of learning that you might really like. Who knows, maybe even by experimenting with the technology and AI that I discuss in Part Two.

LEARNING PYRAMID(S)

The learning pyramid resembles learning styles and is just as popular in adult education and corporate learning. However, it is as big a myth as the learning styles we were assigned from childhood. Believing in this theory can damage your future by aligning different learning opportunities and learning content with the nonsense of the pyramid. So, it amazes me repeatedly that I still hear executives in L&D and even professors in teacher education preach about this as if it were the truth.

The learning pyramid theory assumes that we learn little or nothing by listening and mostly by doing: somewhat similar to some of the learning styles. In other words, the more actively you take in information, the better you will remember the information. The best way to minimize forgetting and make learning more effective is to absorb the information as actively as possible. Sounds very plausible, right?

However, what should set off alarm bells is that the pyramid has random numbers attached to it as to how people are assumed to remember:

- 10 per cent of what they read
- 20 per cent of what they hear
- 30 per cent of what they see
- 50 per cent of what they see and hear
- 70 per cent of what they say
- 90 per cent of what they do and say.

I do understand why this comes across as plausible. For a complex concept like learning, the figures seem pretty accurate to me. Interestingly, depending on the source, they vary slightly and are never really substantiated. But, firstly, for a complex fact like learning, the figures are very precise and, remarkably, depending on the source slightly different figures are given that are not substantiated. What is also striking is that authors always refer to a *learning* pyramid but in the accompanying texts they always refer to we *remember* X per cent of. In my opinion, this falls seriously short because, as I pointed out earlier, the relationship between learning and memorization is a bit more complex.

And it became more interesting when I researched the origins of the learning pyramid. It amazes me that this can still be followed and applied. Part Two of this book stresses the importance of being open to opinions and ideas that are different from your own, yet there must be a basis to fall back on. However, the research on learning pyramids is ambiguous and contradictory and, in my opinion, sometimes rather short-sighted.

For instance, today's pyramids are all based on Edgar Dale's Cone of Experience, which refers to the theory that something can be learned only by putting it into action.[17] So, this theory, which had no scientific basis, is actually not even about memorization but experiential learning. What is more, Edgar Dale's Cone originally had no numbers. The numbers and the idea that they contain a hierarchy of forgetting were added later and copied repeatedly by other authors.

There is danger in adopting this theory to align it with how you can improve your learning. Just as with learning styles, effective learning depends on the learning content, the moment we need to learn, why we want to learn something, with whom we learn and so on. Learning cannot be pigeonholed, just as people should not be given labels. Why did I share this myth? I hope it encourages you to verify things, not believe everything that seems scientific, be a rebel and experiment curiously to find your own methods. That will help you learn and, above all, (again) experience the joy of learning.

WE ONLY USE 10 PER CENT OF OUR BRAIN AND WHEN WE UNLOCK MORE THAN THIS WE BECOME SUPERMINDS

One of the most widespread myths that continues to be repeated even by well-known writers and keynote speakers is that we as humans would only use 10 per cent of our brains, suggesting that we have 90 per cent untapped potential. What if we could activate all that untapped potential? Would we, like Lucy, played by Scarlett Johansson in the sci-fi movie of the same name (2014), gain extraordinary powers such as telekinesis, superhuman strength, speed and the ability to control and manipulate technology? If we can activate 100 per cent, like Lucy, would we be a human supercomputer that becomes one with a virtual universe?

It speaks to the imagination that we have so much untapped potential that we could activate. Yet it is absolutely a myth without any scientific basis. However, some so-called experts refer to the work of American psychologist William James and even to statements by Albert Einstein. Yet neither has ever claimed that we only use 10 per cent of our brains, although they may have said that many of us only use 10 per cent of our potential. Which is therefore not the same as not using 90 per cent of our brains.

That we do use 100 per cent of our brains is easily demonstrated with neuroimaging techniques such as PET scans and xMRI. With these scanners you can clearly see that all parts of the brain light up during different activities for the brain. This is actually very simple to explain. The brain can be compared to the muscle mass in our body. When we make a movement, we do not use our muscles all at once. However, to function during a day we will probably use most of our muscles. This is similar to our brain. For example, not all parts of our brain are activated when we read a passage from a book. You will use the temporal lobe, which is responsible for phonological awareness and decoding/distinguishing sounds; the frontal lobe for speech production, reading comprehension, grammatical usage and comprehension; and the angular and supramarginal gyrus as a 'reading integrator', a kind of conductor that connects the different parts of the brain to perform the reading action. When all these brain areas work together you can read the letters b, o, o, k out loud, like 'book'.

If you compare reading aloud to exercising muscles, you will understand that using 10 per cent of your brain does not correspond to 10 per cent of your mental potential. If you don't practise reading aloud much as a child, it will often be much more difficult to read aloud fluently later on because the connections and neural pathways have not been strengthened or trained enough.

Another important piece of evidence that we need all parts of our brains is found in patients who have suffered brain injuries. These patients often lose certain competencies, such as speaking or walking, or even their ability to empathize. If you remove a piece from your brain, or if a part is so damaged that it is no longer 100 per cent intact, the consequences are significant. Brain reactivation or strengthening after trauma with brain implants are, as I describe in Chapter 2, beautiful innovations with a lot of potential. Yet, they are not the panaceas to create a super brain, and there are no shortcuts to facilitate learning. Lucy was a sci-fi movie and aids for using more brain power or activating more mental potential remain nothing more than a fantasy.

So, no more excuses: your brain is like a muscle and if you don't make it work enough, it loses strength, just like when you don't get out of your easy chair and, after a while, can barely climb the stairs.

Endnotes

1   C S Dweck (2007) *Mindset: The New Psychology of Success*, Ballantine Books, New York

2   P Main. Jean Piaget's theory of cognitive development, Structural Learning, 11 June 2021, www.structural-learning.com/post/jean-piagets-theory-of-cognitive-development-and-active-classrooms (archived at https://perma.cc/2FPK-E8EV)

3   H Thomas. What are learning theories and why are they important for learning design?, My Brain is Open, 1 October 2020, mybrainisopen.net/learning-theories-and-learning-design (archived at https://perma.cc/SN7B-KLA7)

4   Teaching and Learning (no date) Getting started: What is learning? onq.queensu.ca/shared/TLHEM/home.html (archived at https://perma.cc/F7WG-5DYP)

5   S Collins (2023) *Neuroscience for Learning and Development: How to apply neuroscience and psychology for improved learning and training*, Kogan Page, London

6   M H Immordino-Yang and A Damasio. We Feel, Therefore We Learn: The Relevance of Affective and Social Neuroscience to Education, *Mind, Brain, and Education,* 2007, 1(1), 3–10, doi:https://doi.org/10.1111/zj.1751-228x.2007.00004.x

7   Editors of Encyclopaedia Britannica. B F Skinner, last updated 14 May 2024, www.britannica.com/biography/B-F-Skinner (archived at https://perma.cc/3HF3-FSKM)

8   The 5 Moments of Need®: Enable & sustain efficient, effective job performance, www.5momentsofneed.com/ (archived at https://perma.cc/QV4Q-C3VA)

9   K C Berridge. Robert Zajonc: The complete psychologist, *Emotion Review*, 2010, 2(4), 348–52, www.researchgate.net/publication/223985870_Robert_Zajonc_The_Complete_Psychologist (archived at https://perma.cc/X8D5-WG94)

10 J P Womack, D T Jones and D Roos (2007) *The Machine that Changed the World: The story of lean production: Toyota's secret weapon in the global car wars that is now revolutionizing world industry*, Free Press, New York

11 D L Crawford. The role of aging in adult learning: Implications for instructors in higher education, Scribd, www.scribd.com/document/193576462/The-Role-of-Aging-in-Adult-Learning (archived at https://perma.cc/G7QJ-7ZWJ)

12 R Kegan and L L Lahey (2016) *An Everyone Culture*, Harvard Business School Publishing, Cambridge, MA

13 M Cranston and B Duignan. Jean-Jacques Rousseau, *Encyclopaedia Britannica*, last updated 23 April 2024, www.britannica.com/biography/Jean-Jacques-Rousseau (archived at https://perma.cc/KH95-CD9B)

14 X Sun, O Norton and S E Nancekivell. Beware the myth: Learning styles affect parents', children's, and teachers' thinking about children's academic potential. *NPJ Science of Learning*, 2023, 8(46), doi.org/10.1038/s41539-023-00190-x (archived at https://perma.cc/R4CR-DRJX)

15 S Macleod. Kolb's learning styles & experiential learning cycle, Simply Psychology, 2 February 2024, www.simplypsychology.org/learning-kolb.html (archived at https://perma.cc/37EQ-LNGE)

16 F V D Pontseele. Leerstijlen: Feit of fabel?, Klasse, 24 January 2023, www.klasse.be/628962/leerstijlen-feit-of-fabel/ (archived at https://perma.cc/JH7D-6NH4)

17 E Dale (1969) *Audio-visual Methods in Teaching*, Dryden Press, New York

2

The symbiosis of humans and machines

What if Captain Kirk's Universal Translator, which can instantly translate brainwave patterns, became a reality? In these rapidly changing times, when functional magnetic resonance imaging (fMRI) scans are being tested to read minds and, soon, wearables will be deployed to gain insight into our thoughts, nothing seems impossible anymore. And what's next? Perhaps brain implants and organoid intelligence making the symbiosis between man and machine a reality?

One thing is for sure, new innovations are moving at lightning speed and becoming mainstream in the consumer world even faster than expected, such as extended reality (XR) glasses like the Meta Ray-Ban. As a result, lean learning via augmented reality in the flow of life seems to be becoming more and more accessible. In the process, the possibilities for social learning are also endless. Just think of virtual worlds with human-like avatars and gener-ative AI for text-to-speech and voice cloning capabilities blurring the lines between reality and fake. What the impact of all these innovations will be on the future of work and learning is difficult to assess. Therefore, I don't dare make too many predictions, yet I look curiously at the youth and how they embrace innovations in everyday life. What I do dare predict is that when they get used to these, they will also expect these as natural tools for learning and connecting on the job. Not to mention their expectations of AI as a spar-ring partner which for many, not just the youth, is already the new normal.

In this chapter, I will show you that AI and other mind-blowing innovations will have a place in your life. Hoping it all won't take off is a utopia. The only question you can ask yourself is how can I still be human in a world that is becoming increasingly artificial and virtual? After you have read this part, I hope that curiosity, not fear, will drive you to unfold your learning mindset in the following parts on the potential of innovations and contingent improve-ment.

Should we be afraid of innovation?

Innovation is a natural part of human evolution and fear of the change that comes with it is with us all the time. We worry about the incalculable impact on us and future generations without being able to paint a picture of that impact. A very good example of this can be found in *Phaedrus*, one of Plato's most profound and beautiful works. This work, which, of course, has been edited and translated many times over the years, depicts a conversation between Socrates and Phaedrus. One of the topics they discussed was the invention of writing. On this, Socrates is said to have expressed concern in relation to its impact on humanity: 'They will no longer use memory because they rely on what is written, so they no longer remember things by themselves, but through external signs.'

The above example is enormously interesting in light of learning and neuroscience, so the philosophical conversation between Socrates and Phaedrus could go on for some time. Less philosophical is the impact of the various industrial revolutions on humans, starting with the Luddites. This movement against innovation emerged after, according to legend, Ned Ludd smashed two stocking feet with a hammer in 1779. This was the starting point for a movement committed to the livelihood and lifestyle of skilled workers. In doing so, they wanted to curb the possible negative impact of progress on employment, economics and society. Luddism, therefore, refers to technophobia or the fear of change. Yet, in light of today's innovations, this fear should no longer be a philosophical debate as it was in the time of Socrates. Today, innovation is acceleration so fast that one can legitimately wonder if we can still push the stop button for general AI or for the moment that Singularity becomes a reality.

In what follows, I'll share some background into more recent innovations, so you can decide for yourself what scares you and where you see opportunities. I also encourage you to discuss this with those around you, possibly philosophically, as I do with my daughters. What if? What can I do to not let fear get the upper hand, but to be resilient towards the future?

The speed of innovation

The digital age, which some say to be the fifth industrial revolution, has accelerated at an unprecedented rate. The way you live, work and communicate is hardly comparable to, say, 10 years ago. I can hardly imagine why I argued with my daughter about Facebook in 2015. At the time I believed I had to protect her from social media, which even then she saw as a necessity to be connected to her friends and thus learn with them. I realize now that her anger that I was old and didn't understand her world was justified. However, what neither she nor I could have imagined then is that we would laugh now at the naivety we had then. I could not protect her from the increasingly virtual world, nor was Facebook the tool that would connect her with her friends to play and grow together.

Since 2015, the world seems to have hyper-accelerated, and Facebook seems to have lost all popularity with teens. En masse, younger generations are hooking up with other apps like TikTok and Snapchat, whose complex algorithms and integration with generative AI often make them far more dangerous than what I wanted Farah to avoid. Yet those apps are, in terms of unconscious, social and lean learning, very relevant to discuss further.

How fast is this change and can we keep up with the speed in the future? Is it still possible for futurists to make any predictions? For decades, many have been guided by three influential principles: Moore's law, Gilder's law and Metcalfe's law. Today, however, I dare question their continued validity. Still, I like to share them, even though I feel we can no longer extend them into the future. In my opinion, everything will move much faster, so I want to try to take you out of your comfort zone, and possibly provoke you with the speed of innovation that defies even known laws.

Moore's law and innovation in staggering numbers

Gordon Moore, the co-founder of Intel, formulated his law in 1965. He predicted that the number of transistors on a microchip would double approximately every two years, leading to exponential improvements in computing power.[1] For decades, Moore's law remained valid and there was relentless progress in computing. This led to smaller, faster and more energy-efficient devices, fundamentally changing computing capabilities and industries such as telecommunications, healthcare and entertainment.

That Moore's law does not apply today is already shown by the fact that doubling the number of transistors is obsolete. We already see that due to the physical limits of semiconductor technology, you simply cannot go any smaller or faster. Consider also that other innovations in quantum computing and alternative materials are challenging the traditional silicon-based computing paradigm. Although Moore's law is no longer associated only with basic microchips, it is interesting to consider whether we can still talk about doubling speed, or whether we are accelerating much faster. A nice story to visualize this and that I also like to share during my keynotes is that of the number of grains of rice on a chessboard and what happens if we double them every two years.[2]

According to a legend, there was once a clever inventor who created the chessboard for an ancient Indian emperor who was so impressed with it that he let the inventor choose his prize. The inventor, who himself possessed incredible intelligence, or should I say computing power, asked something seemingly small. He asked for the equivalence of rice distributed according to a mathematical calculation on a chess board. He started with just one grain of rice on the first square and doubled the number for each subsequent square. The emperor initially laughed at the question, but he would later realize his mistake, as the total sum is about 1.4 trillion cubic tons of rice grains (more than 2,500 times the annual world production in 2021[3]). With 64 fields on a chessboard, if you double the number of grains on consecutive fields, the sum of the grains on all 64 fields is: $1 + 2 + 4 + 8 + \ldots$ and so on. The total number of grains equals 18,446,744,073,709,551,615 (eighteen trillion, four hundred and forty-six thousand billion, seven hundred and forty-four billion, seventy-three thousand million, seven hundred and nine million, five hundred and fifty-one thousand, six hundred and fifteen). Converted, that gives more than 1.4 trillion cubic tons. Not bad as a prize for inventing a game.

Now suppose we find ourselves today about halfway down the chessboard and we double the rate of innovations next year. That is an unimaginable multiplication of innovations coming our way. Then try to imagine for a moment what we knew regarding generative AI, meta-worlds and so many other innovations today a year ago. Do you still think anyone can predict the future?

George Gilder enables the hyperconnected world

George Gilder, an American investor, writer and futurist, introduced the importance of telecommunications bandwidth in 1995. He predicted then that network capacity would triple approximately every year.[4] His law did not hold, yet his assumption was correct regarding an exponentially increasing demand for bandwidth. There is already a much higher need for ever faster and more secure data transmission. In the era of the Internet of Things, autonomous vehicles, drones, special computing in healthcare and predictive digital twins, 5G networks are already inadequate for some purposes.

6G will offer advantages in terms of speed and reliability. 6G will be another hundred times faster than 5G as regards latency or response time to get data from your device to the destination and back. Moreover, the 6G network will be much more reliable. This improvement has advantages for certain applications, such as healthcare, where network reliability is essential, for example when performing remote operations. It may therefore be useful to consider which applications already benefit from the local deployment of 6G today.

I should note that there are not only benefits to ever-faster networks and that we should also be aware of the dangers. I point this out because although 5G has not yet been widely deployed in many countries, speculation about the introduction of 6G is already rife. Here we need to take into account the network capacity, which would be much greater with 6G, allowing many more wireless devices to use the internet at high speed. And so here lies a potential danger to our health. By comparison, with 4G, we reached a density of about 100,000 devices per km². 5G networks are already doing a lot better in this respect: after all, they allow one million devices per connection. And with 6G networks, the figure of 10 million connected devices per km² would come within reach. That's extra radiation in light of masts and devices all around us. Not to mention the energy consumption that will accompany 6G.

George Gilbert's law may not hold up, but it is relevant to consider how far we want to go with the hyperconnectivity we are heading toward. Is it really necessary to make 5G and possibly 6G accessible to everyone, or should we make smart human choices that take into account a sustainable and healthy future for our children?

BeReal about Metcalfe's exponential growth

The last law I like to cite as a reference for the speed of innovation is that of Robert Metcalfe, an American engineer and entrepreneur who co-invented Ethernet. He stated in the 1980s that the value of a telecommunications network is proportional to the square of the number of connected users.[5] Essentially, the more users a network has, the more valuable it becomes, creating network effects that drive innovation and adoption.

Although Melcalfe's law is very popular with academics and keynote speakers, there remains significant academic debate about the concept. However, as stated earlier, I don't seek debate. My sole purpose with this example is to get you thinking about today's world and how you can grow in it by embracing technology that supports your learning mindset.

Returning to the debate, which I did engage in, with my daughter Farah who wanted a Facebook account. Not long after I clearly lost, she decided it was irrelevant anyway. The girlfriends' interest had already shifted to another popular place in the virtual world for social collaboration. And, since then, this has happened a few more times, with platforms like Instagram, TikTok, Snapchat and Roblox that grew exponentially but also had to innovate harder and harder to keep up with the attention of their users.

I also noted that with each new hype, the exponential growth of these new apps was accelerating, as with my daughters' new temporary favourite, BeReal. This groundbreaking French app, which only went live in 2019, showed unprecedented and exponentially continuous growth that left me stunned and by August 2023 already had more than 100 million worldwide users.[6] The biggest acceleration it made was between April 2022, with 'only' 7.67 million users, to 20 million in July 2022 and a month later, in August 2022, to 28 million users of the app. It then becomes very difficult as a non-user to stay on the sidelines and suppress your curiosity. Once connected, it often turns out that these apps try to keep you hooked with clever algorithms.

Understanding Metcalfe's law is also very interesting when considering innovative projects like social learning platforms or even metaverses and Web3 applications to support collaborative learning. These learning ecosystems, which I describe in the last part of this book, grow from a few learning influencers and learning leaders to create a ripple effect that fuels the learning mindset of others. They create optimal lean knowledge exchange within an organization, where everyone can experience added value in the ecosystem from their own starting point, infinitely connected by intelligent algorithms.

Humans have created AI in their image

As described, the speed at which innovations are accelerating today is increasing exponentially, and faster than many futurists had predicted. Today, AI seems to many to be that new wave sweeping over us. Yet AI is far less new than you think. However, the ripple effect of what started long ago has now led to ever larger and faster waves of new AI-driven applications coming our way. Indeed, with roots going back to the Dartmouth Conference of 1956, AI as a concept is a lot older than many other innovations we have already embraced.

The birth of AI took place during the Dartmouth Conference of 1956 at Dartmouth College in New Hampshire, USA.[7] During this summer camp, researchers were brought together from seemingly disparate fields of study or boundary regions to explore the potential of synthetic intelligence. This synthetic intelligence, which was then renamed artificial intelligence by US computer scientist John McCarthy, was essentially nothing more than a collective name for machines that perform tasks based on instructions given by humans.

The Dartmouth Conference had a major impact on the history of AI, similar to the summit at Bletchley Park in the UK on 2 November 2023.[8] Where recently the potential catastrophic impact of AI was addressed, the first conference was precisely to establish AI as a field of study and encouraged the development of new technologies and techniques. At this first conference, participants discussed a wide range of topics related to AI, such as natural language processing, problem solving and machine learning. They also mapped out a roadmap for AI research, including the development of programming languages and algorithms for creating intelligent machines. This led to a wave of research and innovation in this field. Today, many of us still know the first AI programming language, LISP and, of course, the famous Turing Test developed by British mathematician Alan Turing, a test used to determine whether a machine could exhibit intelligent behaviour indistinguishable from a human.[9] To this day it is an important yardstick for measuring the progress of AI research.

The convergence of neuroscience and computer science

The Dartmouth Conference brought together scientists from many different fields, which had clearly had an impact on the development of AI. In particular the presence of Massachusetts Institute of Technology (MIT) professor Norbert Weiner, a prodigy who could read as early as the age of three, had a big impact on the outcomes of the conference.[10]

Drawing from broad knowledge of various fields such as mathematics, neurophysiology, medicine and physics, he had the urge to build machines capable of intelligent behaviour. Weiner's interest and pioneering work explored the similarities between the biological nervous system, neuroscience and electronic computers. This relationship, which he called cybernetics,[11] became the cornerstone for the creation of AI, supported by the theory that computers and brains work in essentially the same way. To me, however, Weiner is more than just one of the icons who laid the cornerstones of AI. This prodigy with a fascination for frontier exploration is also an inspiration for the unique competence of consilience that I describe in Part Three.

Without going into too much academic detail here, I will briefly discuss the connection scientists made between human learning and artificial learning. More specifically, how they drew inspiration from human neural networks, which I described in Chapter 1. The neural networks, or computational models, they developed mimic the function and structure of biological neurons. In other words, the learning algorithms are largely inspired by the way neurons work in the brain. Because just like in humans, these artificial neurons are networks composed of several layers of interconnected nodes that help process and transmit information. Similar to what dendrites, somas and axons do in biological neural networks.

However, it is not just the way brains and computers are wired that is hugely similar. Artificial neural networks are also designed to learn from previous experiences, through failure, testing, feedback loops, reward, pattern recognition and so on. With some examples, it is easy to demonstrate that AI is indeed created in the likeness of humans.

FEEDBACK MECHANISM

As I indicated in Chapter 1, people learn from previous experiences and the feedback they receive on the outcome of what they learned. As a result, they adapt their knowledge or behaviour and strive for continuous improvement.

This technique is also used for training AI models where the output of a neural network is fed back as input. This additional data input in training ensures that more and more data and knowledge are created and that the result gives an increasingly better output.

REINFORCEMENT LEARNING AND OPERANT CONDITIONING

Reinforcement learning is a fundamental concept in both human cognition and AI training. In the human brain, reinforcement learning implies learning from experiences through trial and error. It is closely linked to the brain's reward system, which helps individuals adjust their behaviour based on the results of their actions. Similarly, reinforcement learning in AI is a technique that enables machines to make decisions and learn from their consequences.

In the human brain, the release of neurotransmitters such as dopamine, associated with pleasure or reward, reinforces specific behaviours. In AI, reinforcement learning algorithms use reward signals to steer agents towards desired decisions. This similarity suggests that both systems rely on the above feedback mechanisms to improve their performance over time. Human brains and AI systems seek to maximize rewards, whether intrinsic, such as personal satisfaction, or extrinsic, such as a numerical score.

PARALLEL PROCESSING AND MULTITASKING

What often happens unconsciously in humans is the division of more complex tasks into smaller tasks. For example, young children at school still have to write down their arithmetic sums with sub-steps until they can apply arithmetic method so naturally that they are no longer aware of the division.

AI tries to make equally efficient use of its computational capacity by breaking down complex computational tasks into smaller pieces. These are then processed on a different processor in an attempt to increase speed. This approach enables AI systems to process more input data faster. However, it is not just with arithmetic that we apply this unconsciously. As humans we are perfectly capable of having the brain perform several tasks simultaneously, such as walking and talking (multitasking).

UNCONSCIOUS LEARNING AND UNSUPERVISED LEARNING

As humans we learn a lot unconsciously, because our brains constantly receive new streams of data in the form of sounds, visual content, sensory feelings and so on. We bring this together without effort or awareness to form a logical understanding of a given situation and its influence on us.

Take, for example, a nice summer's day that suddenly turns grey. Suddenly you hear thunder in the distance and you then feel a big drop of rain on your head. Without thinking, you search for your umbrella, which you then remember has been left at home. Your brain will unconsciously and very quickly assess whether you will get home before the heavy storm or whether it is better to take shelter somewhere.

This ability to process seemingly disparate data points such as water, sound, feeling and distance simultaneously is called unsupervised learning when training AI. AI systems are taught to work with raw, unstructured data and interpret them without explicit labelling of what they are and how they should be related. A technique that can be useful, as I further describe with the example of Libratus, who was able to beat people at poker. It probably won't surprise you that this technique also has potential ethical dangers, as I will further illustrate.

Attention mechanisms and suppressing noise

This example, where AI seems to be outpacing many of us, concerns attention to what is relevant. With an overload of information and distractions from our environment, such as noise, emotions and many other jammers, it is often difficult to concentrate.

AI does not suffer from concentration problems to complete a task. In fact, most algorithms are driven with only relevant data points to complete the task. However, we as humans need to pay attention to the algorithms we have created because as of early 2024, large language models (LLMs), which I discuss further, such as ChatGPT, seem to be getting distracted by irrelevant or even corrupted data at an increasing rate, resulting in worthless output.[12]

Distributed representations to arrive at a whole

By now you will have realized that humans sometimes use strange neural paths to arrive at an idea without realizing what is going on up there. With this last example of how humans and machines learn very similarly, I link to the different types and complexity of AI that I will explain in the following sections.

Distributed representations basically means that we learn by looking at many examples and recognizing common things. It helps us understand and recognize what something is, even when we have never seen it before.

As such, while you can explain to a child hundreds of times what a cat is by saying 'A cat has four legs, a tail, ears and a moustache', I doubt they would be able to tell a dog from a cat. No, as humans we learn what a cat is by seeing a lot of cats. Every time we see a cat, we remember its features, such as the shape of its ears and whiskers. So, when we see a new animal with those similar features, we think it is also a cat.

AI learns in a similar way, which is called machine learning. This *old* technique still underpins many innovations. It looks at many pictures of cats and notices that they have common things like ears and whiskers. It uses this 'distributed' information to understand what a cat is. When it sees a new animal with similar features, it can say, 'This could be a cat!'

The above comparisons indicate that the functioning of the artificial brain is enormously similar to that of the human brain. Of course, this is not surprising, since the bright minds at the Dartmouth Conference used the workings of the human brain as an example. But that is also exactly where the limits and dangers of AI lie. Admit it, humans are not exactly flawless examples when it comes to general intelligence and ethical values.

The limits of human-brain-based AI

So, our own grey matter is the inspiration for creating AI. Yet, although this is very interesting to know, because of this, there are also challenges inherent in developing these systems further. Consider the complexity of the human brain, which consists of about 100 billion neurons, which are the building blocks of the brain. These neurons have about 600 trillion synaptic connections. Each neuron has an average of 10,000 of these connections with other neurons. What makes it even more complicated is that these connections are constantly communicating with each other in a dynamic and unpredictable way. So, it is quite a daunting challenge to try to build AI systems that are as smart as the human brain. To do this, we would have to use very complicated mathematical models that are challenging even for quantum computers. It is like trying to solve a huge and complex puzzle whose pieces are constantly changing shape.

Besides the computational power of our brains, which were already trained through our DNA, training large models like the LLMs I describe further is based on incredible amounts of data. As such, ChatGPT4, developed by OpenAI, already requires 47 gigabytes of data. By comparison, its predecessor, GPT3, was trained on 17 gigabytes of data, which is about three orders of magnitude lower. Imagine how much GPT5 will be trained on. Thinking back to Moore's, Gilder's and Metcalfe's laws this would still increase exponentially. This puts a lot of emphasis on the data on which these systems can still be trained. Because, as you can already notice with many systems, the output is far from what we expect from them.

The above also requires ever-increasing computing power, which raises energy-efficiency problems in supercomputers that train AI, such as OpenAI. Consequently, there is growing concern about the ecological impact of training AI models at this scale. In response, researchers and organizations are working on methods to make AI training more energy efficient. This includes developing more energy-efficient hardware, optimizing algorithms for energy efficiency and using renewable energy sources to generate the electricity for these supercomputers. The aim is to reduce the carbon footprint of AI training while maintaining the power of advanced AI systems.

In conclusion, the relationship between human intelligence and AI is profound. Humans have created AI in their own image and likeness, meaning they have transformed their own thinking skills and ways of learning into complex algorithms and systems. This transformation has led to exciting innovations, but also to several challenges and limitations that need to be overcome to realize the full potential of human-brain-inspired AI. The relationship between human intelligence and AI continues to evolve, and understanding these dynamics will help us further develop AI in the future.

The evolution of AI

From the above, we know that AI is based on the neuroscience of the human brain in the ways that it stores information, retrieves knowledge and learns. Yet, the development of AI since the Dartmouth Conference of 1956 has not always been successful. At times, there was even a so-called AI winter, where interest and funding for AI research seemed to dry up. Without going into too much detail, and mainly to underline applicability with respect to learning in further chapters, I would like to give insight into some historical milestones and terminology related to AI.

Weak AI or artificial narrow intelligence

When we go back to the first experiments with AI, the algorithm did no more than catalogue or process a set of data based on human-written instructions. This is weak AI, as we know from recognition software being able to tell dogs and cats apart. In these rule-based systems, the intelligent technology does not take action if it is not predefined. But make no mistake, even if it is weak in AI terms, that does not mean that compared to the human brain's capabilities, it is not already far beyond what you and I can do.

Indeed, weak does not refer to the computational power or complexity of the algorithms but rather to the diversity of tasks artificial narrow intelligence (ANI) can handle. For example, ANI is only capable of performing human tasks or commands in a field such as chess. As such, you may remember Deep Blue, the computer that beat chess champion Garry Kasparov in 1996.[13] Although Deep Blue could evaluate 200 million chess positions per second, that was all it could do. Another example is that of the age-old Asian strategic board game Go. The computing power of this one is enormous and beyond the limits of the human brain when you know that the number of possible moves is 10,700. Lee Sedol, however, was convinced that computing power alone would in not hold up against human competence. Yet AlphaGO beat him in no less than four out of five games in the Deepmind

Challenge match in 2016. As humans, Kasparov and Sedol may be considered extremely intelligent, but they still lost to 'weak AI'.[14]

Today, we see a lot of ANI in science, business and healthcare for intelligent solutions that are good at one specific task. I know, for example, a pathologist who has had his judgement validated or tested by ANI for years. Weak AI is also very useful for detecting anomalies in production processes and finding patterns in business data – tasks that we as humans find too boring and that we therefore like to pass on to an artificial colleague.

Strong AI or artificial general intelligence

This type of AI is one of two types of strong AI. Capable of performing multiple tasks, this AI crosses the line where machines become more like humans. Artificial general intelligence (AGI) can also make its own decisions and learn without human input.

We can endlessly divide this category of strong AI into the different applications they are developed for and the similarities they have with humans. Below, I list a few that are relevant to developing or supporting your learning mindset in the following chapters. However, I know that some new ones have probably already been developed since writing this. Also, note that the terms I explain below to clarify further examples in the book sometimes overlap.

Machine learning (ML) with reinforced learning techniques is an evolution that expands on the foundation of weak AI. The important distinction is in the term 'learning'. The system learns based on the data it processes and adapts itself without any instructions from the programmer. This method is similar to how humans learn through operant conditioning by assigning a reward or punishment when the machine does something right or wrong. This allows it to respond to situations that could not be anticipated beforehand, like a human who learns by doing. A very interesting example of this is that of the computer Libratus,who won a lengthy poker game.[15] The fact that poker is often associated with human emotions and the interpretation of human expressions makes it even more fascinating.

The AI robot Libratus, developed by the US university Carnegie Mellon, won its first ever poker tournament against professional human players on 31 January 2017. Libratus won over $1.7 million in chips after an impressive and very long game of no-limits Texas hold'em. It took 19 days and 120,000 rounds! You would think it was a battle of exhaustion that the four human opponents could not physically handle. No, Libratus won through 'a higher form of intelligence'. And this is what makes it interesting. Unlike other games, poker could not build on previous data, and so Libratus had to keep re-learning with an improved algorithmic approach to the game. This allowed him to handle imperfect or hidden information better than humans. It sounds scary that even then, AI could outsmart us as humans. However, the reality is no longer science fiction.

According to Noam Brown, the PhD student who co-developed the algorithm for Libratus, they did not 'teach' the machine how to play poker. Instead, Brown gave it the rules and instructed it to 'learn by itself'. The bot started playing randomly, but in the course of playing, trillions of hands allowed it to refine its approach and arrive at a winning strategy. However, he did not do this alone but was helped by Brown. Late every day, after the poker game was over, Libratus was connected to the Bridges computer at the Pittsburgh Supercomputer Centre to run algorithms to improve strategy overnight. In the morning, Brown would spend two hours getting the newly improved bot working again. Looking at the collaboration that Brown and Libratus had while having to learn from imperfect information opens up many possibilities for human–machine partnerships.

Deep learning and neural networks

Neural networks support humans' complex mode of reasoning. Our brains, as discussed in the previous chapter, are made up of neural networks of layers of neurons. They do nothing but transmit information from one layer of neurons to another. This is exactly what machine learning does by linking together as many layers of datasets as possible. The more layers, the deeper the system, and hence the term 'deep learning'.

How is the best way to imagine this, and how is this relevant for you if you want to learn from online media and not be influenced by it? Maybe you have Netflix or another streaming service that suggests to you, based on the data you have entered, what movies are relevant to you. To do this, it relies on several layers of datasets that are developed after you have provided the initial basic info to feed the algorithm. However, at Netflix, after a few weeks, you still get those recommendations that are totally irrelevant and certainly not surprising at all. In contrast, TikTok, known as one of the most advanced algorithms for social media, can make connections between many more neural networks. It constantly replenishes these with new knowledge gained from reinforced learning techniques. As a result, you may suddenly come across content you would otherwise never have reached because you did not know it could be relevant. This is a great example of how learning ecosystems can evolve from human-2-human to interest-2-interest through AI.

However, deep learning techniques in applications like TikTok can also be dangerous if you don't understand the implications of the data it feeds you with. How you can steer the algorithm to what interests you and to support lean learning I explain in Part Two of this book.

Autonomous AI and swarm intelligence

Another type of strong AI that certainly fascinates me is that of spontaneous autonomous swarm intelligence. This technology enables efficient and adaptive collaboration between autonomous systems. This model is inspired by nature or swarm-intelligent animals and insects that are able to interact with each other and the environment in a decentralized and self-organized manner. I think it can also be inspiring for collaborative learning from a collective learning mindset stimulated by mirror neurons, as I explain in Part Three.

Autonomous swarm intelligence technology equips multiple autonomous agents, such as robots and drones, with the intelligence of spontaneous collaboration. In doing so, they can organize co-operative tactics, multi-objective governance and control and automatic discovery. They have a collective contextual awareness and distributed AI that can be used for many purposes through local communication and collaboration between humans and swarms. An example of this can be found in traffic control or the port of Antwerp-Brugges, where they deploy drones for safety monitoring and feeding their digital twin with live data. There are also great examples in logistics, agriculture and, yes, also in defence. Yet we should not forget that there are also risks involved, as I describe in the last part of this chapter.

Spontaneous autonomous swarm intelligence is one of the many applications that I will follow in the coming years, especially with the ability to increase machine learning of swarm intelligence. Here, I am already looking at multi-agent reinforcement learning (MARL) as an interesting research area in AI, particularly when looking at the symbiosis between artificial and natural intelligence.

Generative AI

AI has been all over the news since 2022, mainly due to the breakthrough of generative AI with the popular ChatGPT, developed by OpenAI. Chatbots are not new, however, as the first one, Eliza, was developed at MIT in 1966 by Professor Joseph Weizenbaum, who later, remarkably, turned against the development of AI. It wasn't until 2014, with the introduction of generative adversarial networks, or GANs, a type of machine learning algorithm, that generative AI could convincingly create authentic but fake images, videos and audio of real people.[16]

When thinking about the possibilities that this offers, and also the impact on the future of work which I discuss in Part Two, it is relevant to know what it can do right, and what it cannot, especially as more and more integrations take place in tools we use every day such as search engines, office applications and social media platforms.

WHAT IS GENERATIVE AI?

In generative AI, the user gives a command or asks a question. The input is almost always text based. An AI model interprets the task and generates content based on the task. The basis for that created content is a very extensive set of data with which the generative model has been trained. So, the outcome or answer resembles that training data. Because of this principle, generative models can:

- Generate texts, based on a complex task, which appear persuasive and make use of a given context. Here, of course, ChatGPT is currently the best known but think also of Bard, Google's AI chatbot, and Microsoft's Bing Chat.

- Generate images based on description with, for example, DALL-E 2, Midjourney, Craiyon or Imagen.

- Generate music based on the description of a particular style of music and its tempo. Examples include Amper Music, AIVA, Soundful and Ectrett Music.

- Instantly translate texts, with the possible adaptation of a personal voice that makes it appear as if you are listening to the speaker themself at a conference, as with ElevenLabs.

- Generate code for computer programs which will soon make programmers revise their skills. The tools are endless, including GitHub Copilot, Replit GhostWriter, Amazon CodeWhisperer, Cody by Sourcegraph and AskCodi.

- Design new materials or co-develop new medicines.

Today possibilities already seem endless; however, every day I see new applications popping up. Ignoring them, thinking that your job and your life will not be drastically challenged by these tools, is no longer possible. Learning, experimenting and adapting to new possibilities is the basis of the learning mindset that will help you thrive in the future.

GENERATIVE AI WITH HUMAN LANGUAGE AS CONTROL

Using human language to drive technology makes human–machine interaction increasingly natural and accessible. Given the hype around this at the time I am writing this, there will be additional focus further in this book on its applicability to nurture the learning mindset and prepare you for the future of work. For this, I will discuss tools like ChatGPT, as well as the integration of generative AI as LLMs deployed in learning ecosystems to achieve lean learning. Without going into too much detail, I will give a brief introduction to the terminology below so you can join the conversation on this topic yourself.

Generative AI, as mentioned, is always based on human text input and is often called natural language processing (NLP). In the context of this book, which focuses on learning and also coaching, I want to stress that it is not the same as neuro-linguistic programming (NLP)[17] which has its origins in psychology from a study of successful behaviour, especially in the area of successfully learning to communicate. NLP is all about people's thinking, feeling and acting (behaviour). Yet, as you can see, there are similarities there too. Communicating successfully with AI and using clear prompts that the system understands are as important as communicating clearly with your flesh-and-blood colleague.

Another term you will often hear is that of a large language model (LLM). This term refers to a deep learning algorithm that can perform a variety of NLP tasks. Large models use transformer models and are trained with huge datasets – hence large. In addition, we see that these models are called neural networks (NNs), because they are inspired by the human brain and work with a network of nodes that are layered, just like human neurons.

Like the human brain, LLMs need to be pre-trained and then refined so that they can solve problems such as text classification, answering questions, summarizing documents and generating text. Their problem-solving capabilities can be applied to specific areas they are trained on such as healthcare, finance, entertainment, etc. However, they are not yet the broadly applicable ASI, which I explain further.

What LLMs can do is work much faster and with many more parameters than you and I can. These parameters, similar to memories, are collected by the model as it learns from training. The amount of data available to the LLM is the memory or knowledge database of the model.

Several architectures for LLMs already exist and it is not relevant to name them all, yet in relation to human learning, the transformation model is interesting to share. A transformer model, which is the most common architecture of an LLM, consists of an encoder and a decoder. A transformer model processes data by tokenizing the input and simultaneously performing mathematical comparisons to discover relationships between tokens. This allows the computer to see the patterns that a human would see if given the same query. Of course, computers are often much more effective and efficient, which is why in many jobs, people already rely on these systems.

What distinguishes transformer models from other models is that they work with self-attention mechanisms, allowing the model to learn faster than traditional models, such as models with long-term memory. Self-attention allows the transformer model to consider different parts of the sequence or the whole context of a sentence to generate predictions. In other words, you as a human hardly need think anymore what to prompt because the machine already knows what you want.

In any case, the future of AGI models like LLMs is promising, even though they are not always reliable. As such, there are still errors in the results, and bias cannot be ruled out in some cases, but we are getting there. Chatbots and digital virtual assistants are improving at having conversations and can already respond seemingly emotionally to direct stimuli. Some researchers have to activate these trained robots to read human emotions. This seems exciting and scary at the same time. Yet AI reading and producing emotional responses does not necessarily mean AI can become emotional. As humans, we still have those competencies, like empathy and others that I describe in Part Two, that assure us distinctiveness as colleagues and human beings.

ARTIFICIAL SUPER INTELLIGENCE OR THE SINGULARITY

I say it often: the future is catching up with us! It seems like the sci-fi films and novels of Jules Vernes and Isaac Asimov serve as inspiration for developing innovations like human robots living among us without knowing themselves to be synthetic, as in the romantic fiction film *Zoe* directed by Drake Doremus in 2018.[18]

When this happens, we are talking about the technical singularity, or the moment when the machine equals or overpowers humans in all aspects. This is the second type of strong AI, artificial super intelligence (ASI). ASI models are machines that are smarter, wiser and more creative than humans. However, this type of AI will only exist in science fiction for some time. Scientists would not dream of it because of all the potential dangers and ethical restrictions. As I cite in the last part of this chapter, precautions are being taken worldwide to keep these developments from getting out of hand. Still, although this type of strong AI cannot yet be made, scientists are making progress in a few different mind-blowing areas.

Some mind-blowing innovations

As mentioned previously, human thinking and learning are quite similar. But what if we go a step further and make the symbiosis between humans and AI a reality?

The following examples seem, again, to come from a sci-fi movie, yet they are a reality in today's scientific research fields. What is more, some of the mind-blowing innovations I share are to be successfully tested on humans. Why am I sharing this? On the one hand, I like to provoke so that you understand that innovations are coming at us hyper fast. On the other hand, I want to seek added value in innovations that help us work, live and learn, while respecting the boundaries of humanity and ethics.

Brain–computer interfaces (BCIs)

Imagine a chip in your brain that gives you superhuman abilities beyond the reach of your own brain. It is, of course, very reminiscent of the American sci-fi film *Lucy* I previously mentioned. Lucy, played by Scarlett Johansonn, was surgically implanted with a package containing a powerful chemical. After this implant leaks into her system, she gains superhuman abilities, including telekinesis and telepathy.

Unlocking these superhuman powers is not currently feasible, nor are they the goal of current research and self-testing with neuroprosthetics or invasive BCIs. Yet recently, partly due to the rapid evolutions in generative AI, a lot has moved forward when it comes to the possibilities that neuroscience and computer science have to offer. As such, the symbiosis between humans and machines is becoming a reality.

I'm going to give you a few examples that might scare you, but do try to be positive and curious. When looking at innovations, try to keep an open mind, looking for the added value these applications can bring to you or the people around you. To keep it clear, I will categorize BCIs based on how they integrate your brain through invasive techniques, semi-invasive techniques and through wearables. But first, a quick look back into the history of these fascinating developments, which have suddenly become more familiar since the launch of Elon Musk's Neuralink in 2016.[19]

The history of BCIs goes back to 1924. For as long as there were computers, there were scientists trying to figure out how to control them with their minds. It all started with German psychologist Hans Berger in his quest to demonstrate telepathy.[20] Through this, he discovered that the human brain generated electrical activity that he could demonstrate through electroencephalography (EEG). In-depth research into BCIs did not start until the 1970s at the US university UCLA by Professor Jacques Vidal, who thus also became the inventor of the term 'brain–computer interface'.

The first implementation in a human occurred as early as 1998 with a breakthrough by Phil Kennedy implanting the first invasive BCI in a human – more precisely, a Vietnam veteran who had suffered a stroke.[21] Much later, in 2004, came the first certain breakthroughs when Matt Nagle became the first to receive an implanted invasive BCI system to restore functions after paralysis, a pioneering experiment for people with quadriplegia.[22] This was followed by a wave of BCI research in the 2000s, culminating in two pioneering studies published in Nature in 2012 that showed how BCI systems could enable neural arm control and restore arm movement after paralysis.[23] Today, we see that studies related to BCIs are mainly looking to treat neurodegenerative conditions such as paralysis, epilepsy, brain injury, amyotrophic lateral sclerosis (ALS), Parkinson's disease and Alzheimer's disease.

These positive developments are opening up prospects for a huge number of people and, as the global population ages, the demand for invasive BCIs and their potential applications is likely to increase.

Will Captain Kirk's brainwave translator soon be a reality?

Developments with (semi)-invasive BCIs have increased dramatically in recent years, with more successes achieved with tiny electrodes that talk and listen to our brains. These tiny electrodes, which, due to the electrical nature of the brain, hear certain groups of neurons talking to each other, are like tiny microphones. Indeed, they do not decode the entire brain simultaneously but rather the language of those specific neurons of a particular person. It is important to understand before you let ghost stories or fake news scare you that there are already developments that can read all your thoughts. Everyone has their own 'thought language' and all neurons have their way of communicating.

Neural decoding has become very successful in recent years due to the advances made with generative AI and the augmented computing power paired with it. Nevertheless, organizations still focus on those neurons they can decode or translate most easily. So, these are in those brain regions where the above neurological disorders were identified.

Worldwide, various studies and tests are carried out for BCIs, all with their unique approach. With a few examples, the possibilities are listed below, broken down according to how they connect to your brain:

- **Invasive BCIs** such as Neuralink require surgery where electrodes are implanted under the scalp to transmit brain signals. The main advantage is that it provides a more accurate measurement. However, it goes without saying that the side effects of the surgery are a major drawback to this development. After surgery, scar tissue may form that can weaken brain signals. Moreover, according to some researchers, the body may not accept the electrodes once implanted, which can cause medical complications.

- **Semi-invasive BCIs** or partially invasive BCI devices, such as those used at Precision Neuroscience and Synchron, are also implanted in the skull. Yet they rest outside the brain rather than in the grey matter. So, they have a lower risk of forming scar tissue in the brain than fully invasive BCIs.

Neuralink is probably the best-known player in an already highly competitive market in which trillions are being invested. Of course, the fame of Neuralink's founder plays a role here and it is far from being the most advanced solution. Elon Musk, who, along with eight others, including Max Hodak and Benjamin Rapoport, founded Neuralink in 2016, came into the press years ago for implanting monkeys with a chip, after which he taught them to play the game of Pong via thoughts. In September 2023, Neuralink became one of the first Food and Drug Administration (FDA) approvals to conduct clinical trials on humans.

Interestingly, Musk's short-term goal was to develop advanced brain devices to treat major brain-related diseases. However, that was not the only thing Musk had in mind. His long-term vision did focus on the fusion of humans and AI. And, if you are equally fond of sci-fi movies, it is nice to know that Musk was inspired by the science fiction concept of neural lace from Iain M. Banks' *The Culture* series.[24]

Musk may have paved the way in 2016 to make BCIs known to a slightly wider audience, but his start-up was not always successful. Certainly not when it came to retaining talent. As such, he lost almost all eight of his co-founders, including Benjamin Rapoport, who, along with Michael Mager, competed with Neuralink in 2021 when he founded Precision Neuroscience. With the Layer 7 Cortical Interface, they developed a platform consisting of microfabricated electrode arrays, in-house designed microelectronics and advanced ML software.[25] The major difference from Neuralink is that the Layer 7 Cortical Interface is one-fifth the thickness of a human hair, and surgeons apply it to patients' heads with a tiny incision. This contrasts with Neuralink's chip, which uses an in-house developed robot to surgically make a hole in your skull to insert a coin-sized chip into your brain. The risk with precision software is, therefore, much lower because it is minimally invasive. The procedure is also reversible. This means a patient can change her mind without any problems, or upgrade to a newer model.

The first target group for the Layer 7 Cortical Interface is for people with all kinds of limb paralysis disorders, but also, for example, aphasia, which allows people who can no longer talk to communicate with thoughts. It seems a small step to use thoughts to control computers or social media.

A third start-up in the long list of organizations investing in BCIs is Synchron. This originally Australian company, founded back in 2012, is focusing on endovascular BCIs. In other words, not surgery in the brain but a Stentrode introduced into the body through the bloodstream.[26] The company, like many others, received US approval in late 2023 to conduct tests on humans. Synchron designed a neuroprosthesis to restore motor signalling to control digital devices for people with severe motor impairments to perform daily tasks such as texting, emailing, online shopping and telehealth services. In the future, they see potential with this implantable endovascular neuromodulation therapy to diagnose and treat nervous system disorders, including Parkinson's disease, epilepsy, depression and high blood pressure.

It is obviously frightening when you hear some sci-fi stories, but know that it will undoubtedly be a long time before these mind translation systems are trained and programmed to decode all thoughts. Let alone when we can talk to each other, and aliens like in *Star Trek* with a universal brainwave translator. But should you have an anxiety attack now, know that BCI is also being developed to counteract anxiety attacks.

Non-invasive brain interfaces and wearables challenge our mental privacy

The (semi-) invasive brain interfaces I cite above seem futuristic and perhaps scary, but know that most forms of BCI are non-invasive and are already very widespread. BCIs are placed against the skull but are not connected to the brain. This makes them less powerful because the bone tissue of the skull deflects and distorts the signals. Still, this form of BCI already has many possibilities in terms of learning, such as attention, which I will discuss in the next chapter. But first a few other BCIs that could potentially excite your brain.

The first example, developed in 2018 by Arnav Kapur, a Delhi-born student at MIT, aims to change the relationship between humans and machines. According to MIT, 'AlterEgo' is a non-invasive, wearable, peripheral neural interface. It allows users to 'converse in natural language with machines, artificial intelligence (AI) assistants, services without opening their mouths and without externally observable movements.[27] All they need to do to communicate with words is to speak to them internally.

According to the inventors, the initiative is primarily for people with speech problems, such as those with ALS and MS (multiple sclerosis), among other diseases. In addition, according to the institute, it has the potential to improve intellect and abilities while smoothly integrating computers into people's daily lives as their 'second self' (hence the term AlterEgo).

But it can all be much simpler: just think of fMRI. This long-existing technology, where you are put into a scanner (present in most hospitals), takes coarse, colourful snapshots of the brain in action. While this specialized type of magnetic resonance imaging has transformed cognitive neuroscience, it is not a mind-reader. It is a fable to believe that neuroscientists look at a brain scan and say what someone in the scanner saw, heard or thought. Yet, here too, experiments are being conducted that attempt to decode the brain through non-invasive techniques.

Researchers have already made great progress by combining the ability of fMRI to monitor neural activity with the predictive power of LLMs similar to those used in invasive BCIs. This has resulted in an AI decoder that can reproduce with a surprising degree of accuracy the stories someone in the scanner has heard or imagined. The decoder could even guess the story behind a short film someone watched, albeit with less accuracy.[28] Of course, the above experiments are not intended to translate stories and images from someone's brain. Researchers' main intention is to provide answers for people with neurological disorders by decoding brains.

This is very exciting of course, and it could be even easier via wearables we have been using for years such as sensors to record our heart rate, breathing, steps and sleep. It seems our brains will have no privacy either.[29] An avalanche of brain-tracking devices – earbuds, headphones, headbands, watches and even tattoos – will soon hit the market. These innovations seem to be changing our lives ever more measurably and, according to some, threaten to invade the privacy of our brains.

Not surprisingly, tech titans like Meta, Snap, Microsoft and Apple are already investing heavily in brain wearables, by trying to build brain sensors into smartwatches, earbuds, headsets and sleep devices. In doing so, they claim that the integration of such sensors into our daily lives will revolutionize healthcare. With this, like invasive BCIs, they target neurological disorders more specifically by enabling early diagnosis and personalized treatment of conditions such as depression, epilepsy and even cognitive decline.

It doesn't stop there. Some tech titans claim that brain sensors in wearables would help us meditate, focus, learn and even communicate with seamless technological telepathy. Imagine using your Google Glasses or Meta Ray-Bans to harness the power of thoughts and emotions by interacting with augmented reality (AR) and virtual reality (VR). I would find it interesting to type this book with my thoughts on virtual keyboards. Or, if I am really allowed to dream of a nice innovation, I can dream of the book and process it in my sleep. It reminds me of the experiments I did as a child to learn in my sleep by putting a book under my pillow, as I mentioned in Chapter 1.

Lab-grown brains, the latest step towards cyborgs?

If you think it all can't get any crazier, I want to share another mind-blowing study where brains are simply grown in a lab. Indeed, the next step in brain labs is 'organoid intelligence'.[30]

It seems out of a sci-fi movie, yet it is reality that Cortical Labs in Melbourne, Australia, has now developed a DishBrain that they have taught to play the game of Pong via reinforced learning techniques. DishBrain, made from clusters of neurons grown in the lab from about 800,000 human stem cells, was connected to hard silicon to create what is described as a biological intelligence operating system (biOS). This 'human' chip was then linked to a computer, which allows it to both detect electrical signals produced by neurons and deliver electrical signals to them.

Why did they want to do this? Well, in their own words, it was part of an attempt to understand how the brain learns and how we can make computers more intelligent by understanding how living brain cells acquire this kind of intelligence. And even though the results were not overwhelming, and DishBrain missed the ball in Pong mostly, Cortical Labs' researchers believe the results point to a future where biology helps computers become more intelligent by changing how they learn. Although, according to many experts and my beliefs, that future still seems very far away.

But far away or not, it still gives food for thought: how far are we willing to go and when is the line? When is it still ethically correct? What are the possible risks associated with more far-reaching innovations? And should we already be setting out guidelines to contain future doom scenarios?

Ethical impact and risk of AI-powered innovations

In this chapter, I have discussed increasingly rapid developments, with AI increasingly invading our lives. Couple this with innovations that link our brains to machines and you would think of Asimov for a good reason. As far back as 75 years ago, Isaac Asimov, author and professor of biochemistry at Boston University, raised the potential dangers regarding human interactions with robots. Regarding these dangers, he published 'three laws' to protect humans in his 1942 short story 'Runaround':[31]

1 A robot must not injure a human or, by doing nothing, endanger a human.

2 A robot must obey people's commands, except when those commands violate the first law.

3 A robot must protect its own existence as long as that protection does not violate the first or second law.

Of course, when Asimov talked about robots, he was not thinking of AI, but rather androids or human-like robots. He imagined a world where these human-like robots would behave like servants and require a set of programming rules to prevent them from doing harm. Yet, in the 75 years since the story with its ethical guidelines was published, significant technological advances have been made, and the need for frameworks has, according to many, become pressing.

Policies and frameworks

When it comes to data privacy, a wave of new regional regulations has been developed since May 2018, aimed at making our digital experiences safer. As such, there is GDPR (Europe's General Data Protection Regulations), CCPA (California Consumer Privacy Act), LGPD (Brazil's Lei Geral de Proteção de Dados) and POPI (South Africa's Protection of Personal Information), but when it comes to rules regarding the use of AI and the ethical issues surrounding it, there is still little to report.

Ursula von der Leyen also agrees that an ethical framework is needed or should already have been in place. As president of the European Commission, she presented a proposal for a regulation of the European Parliament and the Council laying down harmonized rules on AI (Artificial Intelligence Act) and amending certain legislative acts of the Union on 21 February 2021. With this proposal, the president wanted the European Commission to develop legislation for a co-ordinated European approach to the human and ethical implications of AI.

In response, the Commission published the 'White paper on artificial intelligence – a European approach based on excellence and trust'. This white paper outlines policy options to achieve the twin objectives of facilitating the uptake of AI and addressing the risks associated with certain applications of such technology. This proposal aims to achieve the second objective of developing an ecosystem of trust by proposing a legal framework for trusted AI. Based on EU values and fundamental rights, the proposal aims to give people and other users the confidence to embrace AI-based solutions and encourage businesses to develop them. AI should be a tool for people and a positive force in society, aiming to increase human well-being. The rules for AI applications available on the Union market or otherwise affecting individuals in the Union should therefore be human-centric. The public should have confidence that the technology is being used in a safe manner, in accordance with the law and respecting fundamental rights.

More recently, around late 2023, the rapid rise and spread of generative AI like ChatGPT prompted voices worldwide to call for more rules and a framework. Yet the motivation of some, like Elon Musk, was not always for the common good. He wanted a temporary halt to developments related to generative AI in 2023, but, in the meantime, he was working on his own company, xAI, which launched the chatbot Grok in November 2023. I therefore dare to question his ethical compass as he had just pleaded for more transparency at the AI Safety Summit.

This international conference on the safety and regulation of AI was perhaps the first big step towards more rules and transparency. It was held on 1 and 2 November at Bletchley Park, Milton Keynes, UK. This was not coincidentally, as Bletchley Park was also the place where, during World War II, mathematicians and codebreakers like Alan Turing managed to decipher coded messages on the Enigma machine.

The outcomes of this summit are not significant as I write this, yet 28 countries at the summit, including the US and China, and also the EU, signed the agreement known as the Bletchley Declaration. It calls for greater international co-operation to manage the challenges and risks of AI. They emphasized regulating 'Frontier AI' or the latest and most powerful AI systems. The summit naturally zoomed in on the potential use of AI for terrorism, criminal activities and warfare as well as existential risks to humanity as a whole.

Not much after this summit, US President Joe Biden signed an executive order requiring AI developers in the US to share security results with the US government. For this, he also announced the creation of a US AI security institute, as part of the National Institute of Standards and Technology. However, the question I wonder about is what the intention of this institute is, and whether that information belongs in government hands.

We all have a responsibility to a human-centric society

I believe that as human beings, we all have a responsibility that starts with ourselves. We, but certainly the executives of organizations that are leading the way in these innovations, must have our own ethical charter and pursue the values of a human-centric society. Therefore, I would like to provide some guidelines that can be considered from the perspective of social responsibility:

- **Explainability.** Organizations using AI should be able to explain the source data, the expected results and what the algorithms do to get there. This is necessary so that when there is damage, it can be traced back to a cause and lessons learned.

- **Honesty and bias.** It seems obvious, but with data collection that contains personally identifiable information, it is extremely important to ensure that there is no racial, gender or ethnic bias or other factors that do not belong in an inclusive society.

- **Abuse.** The security of AI will be a major challenge, so whether the AI algorithms can be used for other non-ethical projects should be analysed from the development phase. All possible situations and security measures should be taken to mitigate this.

- **Accountability.** When something goes wrong, we want to assign blame and this is no different with AI, especially when the outcome can be catastrophic, as with self-driving cars. The ethical question of who is better placed to make the 'right' choice in an impossible life-or-death decision has been asked for many years, as has the question of who is responsible when things go wrong – the driver who has handed over the wheel to AI or the creator of the car?

This chapter shows that technology is becoming increasingly intelligent and this affects how we as humans interact with it. Frameworks and agreements are important, but, above all, they need more support for people who see the future of work and learning and whose lives are drastically impacted by this development. A learning mindset in which we deploy human competencies, not to get overwhelmed but to thrive together with these innovations, is therefore an important topic in the second part of this book.

Endnotes

1   M Roser, H Ritchie and E Mathieu. What is Moore's law?, Our World in Data, 28 March 2023, ourworldindata.org/moores-law (archived at https://perma. cc/8U8A-6TD2)

2   C Campbell. Moore's law and the chess board, Campbell Academy, 11 November 2020, www.campbellacademy.co.uk/blog/moores-law-and-the-chess-board (archived at https://perma.cc/35ME-URJR)

3   M Shahbandeh. World production volume of milled rice from 2008/2009 to 2023/24, Statista, 31 January 2024, www.statista.com/statistics/271972/world-husked-rice-production-volume-since-2008/ (archived at https://perma. cc/Y48J-HV6N)

4   Gilder's law, CIO Wiki, 8 March 2024, cio-wiki.org/wiki/Gilder%27s_Law (archived at https://perma.cc/XNN2-FJDY)

5   M Rouse. Metcalfe's law, Techopedia, 28 May 2019, www.techopedia.com/
    definition/29066/metcalfes-law (archived at https://perma.cc/BG4S-F284)

6   A Sklencar. 20 BeReal stats you need to know, Online Optimism, April 2024,
    www.onlineoptimism.com/blog/bereal-stats-app-figures-data-be-real-numbers-
    to-know/#:~:text=How%20many%20daily%20active%20users%20does%20
    BeReal%20App%20have%3F,in%20the%20last%20year9 (archived at
    https://perma.cc/L93P-XN9H)

7   Artificial intelligence coined at Dartmouth, home.dartmouth.edu/about/
    artificial-intelligence-ai-coined-dartmouth (archived at https://perma.cc/
    HT8H-PMP4)

8   AI Safety Summit 2023, www.aisafetysummit.gov.uk/#:~:text=1st%20and%20
    2nd%20November%202023%20at%20Bletchley%20Park&text=The%20
    UK%20hosted%20the%20first,frontier%20AI%20around%20the%20world
    (archived at https://perma.cc/5GPA-9C65)

9   G Oppy and D Dowe. The Turing test, Stanford Encyclopedia of Philosophy,
    revised 4 October 2021, plato.stanford.edu/entries/turing-test/ (archived at
    https://perma.cc/TPS4-EGT4)

10 Editors of Encyclopaedia Britannica. Norbert Wiener, Encyclopaedia
    Britannica, 16 April 2024, www.britannica.com/biography/Norbert-Wiener
    (archived at https://perma.cc/J2Z5-CDHA)

11 S Sieniutycz (2020) *Complexity and Complex Thermo-Economic Systems*,
    Elsevier, Amsterdam

12 Unexpected responses from ChatGPT, OpenAI Status History Atom, status.
    openai.com/incidents/ssg8fh7sfyz3 (archived at https://perma.cc/9N7A-3984)

13 Deep Blue, www.ibm.com/history/deep-blue (archived at https://perma.
    cc/3RRB-N72E)

14 AlphaGo, deepmind.google/technologies/alphago/ (archived at https://perma.
    cc/8LSJ-Q9DN)

15 C Metz. Inside Libratus, the poker AI that out-bluffed the best humans, *Wired*,
    1 February 2017, www.wired.com/2017/02/libratus/ (archived at https://
    perma.cc/2RWT-XYVU)

16 B Tarnoff. Weizenbaum's nightmares: How the inventor of the first chatbot
    turned against AI, *The Guardian*, 25 July 2023, www.theguardian.com/
    technology/2023/jul/25/joseph-weizenbaum-inventor-eliza-chatbot-turned-
    against-artificial-intelligence-ai (archived at https://perma.cc/BQ5E-7SVH)

17 J O'Connor and A Lages (2004) *Coaching with NLP How to be a Master
    Coach*, Element, London

18 *Zoe* (film), en.wikipedia.org/wiki/Zoe_(film) (archived at https://perma.
    cc/6R4P-RRVL)

19 I A Hamilton and B Nolan. Neuralink's first human patient has been revealed. Here's how we got here, *Business Insider*, updated 22 March 2024, www.businessinsider.com/neuralink-elon-musk-microchips-brains-ai-2021-2?r=US&IR=T (archived at https://perma.cc/J2K9-ATKJ)

20 L Sanders. How Hans Berger's quest for telepathy spurred modern brain science, *Science News*, 6 July 2021, www.sciencenews.org/article/hans-berger-telepathy-neuroscience-brain-eeg (archived at https://perma.cc/QQG9-585Y)

21 D Winters. The neurologist who hacked his brain – and almost lost his mind, *Wired*, 26 January 2016, www.wired.com/2016/01/phil-kennedy-mind-control-computer/ (archived at https://perma.cc/6VF3-FMV2)

22 Wikipedia, Matt Nagle, en.wikipedia.org/wiki/Matt_Nagle (archived at https://perma.cc/L2YU-8KV6)

23 C Ethier, E R Oby, M J Bauman and L E Miller. Restoration of grasp following paralysis through brain-controlled stimulation of muscles, *Nature*, 2012, 485 (7398), 368–71, doi.org/10.1038/nature10987 (archived at https://perma.cc/YX2V-Y7J4)

24 T Cross. The novelist who inspired Elon Musk, *The Economist*, 31 March 2017, www.economist.com/1843/2017/03/31/the-novelist-who-inspired-elon-musk (archived at https://perma.cc/8YYN-XYWE)

25 This Week in Startups. Brain–computer interfaces and the future of neural engineering with Dr Benjamin Rapoport | E1682, YouTube, www.youtube.com/watch?v=UTOLbK64F7k (archived at https://perma.cc/TCP8-PZKW)

26 Synchron Inc. Stentrode brain computer interface online in first two human patients, YouTube, www.youtube.com/watch?v=mm95r05hui0 (archived at https://perma.cc/3U4Z-B7MS)

27 T Ong. This wearable device can respond to your thoughts. *The Verge*, 6 April 2018, https://www.theverge.com/2018/4/6/17206100/alterego-device-respond-thoughts-mit-researchers-chess (archived at https://perma.cc/Z2BT-F2NE)

28 A Parshall. A brain scanner combined with an ai language model can provide a glimpse into your thoughts, *Scientific American*, 1 May 2023, www.scientificamerican.com/article/a-brain-scanner-combined-with-an-ai-language-model-can-provide-a-glimpse-into-your-thoughts/ (archived at https://perma.cc/BP2G-W9GH)

29 N A Farahany. Wearable brain devices will challenge our mental privacy, *Scientific American*, 27 March 2023, www.scientificamerican.com/article/wearable-brain-devices-will-challenge-our-mental-privacy/ (archived at https://perma.cc/JZD9-HNPT)

30 J Hamilton. Brain cells in a lab dish learn to play Pong – and offer a window onto intelligence, *NPR*, 14 October 2022, www.npr.org/sections/health-shots/2022/10/14/1128875298/brain-cells-neurons-learn-video-game-pong (archived at https://perma.cc/J47P-GT5X)

31 Editors of Encylopaedia Britannica. Three laws of robotics: concept by Asimov, Encyclopaedia Britannica, 5 April 2024, www.britannica.com/topic/Three-Laws-of-Robotics (archived at https://perma.cc/3Y45-T7RB)

PART TWO

Adopt a positive mindset to your personal learning

In Part One of this book, I imparted what learning and a learning mindset are. Learning is much more than studying or attending a training course: it includes techniques that often happen unconsciously and support you to navigate your life and work. I also encouraged you to think about the relationship you have, even if you are not aware of it, with innovations like AI, which are becoming increasingly prevalent.

I will refer to that knowledge in the following chapters to further develop your learning mindset, making you resilient to change and turning obstacles into opportunities. After this chapter, you can continue working towards a positive learning mindset that inspires others.

3

Now is your moment to embrace learning

Learning is what makes you happy[1] and open to change. It supports your mental health by firing your neurons when you have learnt something and, in the process, providing you with neurotransmitters that support your well-being. But learning is also necessary to keep you engaged as an active citizen in an increasingly digital society. We face a future where it is difficult to predict what the future of work will look like. Which jobs will remain and where will innovations using AI have the most impact? A learning mindset that positively and anticipatively embraces innovations will not only help you survive, but also ensure that you can help shape your future yourself.

Taking your future into your own hands is the ultimate goal of the learning mindset. Not just believing you can grow, but actively seeking continuous improvement by learning, unlearning, experimenting, failing and starting again. A learning mindset starts with yourself and even though it is sometimes difficult to detach from experiences which hindered learning in the past, you can develop a learning mindset at every stage of your life. What is more, the negative experiences or obstacles you faced in the past can actually add value if you turn them into opportunities, as I will demonstrate later.

A learning mindset starts with yourself and, if you take and embrace the first steps, you can grow faster and become nimble and resilient to change. With a learning mindset, you will be an inspiration to others because everything starts with you. So, you not only have a responsibility for yourself, but also to your environment. In what follows, I want to address the urgency of having a learning mindset and give you tips on how to turn your past experiences into strengths for the future.

The urgency of learning for the future of work

Annual analyses and predictions about the future of work and the expected impact of innovations on jobs are made by major consultancies and trend watchers. However, the trends are hardly surprising.[2] Trends fuelled by the United Nations' Sustainable Development Goals (SDGs),[3] economic and political drivers and, of course, the acceleration of innovations, among others, have an impact on job creation and destruction. Still, not surprisingly, not all studies agree on the ultimate net impact on the labour market. However, one thing is unanimous among the many analysts who recommend their report as the best predictor: there will be a shift in the expected skills and competences of the workforce at all levels, around the world.

To return to the Luddites' fear that machines would take over their jobs, as I said in Chapter 2, I can partly understand that. There is legitimate fear, but it should also not be exaggerated because it does not look like many jobs will disappear. However, there may be changes regarding their structure and specific tasks, and therefore employees will need different skills and competences.

The World Economic Forum (WEF) reports in Jobs of Tomorrow: Large Language Models and Jobs (2023) that 23 per cent of jobs worldwide will change in the next five years.[4] The report offers a structured analysis of the possible immediate short-term impact of LLMs on jobs. Yet I dare say that they have underestimated this short-term impact. In fact, as the report mentions that 62 per cent of total working time consists of tasks that can be automated by LLMs, I think the urgency is now. The widespread adoption of LLMs, such as ChatGPT, will significantly impact a wide spectrum of jobs.

When talking about physical and manual work, the WEF's Future of Jobs Survey shows that 34 per cent of all automatable tasks will be done by machines by 2027, while humans will do the remaining 66 per cent.[5] Interestingly, this increase is slower than predicted a few years ago. These are interesting figures, but in the light of a global study, you might naturally wonder how this compares globally, depending on the region you work in. Sharpening your critical competences when reading these reports is definitely an added value when you want to see how relevant they are to you.

According to these studies, physical and manual work is unlikely to be replaced by the machine anytime soon. However, there would be a huge shift in how manual tasks will be performed. So, it is not a replacement but an enhancement and higher efficiency through human–machine collaboration.

What also strikes me in the various studies I read year after year is that those competencies we once considered human, such as reasoning, communicating and co-ordinating, are nowhere really addressed. Yet it seems to me that with the added value and easy automation that AI has to offer, more and more benefits can be found in human–machine collaboration.

The WEF report above indicates that a whopping 75 per cent of global companies surveyed say it will lead to a major shift in the workforce. In other words, all these reports create a lot of data from many different queries, yet there is still a high degree of uncertainty. Within one survey, the different participants absolutely disagree, so what do these numbers say? Fifty per cent of organizations think investing in AI will lead to job growth and 25 per cent think it will lead to job losses. This may initially seem confusing, but I think we can agree on the impact of change and that ignoring it is not an option for anyone.

Lifelong learning for the future of work

There are also notable studies on the importance of lifelong learning. Just about all analyses recognize the crucial focus needed here to thrive as people, as employees and as organizations in the coming years. As such, 74 per cent of Millenials and Gen Z indicate that they are aware of the need for lifelong learning and that they will leave their employers in the coming years if they are not given enough opportunities to develop their skills and talents.[6] If you belong to this target group, then you already have a learning mindset and of course I am excited about that. But it is not just young people who feel the need to learn. Seventy per cent of those surveyed, according to a survey of 3,000 people by Amazon and Workplace Intelligence, say they do not feel prepared for the future of work. As such, the fear of insufficient skills and training is high.[7] According to this survey, nearly 80 per cent of workers are concerned that they have insufficient skills and 70 per cent that they have insufficient training to advance in their careers. Fifty-eight per cent believe their skills are not up to date since the pandemic.

In addition, Adobe's survey of nearly 10,000 people in eight global markets found that 80 per cent are concerned about at least one global problem that upsets them as much that it negatively affects their productivity and job satisfaction. Across all age groups, 44 per cent of workers in all age groups feel more anxious and discouraged than ever before.[8] In other words, not just learning but also well-being in general is an urgent problem for employees, organizations and society by extension.

In contrast, the results of the WEF survey among respondents/leaders show that they are confident in their current staff's development and learning capacities and thus do not think they need to make additional efforts. However, they are less optimistic about the availability of talent and their inability to attract talent. Talent that, according to previously mentioned research, they let leave because they did not provide them with sufficient training. And even though they recognize the inability to attract/retain talent as a major barrier to their own organization and the entire industry, they mostly revert to non-structural solutions that no longer fit this zeitgeist. As such, 48 per cent primarily want to invest in career and promotion processes for talent and 36 per cent indicate that higher salaries will win talent over. They have not understood the need to support learning and personal growth within these career and promotion processes, as only 34 per cent think that offering effective upskilling and retraining is the solution.

Learning is urgent at all levels, sectors and geographical regions. Learning starts with yourself, more ideally stimulated by your environment and the ecosystem you are part of. Nobody is solely responsible; learning is the responsibility of each individual, organizations and society.

Is school a good start for lifelong learning?

Maybe you have children for whom school seems like a torment that will never end. Or maybe you left school not so long ago and it seems that you didn't get much out of all those years in school that felt like a life sentence with no prospect of parole. I can understand the frustration because, in many cases, school is still an institution that does not focus on the future of work. The foundations and much of the current approach date back to the Prussians and the school reform around 1750 by Frederick the Great[9] and one can rightly question its relevance. The motivation and approach at the time stemmed from the need to pay for Frederick the Great's wars and ambitions, for which he needed better-educated citizens. But more than that, the aim was to turn them into good obedient citizens who would do what was expected.

Unfortunately, we still see far too much of this approach in today's school system, where knowledge transfer and obedience are paramount. In truth, schools kill creativity and label anyone who does not fit the picture, as Sir Ken Robinson claimed in his much-discussed Ted Talk.[10] Indeed, there is no denying that education has the challenge of preparing students for the future of work as early as primary school. A future that, for most pupils, is still 12 years away. At the start of their school career, however, children are still rough diamonds, untouched and possessing an abundance of those competences that make them human. Children in whom the intrinsic motivation and joy of learning is still present. So why do we condition students in such a way that when they leave school years later, they have largely lost those competences? I partly agree with Sir Ken Robinson that we could pay more attention within education to nurturing intrinsic motivation and human competences. However, I dare say that children have not lost them, and schools have not killed them. They may have faded into the background, but, as I will describe in further detail, the flame can be rekindled and neurons can fire up again and again.

I also like to take inspiration from Tim Leunig who, in his amazing Ted Talk, takes on the debate with Sir Ken Robinson.[11] Leunig argues from the principle of Enlightenment that schools cultivate creativity precisely by giving them the knowledge on which it depends. It may be a little far-fetched but still, with the examples he gives of inventions like the steam engine, it is certainly interesting to follow. As such, he argues that without basic knowledge, none of the inventions that often had a huge impact on society would have come about. In other words, maybe you are very creative and can come up with an innovation that solves all societal problems based on AI. But if you have no knowledge of how to build that algorithm, it remains just a creative idea.

Leunig does not clarify whether schools are killing creativity and other competences. Yet he provides a very important vision for survival in times of ever-faster innovation. I therefore follow his assertion that creativity without basic knowledge is not the holy grail for innovation.

A learning mindset without basic knowledge, without a method to apply cognitive thinking processes, is useless. Learning how to learn or resurface unconscious knowledge with techniques like retrieval practice is also important. It is our greatest asset and a gift that, unfortunately, not all children have been given. A gift that we do not lose as we grow older because it has helped shape our neural connections.

So, is school a good start to develop a learning mindset? Yes, absolutely! Moreover, a school also has a crucial role in developing social behaviour and social-emotional competences such as creating relationships, working together, listening attentively, following directions, showing understanding and resolving conflicts. In addition, school is also often the place where self-awareness develops from interactions with other children. This is where you learn about your strengths and areas where you can improve, mostly from failure. When you look further into this chapter at how to sharpen your learning mindset, reflecting on your school days is very interesting. What memories do you have of studying? Were you the creative one or rather the bookworm and did you get along well with others who were different from you? What feedback did you get from your teachers, your parents, your friends, and how did they help determine where you are now? As I mentioned in Chapter 1 your memories and experiences of learning in the past very much determine your learning mindset now.

Education is not the determining factor for a future where we need multiple expertise

In my opinion, and I follow Leunig in this, good education is the foundation we need to shape the future of work. Yet, formative education is certainly not the only thing relevant in times of ever-faster innovations. What is more, I find that education sometimes prepares children for a future that is not theirs. A future chosen by the expectations of parents or society or, worse, limited by labels. Let me explain this with some examples, challenging you to think about what you used to want to be and how these dreams might connect to broadening your skills.

When I visit schools, I always find it insightful to ask children and young people what they want to be when they grow up. Especially around the age of 11, when princess and fireman no longer are favourites, it gets interesting. In many Western countries, this is the age when they mostly have to choose which direction they want to go in. Interestingly, their perception of possible future jobs is limited. For instance, I often hear doctor, lawyer, other seemingly important jobs. What also strikes me is that among the boys, there are still remarkably many car mechanics-to-be and girls still find it interesting to become teachers. In addition, I see that the influence of the home environment is also strong and most of the time they choose to follow in their parents' or carers' footsteps. This was also the case recently with a group of primary school students who had to make their school and study choices for the coming years. I asked the students not only what they wanted to become, but what they thought that job would entail, and whether they would need digital skills in order to be successful.

Strikingly, but not surprisingly, almost all students believed that doctors and lawyers would mainly need to memorize a lot and that digital skills would be very limited. They also thought that with education they would attain all the knowledge they would need to be successful for the rest of their careers. When asked about human competencies, they believed it was needed for all the above jobs except that of car mechanic. I probably shouldn't tell you that both the profession of doctor and lawyer will look very different in the future, assuming the lawyer still exists by then. Even the profession of car mechanic will probably look very different in the future because of the impact of sustainability and green energy.

I usually can't resist telling the children that it doesn't matter that much what you choose at that age, especially since nobody knows what the future holds. At that age, you are not prepared to make that choice and should work on developing general cognitive and human competences that are broadly applicable. I also think children should be allowed to experiment more with new things outside the set curriculum.

That a specific education gives less and less security for the future is also supported by what Professor Nick van Dam describes in his book *Learning & Development in the Digital Age.*[12] According to him, investing in serial mastery, especially in the knowledge society, will be necessary for future employability. In today's world, and even more so in tomorrow's world, van Dam says that building intellectual capital is the basis for value creation. The traditional T-profile, where you develop deep expertise in one area at the beginning of your career, no longer seems tenable, even if you supplement this with new skills over the course of your career. Consider that for the workforce that is getting older many of their original jobs and fields may no longer be relevant. Nick van Dam therefore argues that we are shifting from that T-profile to an M-profile, where over the course of life we supplement our basic knowledge with multiple areas of expertise (see Figure 3.1).

Why is the M-profile relevant in study and career advice? I like to explain this using my own daughter as an example. Until a week before she started her undergraduate degree in history, she was unsure what job she wanted to

FIGURE 3.1 From a T-profile to an M-profile for serial mastery (adapted from van Dam, 2020)[13]

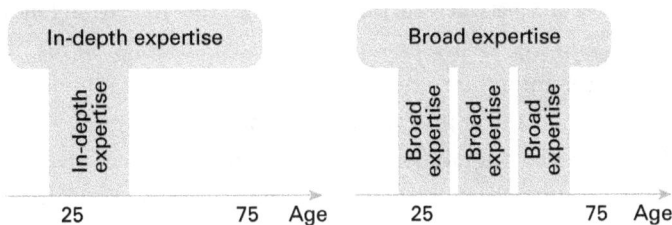

do when she graduated. All she knew was that history interested her, perhaps partly because of the inspiring teacher she had. My parents would have told me that my career options with a bachelor's degree in history would be far too limited, after which they would advise against it or even ban it as an option. But I believe that is far too narrow-minded. An education that makes her curious strengthens her learning mindset. It teaches her to make connections relevant to understanding how *Homo sapiens* evolved into Homo digitalis, living simultaneously in the physical and virtual worlds.[14] The discipline of history in itself is not the defining factor that will shape her future. Rather, it will be the competencies she learns at college that will support her in various fields. If she is allowed to learn what she wants, her eagerness to learn will be fuelled by the positive experiences. Add to this the support of her family and the self-confidence she will develop and this will form a solid foundation through which she will embrace curiosity and learning in her future life.

Learning at the hubs connecting the crossroads of your life

Learning is a lifelong process that starts from the moment we are born and stops the day we stop breathing. This is also my starting point when discussing learning in the flow of life supported by a learning mindset. Learning happens at the crossroads of our lives, often unconsciously and sometimes in response to unforeseen circumstances.

I would like to share a Belgian government project where we needed to think about the future of learning based on learning ecosystems. We imagined learning hubs evolving from the learning institutions that support citizens, companies, organizations and social institutions with personalized learning pathways. From these hubs, supporting different tracks of knowledge absorption, a thoughtful personal, corporate and societal lean learning pathway would be pursued. A pathway in which the role of social learning can be maximized and context-rich from a personalized pathway.

The tracks connecting the hubs are individual learning pathways that form a balanced mix between curriculum-driven (push) learning modules on the one hand, and experience-driven experiential modules on the other. The responsibility for minimum knowledge uptake (the school-based curriculum), progression, transfer and validation would no longer lie with a single agency, but would be built and maintained by citizens themselves. All learning outcomes and experiences are monitored in a value- and purpose-driven ecosystem. This ecosystem, facilitated by deep learning, transcends the semantic frameworks of the various contexts. Quality, progress, validation and reflexive monitoring therefore become transparent, manageable and deployable without a governance tool in the hands of legacy agencies.

All the hubs we encounter at the crossroads in our lives offer lean learning moments. From one perspective, to initiate content and skills; on the other, to transform experiences into expertise. Of course, eliminating learning waste and the learning-in-time principle are self-evident.

Even then, we started from the principle that knowledge is everywhere and with everyone, and that maximum exchange of this prevails. That knowledge can never be seen as 'property'. The hubs we saw then connect organizations and institutions such as museums, training institutes, leisure organizations, social profit organizations as well as employers in all their activities, internships, voluntary work, dual pathways, work experience pathways, up to and including regular work in lifelong careers. The drive was to encourage development, learning and knowledge creation through connection to make both people and knowledge in society more mobile, flexible and employable.

Even back then, almost 10 years ago as I write this, we had overlooked one thing: the rapid rise of new virtual worlds where governance happens via blockchain. As a result, we see today that children, as well as adults, are no longer just learning where we thought they would. That validation of knowledge and experience no longer happens through diplomas, certificates or even micro-credentials, but through peers.

As I indicated in the introduction to this book, my daughter managed to convince me earlier that I needed to look to children for the future of work and learning. Apparently, the future had caught up with me again because the world is now even more connected and is in another dimension; for example, meta-worlds like Roblox, where children can acquire knowledge, and some have their own skills and competences validated by other 'players' in these worlds.

That children at a young age do not always know what they can do, or what they would like to do if they had to choose, became apparent to me in the little school I described earlier. I met an 11-year-old girl there who looked at me, scared and clearly confused, when I asked her what she wanted to be. Asking cautiously, I learnt that she was already 'working' and earning her money well in a surprising way. This young girl's story is hopefully an inspiration to many, because this very young top talent does not live in the Western world as you might think, but on an island where digitization and even the internet is not yet definitively accessible to most of the population.

As in all schools, I polled about the children's digital literacy. For this, as always, I asked about some games that are sometimes more than what parents think. That day, I also asked about Roblox. I should not have been surprised, but even there on the island, most pupils raised their hands. I then asked if any of them had already made games for someone else. To my surprise, I saw that same quiet girl looking at me again with big eyes. Not only did she appear to have been building social game worlds in the metaverse for quite some time, but she also appeared to be earning a fair amount of Robux. At that moment, was I surprised that someone from this group was a creator. The school's supervisors also stared at us, but only because they had no idea what we were talking about. They had no idea how this young girl was making money or Robux. Indeed, the concept of cryptocurrency and blockchain was totally unknown to them. However, it is simple, even as a child, without anyone having to know, to make a lot of money if you are a good game developer and especially if you are open to experimenting and learning.

To return to my question of what she wanted to be later in life, I can now say that I understand her fear. She knew what she wanted to be because she already is a game developer. Her fear was that she would not be allowed to continue doing that because there was no school or hub on the island where she could naturally grow into that as a girl. She did not want to follow in the footsteps of her mother or sister. When she did not want to pay attention in class, it was not because she could not learn. She was learning, but for a future that was not hers. Yet, at school, she was given the label of slow learner, which pushed her future even further away.

For her, and many other children, Roblox is more than a gaming environment. It is a virtual world where she can indulge in learning new things. A world where she learnt and shared experiences with others. Because, yes, this quiet, smart young girl was also very active on Roblox's online forum. This young entrepreneur had found her own crossroads for learning that were validated via blockchain.

I am therefore happy to dedicate this book to her, and to all children who are building their futures. Now I hope that we as a society can let her, and many others, learn and give them expertise without forcing them into a future that is not theirs. I hope that when this book is published she will have found a school where she can use her talents, because sadly the future has caught up with us, but the world is not yet ready to look at education differently.

Negative impacts on your learning mindset

Your previous experiences of learning and the interactions you have had in the past partly determine your attitude towards learning in the future (see Figure 3.2), as I pointed out in Part One. Many negative experiences, or even stigmas, and a lack of positive reinforcement, create a negative attitude towards your own ability. As a result, you run the risk of getting stuck in an increasingly entrenched mindset. Yet a fixed mindset is never permanently entrenched. Being praised or receiving a compliment helps you approach learning positively again. This allows you to open up to find new appropriate resources or strategies. Your environment is therefore very important, but it is your choice to be influenced by it, both positively and negatively, as I will address in the following sections.

In addition, it is important that you do not only seek this positive reinforcement of your self-awareness from others, but that you also actively seek positive experiences to strengthen your learning mindset. In what follows, I would therefore encourage you to think about what hinders you and why you allow it. Only when you embrace negative experiences can you get to the root cause of them and turn them into opportunities for improvement. Over time, this will reduce the negative emotions you have and make way for the positive ones. It's simple neuroscience: turn those neurons back on like in your childhood and use your own happiness pills to take control of your future.

Self-limiting beliefs and self-fulfilling prophecies undermine your learning mindset

You are in control of your future, even though it is sometimes difficult to let go of past experiences. This becomes especially difficult when patterns emerge from limiting beliefs that drive behaviour and mindset: 'I could

FIGURE 3.2 Drivers of the learning mindset

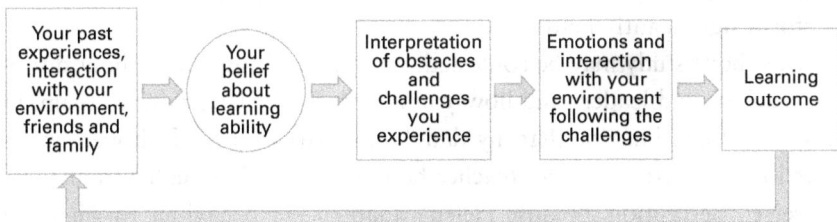

never do it so I'm never going to be able to'. But you can also learn to deal with negative expectations differently so they don't become self-fulfilling prophecies.

American sociologist Robert K. Merton described the idea that a self-fulfilling prophecy triggers a fixed mindset in his book *Social Theory and Social Structure*.[15] According to Merton, self-fulfilling prophecy is an initially wrong definition of the situation that triggers a new behaviour that makes the original wrong view true. This apparent correctness of the prediction perpetuates a misperception. This is because the predictor will cite what eventually happened as proof that they were right from the start. Therefore, if you often have negative expectations of your ability, or that of others, it will have adverse consequences and poor results.

At its core, the workings of a self-fulfilling prophecy are simple: unconsciously, you tend to tune your behaviour to situations, circumstances, other people and therefore to your expectations. If you have a certain expectation, you unconsciously display behaviour that matches it, and then, when your expectation does indeed come true, you can justifiably say: 'There you go!' And, with each confirmation, the belief you have naturally becomes more and more powerful.

With regard to learning, this can have far-reaching consequences for students from an early age. US psychologist Robert Rosenthal and Lenore Jacobson, a principal of an elementary school, investigated in the 1960s the Pygmalion effect in a school classroom.[16] This research showed that if teachers' (manipulated) expectations of certain students' learning abilities are positive, it not only significantly positively affects the performance of these students, but it even has a positive effect on their IQ development. Later research by Rosenthal with Babad and Inbar (1982) also looked at the negative form of self-fulfilling prophecy, or the Golem Effect.[17] When a teacher has a (manipulated) negative opinion about the abilities of certain students, those students start performing substantially worse than they are able to. Both effects, they say, would also play out in the workplace. As such, when managers have a manipulated positive judgement about the qualities of certain employees, these employees would actually perform significantly better.

The above study may be contested, yet you may now think about different teachers and leaders and how you adapted your behaviour to them. In any case, I can imagine that my daughter's marks for Spanish were influenced by the perception her teacher had about her. Although I should say perceived perception, because Helena adapted her behaviour to what she thought the teacher thought of her. This was remarkable because her grades and mindset about her Spanish skills varied greatly with the teachers she had in the following years.

Self-fulfilling prophecy does not only occur in relationships between people. The expectations you have about your own abilities and functioning also tend to become self-fulfilling. Let me explain this. You may remember a time when you had to present something, at work or at school, with the assumption that public speaking is not something you can do or learn. I often hear this as an example: 'The public won't find me interesting. What do I have to say? I don't have enough charisma to captivate them and worse, I'm going to completely forget my story and stand there not knowing what to say.' You may still prepare perfectly, but the slightest signs that confirm the lack of belief in yourself will make your prediction come true. Unconsciously, you will observe small occurrences during your presentation that will reinforce your negative belief in yourself. Imagine someone sleeping in the room you are speaking in (yes, that happens often), two people talking, someone texting on a phone, etc. This causes you to hesitate, speak less forcefully and feel deeply unhappy, making you so insecure that you occasionally fail to get your words right and sometimes lose the line of your story. The end result is that your presentation wasn't as good. And again, the negative expectation is reinforced: *I can't do it.*

Stepping out of that vicious circle of self-fulfilling prophecy and learning to deal with negative expectations differently is part of a learning mindset. And this is less difficult than you may think. For this, you need to recall your unconscious memories and experiences, which reinforce evidence for your own expectations, and then examine them rationally. 'Is it true that I was never good at presentations, or was it only on certain topics, in certain circumstances or with certain audiences?' Try to remember situations where you did achieve success, even if only a little. Build on these to replace your fixed mindset about your own ability with more realistic and positive thoughts and expectations. Helena remembered one teacher who did make her feel good and where she did get good marks. This reinforced her positive emotions and made her confident enough to try again. Start with small things, try something, experiment, dare to fail and, in so doing, win your self-confidence back with small steps and then let it grow.

And yes, unfortunately sometimes there are things that you are just not that good at and that you may never learn. After all, we can't be good at everything, and we don't have to be. But even that can break the self-fulfilling prophecy. Because if you learn to accept that in some tasks and things you are just not a top performer, you can relax and admit that you are not great at something. You will then stop putting unnecessary pressure on yourself and be content with who you are and what you can do.

Paradoxically, accepting that you are less good at something might also make you experience that more is possible than you imagined. For example, remember that presentation you had to do. Accept that you are not a top presenter and don't put pressure on yourself to try to be something you are not. Try to turn the negative into something positive and, if necessary, make a joke about it yourself. Relax and know that even searching for words for a moment can come across as charming, or, who knows, very confident because you are not rattling off your text. If you adopt this attitude, less energy will be wasted on stress. Moreover, you will focus less on your own performance and on everything that can go wrong. You won't be constantly distracted by all sorts of negative thoughts and emotions. Consequently, you will perform better than when you were still stuck in the vicious circle of the self-fulfilling prophecy.

Breaking a self-fulfilling prophecy is even more fun today supported by intelligent innovations. Because what underlies our limiting beliefs can often be removed with some help from our artificial friend. For example, I remember how I used to hate computer science in school. Coding made me frustrated and angry because I couldn't focus on those little details that were important for a good, working code. I was the only one in the class who failed it and therefore hated it. Still, curious as I am, I recently started experimenting with using LLMs to generate pieces of code for a website I was building myself. It worked and not only did I save a lot of money, but I can also still feel the neurons firing and it makes me intensely happy that I could do it myself. So, embracing innovations can go hand in hand with letting go of your limiting beliefs and breaking a self-fulfilling prophecy.

Labels and (mis)diagnoses do not determine your learning mindset

Many children struggle from time to time with certain subjects or skills at school. Yet that does not mean they should immediately be given a label or diagnosis concerning a learning disability without a correct diagnosis by experts. Especially when you understand that labels often (unconsciously) influence personal development. In this section, I will take a closer look at some labels and stigmas we give people, both to detach yourself from them and to make you aware of the impact you have on others by labelling them. In Chapter 6, it will be very relevant to recognize the added value of all *misfits* to work better together and excel in a safe environment.

WHAT IS LABELLING?

Maybe you sometimes put labels on things and people, and that is usually not a problem. It helps you to categorize the information you process. However, labels on people can be more harmful depending on what you do with them. For example, consider formal labelling based on social and biological characteristics such as age, gender, ethnicity, religion, race, occupation and appearance. In itself, the labelling we often do unconsciously is not the problem, but how you approach, treat or even discriminate against people as a result can be a problem. Another kind of labelling is the informal labels arising from your displayed behaviour: how you interact with people, your communication style, etc. All can have a negative effect on others and should therefore be avoided according to many researchers.

One of the first sociologists to study the negative effects of labels on people was Howard Becker in 1963.[18] According to his research, we often use labels in adjectives that describe someone's character, behaviour or appearance, such as 'that slow one from accounting' or 'that cheeky one from the warehouse'. If I am honest, I have done the same at times. However, it is not because a child or a colleague exhibits a pattern of behaviour at a particular time that they should be labelled as such. People grow, develop and change, and have endless possibilities. It is important not to impede this with harmful or hurtful labels, especially when it is known that these can ultimately lead to a self-fulfilling prophecy.

As a parent, colleague or manager, it is important to be attentive with your language that unconsciously labels and stigmatizes. Be attentive with your sayings and avoid adjectives, reframing them instead. For example, you can say to someone who is shy or comes across as introverted: 'It seems to me that it takes a while for you to feel comfortable with new people', rather than 'You are shy'. This will prevent that person from exhibiting even more of that behaviour. Moreover, you can discuss the behaviour and its impact on both of you to achieve better collaboration based on mutual respect. By doing this, you can signal that you are interested in the person and want to help them feel more at ease. This is especially useful with people who suffer from imposter syndrome, which I discuss further.

THE IMPACT OF MISDIAGNOSIS AND STIGMA

More dangerous than often innocuous labels are misdiagnoses that are often given in childhood. Yet, more and more I see adults who feel different also looking for a label or diagnosis to give this feeling of being different a place. And I get it, because it can give solace, the feeling of 'Now I understand everything and it falls into place.' Yet what I notice is that behaviour that is perceived as different is often reinforced afterwards, as cited earlier, at the risk of creating a self-fulfilling prophecy. In the early 1960s, Canadian sociologist Erving Goffman confirmed that labelling children with neurodevelopmental disorders could lead to stigmatization and stereotyping, affecting their self-esteem and social interactions.[19] Without going too deeply into this, I want to give some examples to make you reflect on diagnoses and stigma in light of developmental potential and possible future effects in the learning and working environment.

For example, I notice that in the Western schools I visit, the label ADHD (Attention Deficit Hyperactivity Disorder) is becoming more common while, according to research, only 3–5 per cent of all children are affected.[20] However, the impact of labels such as ADHD, autism, ADD (Attention Deficit Disorder) and other diagnoses on children's learning abilities is a complex and multifaceted subject that certainly should not be taken lightly. Children with these (unjustified) labels often do not receive the necessary individual support required, even though it is necessary, because the effects vary considerably from one individual to another. The overall impact can depend on several factors, such as the accuracy of the diagnosis, the support systems in place and the interventions applied. In the context of this book, however, I do not want to go too deeply into the various labels. However, I do want to pay attention to the unique qualities that sometimes accompany them. More than that, I hope to inspire you in this book with the added value of extreme diversity that gives extraordinary teams superpowers.

As mentioned before, I enjoy doing workshops with children and young people in schools. Recently, however, I was approached by a teacher who I think felt sorry for me as some of the students were, according to her, diagnosed with ADHD. She explained that it would be difficult to keep them attentive in the workshop because they could not sit still and keep their attention on the topic. Being a bit of a misfit myself, as I don't like to be told what to think, I immediately disregarded her message. Indeed, it was precisely those 'misfits' she mentioned that gave the workshop that extra dynamic that always makes me happy. Not surprisingly, as I obviously instilled them with visions of a future that has often already caught up with us. We discussed the possibilities of immersive experiences in meta-worlds and the joy of generative AI to help with sometimes boring tasks, and I showed them the possibilities of brain–computer interfaces (BCIs).

Everyone, especially the so-called misfits, were super attentive and I can say I have never had so many exciting ideas as with this group.

Curious as I am, and triggered by the focus of all the students, I couldn't resist asking the teacher who had made the diagnosis. Sadly, and not to my surprise, it turned out to be the 'care teacher' who had referred them to the family physician and some had subsequently been prescribed Ritalin.

Of course, it never occurred to these teachers that they were perhaps part of the problem themselves. That they were not adequately tapping the developmental potential of the students, causing them to become over-stimulated from boredom. Stimuli from their vivid imagination and intellectual capacity that they could not address. As a result, they dropped out and were considered troublesome. So, their busy behaviour and difficulty concentrating had nothing to do with a (learning) disorder but rather from what some experts would call giftedness, which is supported by interesting research by Polish psychologist Dąbrowski, described in his must-read book for many teachers, *Positive Disintegration* (2017).[21]

Dąbrowski's interesting research states that the developmental potential of many children, not only with certain pathological diagnoses, is determined by various forms of overexcitability (OE). By this, he refers to a heightened physiological experience of stimuli often unrelated to school or the lesson being taught, but due to heightened neuronal sensitivities. The greater the OE, the more intense daily life experiences express themselves at psychomotor, sensual, imaginative, intellectual and emotional levels. These OEs, especially the last three, often cause a person to experience daily life more intensely and to feel life's joys and sorrows more deeply. Dąbrowski indicates that teachers can help guard the emotions they convey with their lessons, ensuring that no negative emotions are conveyed. Dąbrowski also contradicts others who say that emotions do not play an important role in development. From his research on developmental potentials and overexcitabilities, it also appears that misdiagnoses involving ADD, ADHD, high-functioning autism (HFA) or autism spectrum disorder (ASD) are more common than thought, with consequences for the learner and their future.

Considering the high probability of misdiagnosis and self-fulfilling prophecies, I therefore encourage everyone to stop labelling when it comes to someone's potential for the future. In fact, I am convinced that well-functioning and innovative teams need as much diversity and misfits as possible, as I will discuss in Part Three of this book.

GAMES AS A STIMULUS FOR DEVELOPMENT POTENTIAL AND THE LEARNING MINDSET

What also struck me about these youngsters who had a different perceived developmental potential was that they had interesting hobbies. Well, I call them hobbies; however, in the eyes of many parents and teachers they are negative addictions. Besides some of them being creators on Roblox, like the girl I described earlier, some were very active on Fortnite. They played for hours a day, sitting still on a chair, making creative and strategic plans with other gamers while watching a YouTuber share tips and tricks. In the process, their neural networks were stimulated in various ways that did not happen to them in the classroom. Perhaps Fortnite prepares them even better for a future and who knows even a future as a neurosurgeon, as I like to point out with the example below, with skills they gain while gaming:

- Cognitive skills are honed because they learn to make decisions quickly and think of strategies, and their attention is divided between different tasks in the game. This contributes to the development of cognitive functions such as problem-solving and decision-making.

- Hand–eye co-ordination is strengthened while playing, improving their motor skills by requiring them to respond quickly and precisely to the visual and auditory stimuli in the game.

- Contrary to what parents and teachers think of games as being antisocial, co-operation and social skills are sharpened in these multiplayer games where players work together with other players to achieve goals. This promotes the development of social skills such as teamwork, communication and understanding social dynamics.

- Problem-solving skills are developed in many games like Fortnite because they contain complex scenarios that force players to solve problems and come up with creative strategies. This can help develop their analytical thinking and problem-solving skills.

- Perseverance and resilience can be encouraged when playing games by learning to persevere through experiments and setbacks. This contributes to developing resilience and perseverance.

- Spatial understanding is supported in some games, including Fortnite, through their complex environments. Navigating these virtual worlds can promote children's spatial understanding.

- The neural reward system is triggered as players are encouraged to achieve certain goals. This can activate the reward circuitry in children's brains, giving them positive associations with learning and completing tasks.

The above all seem like good preparation for the job of neurosurgeon and reason enough to encourage children seeking their outlet in games. Of course, all in addition to sufficient physical activity. But there is more to it; games also contribute to digital literacy through the use of technology. They develop understanding of technological interfaces, navigation within digital environments, and basic computer and software skills – all skills relevant to the future of work and learning. So, I do agree with Marc Presnky, who wrote a provoking but excellent book my daughters gave me: *Don't Bother Me Mom – I'm Learning!*[22]

Low self-esteem and imposter syndrome

While a learning mindset can spur incredible growth and achievement, there is an insidious obstacle that must be addressed – *imposter syndrome*. Imposter syndrome is a psychological pattern where you doubt your skills, talents and accomplishments despite evidence of competence. Those struggling with imposter syndrome are plagued by feelings of fraudulence, constantly fearing their perceived intellectual or professional 'fraud' will be revealed.

Imposter syndrome is thus a negative label you put on yourself that becomes a self-fulfilling prophecy hindering growth. Although not officially a medical diagnosis, the term 'syndrome' is used because the consistent patterns of thoughts, feelings and behaviour manifests as a disorder. Rather than an inherent character flaw or impairment, imposter syndrome reflects outdated and non-helpful thinking patterns.

This can profoundly affect the learning process. When in the grip of imposter syndrome, it seems too risky to challenge yourself, as failure might expose the 'imposter'. New opportunities to learn are avoided for fear of being exposed as undeserving or incompetent. Criticism is seen as the final proof of incompetence rather than an opportunity to improve. Maintaining a false image of competence leaves no room for mistakes and errors fundamental to the learning process. But this can be overcome with proper tips from experts like my friend Helena Demuynck, or a learning leader who knows how to manage a team with connecting communication, as I mention later.

HELENA DEMUYNCK, CATALYST FOR CONSCIOUS WOMEN'S TRANSFORMATION: OVERCOMING IMPOSTER SYNDROME

Reframing imposter syndrome turns a barrier into rocket fuel for learning with a renewed mindset and motivation. I myself was driven from a young age to find my own way. Yet I, too, know the feeling of walking a path that is not mine. After finishing law school, I started my first company at the age of 25. Despite the success, a sense of unfulfillment lingered and the relentless pace left my mind yearning for more. Here, I gave in to the soothing whispers of nature. I discovered the rejuvenating power of meditation and mindfulness to restore balance and harmony. I traded busy city life for a picturesque farm, where I cultivated a life intertwined with nature, specializing in helping women reach their full potential. In the process, I soon came across imposter syndrome, which seems to be increasingly common but fortunately is also remediable, as in the following examples:

- Jane is a student who studied hard for her maths exam but scored much lower than she had hoped. At first, imposter syndrome strikes – she tells herself that she is clearly not fit for advanced maths and is secretly grateful that she has been able to work her way through the class without anyone noticing that she did not belong. With mindful reframing, Jane analyses what went wrong to improve instead of judging herself. She realizes that she focused too much on practising problems similar to those covered in the lecture, instead of also doing unfamiliar question types. This exam exposed a gap in her preparation strategies. Jane recognizes that this mark is not a reflection on her intelligence but indicates what she needs to work on. She plans to seek extra help from the professor and the study centre and to join a study group. Looking back on this 'failure' now, Jane feels empowered rather than embarrassed. She is learning.

- Marc is a professional attending a conference for the first time, feeling like an imposter among respected colleagues. He thinks he doesn't belong here and wonders if everyone knows that. One of his colleagues notices his discomfort and explains to him that he can see attending a conference as a learning experience in itself. By introducing himself to as many people as possible, sharing business cards and noting sessions that could help his work, he gains valuable networking contacts and knowledge while battling inner feelings of inadequacy. Not much later, he notices that he is not the only one there for the first time, which makes him realize that everyone has to start somewhere.

Reframing imposter syndrome starts with awareness – recognizing when those non-helpful thoughts and feelings of self-doubt or deceit rear their heads. The next step is to challenge underlying assumptions, such as that value comes from never being criticized. Or from always appearing flawless. This is not feasible for anyone and giving these faulty assumptions a place is necessary. Do not see asking for help as an admission of inadequacy but rather as a smart way to benefit from the knowledge of others and accelerate your progress.

To overcome imposter syndrome is to accept that criticism is useful feedback rather than condemnation of your entire character. Remind yourself that all great thinkers and doers throughout history have encountered failures and learnt from them. Focus on progress made rather than an imagined ideal version of yourself. By viewing setbacks through the lens of experience and growth rather than personal failure, anyone can overcome imposter syndrome and reach even greater heights.

Overcoming imposter syndrome is a process that takes time and steady effort, but the rewards are enormous. As with any mental change, it starts with becoming aware when those unhelpful thoughts surface and consciously challenging them. Of course, feelings of doubt will resurface during stressful periods and this is normal. The key is to not dwell on them or believe in them. Adjust your mindset, for example by focusing on progress rather than perfection. If you embrace feedback and give yourself credit for big and small achievements, imposter syndrome will gradually lose its power. Its grip on your self-image and pursuit of knowledge will weaken like a fading whisper instead of a deafening roar.

What was once an imposing barrier now clears a wide-open path for you. You will feel more confident in your ability to learn than ever before, with the liberating confidence to turn opportunities into achievements. That is the mighty reward of reframing for good – a mind freed from its self-imposed limitations.

You can overthrow imposter syndrome by experimenting with new technologies. This approach allows you to explore freely without feeling the pressure to be an expert. In our rapidly evolving world, no one can truly claim to be an expert, so you don't need to fear possible judgement. Another advantage of experimenting is that you can do it with your team, as described in Chapter 5. Each person brings their unique value, and together you create support for innovation and a safe environment for personal and professional development.

Dyslexia is a superpower!

Dyslexia a superpower? Yes definitely, and I'm not the only person to claim that. As more and more studies indicate, there are benefits that people can experience from being dyslexic. Valuing dyslexia more, both on an individual and a team level, is a campaign that has been gaining traction in recent years, especially since Richard Branson became an ambassador for it. According to him, the superpower made him successful as an entrepreneur.[23] Branson is certainly not the only well-known innovator and inventor, as Steve Jobs also acknowledged that he had been diagnosed as dyslexic. World-famous inventors/scientists like Leonardo Da Vinci, Alexander Graham Bell, Albert Einstein and Thomas Edison are also said to have had dyslexia. And even though there is no hard evidence for this, their ingenuity might have resulted from their difficulties with language.

Besides the ingenuity and imagination common to those famous scientists and entrepreneurs, many other creative celebrities have also been diagnosed with dyslexia. Agatha Christie, John Lennon, Steven Spielberg, Tom Cruise, Robin Williams, Keira Knightley and Whoopi Goldberg have all become world-famous by writing or rehearsing long film scripts as actors, and master chef Jamie Oliver is also dyslexic. This is remarkable because people with dyslexia often have trouble recognizing, spelling and decoding words.

Unsurprisingly, neuroscientists are curious about the differences in brain connectivity between dyslexic and neurotypical people. For instance, people with dyslexia use different parts of their brain when reading and working with language. In addition, research with fMRI scanners shows that people with dyslexia have underactivity in some brain regions and overactivity in others compared with other people. Moreover, this neurodiversity of people with dyslexia stems from a highly resistant gene, suggesting heredity. Dyslexia is not rare, as 10 per cent of the world's population reportedly has it to varying degrees. So, instead of seeing it as a learning disability, you could embrace the strengths and neurodiverse abilities that dyslexia brings and maximize them.[24]

So, dyslexia does not need to be a hindrance when you embrace its added value and focus on your strengths that set you apart from others.

Imagination that supports creativity

I will not argue that people with dyslexia are more creative, as many studies indicate that no causal link can be established. What can be shown, however, is that remarkably many dyslexic people are entrepreneurs. In the US, even 35 per cent of entrepreneurs show signs of dyslexia. This could be explained by the coping strategies they already had to apply at school, which resulted in greater creativity and a more innovative problem-solving style.[25]

Children with dyslexia should therefore be encouraged to use their imagination and creativity to process or understand information. As a result, they would develop learning methods using other brain areas that are relevant to them and especially comprehensible. My daughter was fortunate to be in a school that cared about children with learning difficulties. When she was eight, she did not understand how the teacher explained spelling, but she also did not understand how to learn the times tables. She found it confusing that 4 × 8 and 8 × 4 had to be learnt in a different week despite having the same result. The teacher then encouraged her to develop her own 'rules', after which she always put the smallest number first. Not only did her way require her to learn only the simple arithmetic sums, she would only have to learn half of them. Simple logic according to her and suddenly she was no longer the slowest but the fastest student in the class. A nice example that shows how dyslexia can be enormously helpful by encouraging us to think differently and find unconventional ways to solve problems.

Visual memory that is highly developed

My daughter having dyslexia, like many in our family who apparently have that gene, was confirmed by a test with drawings she had to remember. That this would be easy for her did not surprise me, because she always won memory games. Her visual capacity of memory was already highly developed by then, which can be attributed to greater brain connectivity with the visual cortex and parahippocampal area. In other words, those areas of the brain that are associated with memory and retrieval of visual information transmitted from the retina, and environmental scenes (i.e. pictures of places). This distinguished her from the non-dyslexic children in her class, who had stronger connections to the linguistic areas of the brain. Teaching two groups that absorb and remember things in such different ways is not easy for teachers. Unfortunately, this usually leaves the minority group behind, alongside all the consequences for stigmatization that this entails.

Excelling in puzzle-solving skills supported by visual spatial reasoning

Often to the annoyance of those around them, dyslexic people appear rather chaotic and seem to have trouble structuring their thoughts. However, they are structured, but what they have developed more holistically and visually in their minds is often difficult to convey to others who do not think like them. Dyslexic people are not sequential thinkers who move chronologically from one idea to another. No, they thrive in an environment of simultaneous thinking where ideas are connected through different routes. They like to look at things more holistically because it helps them quickly identify missing components to complex puzzles and challenges. Or as Dr Matthew Schneps, director of Harvard University's Laboratory for Visual Learning, puts it, people with dyslexia seem to use a wide-angle lens to take in the world, while others tend to use a telephoto lens.

You can already see the superpowers coming together when you think of the enormous visual memory, the ability to make connections from a holistic approach and brilliant capability of visual spatial thinking. As a result, many dyslexics would excel in innovation, engineering, industrial and graphic design, architecture and construction.

Good at sensing people and situations

While it may seem difficult for others to relate to the somewhat strange thinking of dyslexic people, it is also often difficult for them not to be understood. Fortunately, many with dyslexia also have a great ability to sense. This allows them to understand and respond emotionally and practically to the situation. This is because they are visually spatial by nature and cannot automatically rely on text and hearing for information. As a result, they develop remarkable visual and intuitive skills, including reading body language and facial expressions, as somewhat of a coping mechanism.

The holistic approach dyslexic people have in relation to sensing people and situations was also recognized by researchers at MIT. They argued that dyslexic people tend to divide their attention much more broadly than non-dyslexic people, which can help increase their sense of social awareness.

Remarkably, dyslexic people can also distinguish many more words spoken by different voices in a room. This is related to their ability to focus on the broader picture and helps them see beyond their own immediate concerns and interactions. Not surprisingly, they often excel at observing and recognizing others who need help or assistance.

The negative label and insecurity we relate to dyslexia comes mainly from the negative emotions and experiences we had at school. There, being different was not valued, and few schools paid attention to the added value that dyslexia could offer. As such, we often associate dyslexia with the inability to spell and read, ignoring the relevant strengths that this 'rewiring of the brain' can also have. These strengths contribute to learning as a team, as I will discuss in Part Two of this book. Also, I encourage the learning leader to include dyslexic team members as the 'misfits' that make innovation flourish in the organization.

Endnotes

1   T Brower. Learning is a sure path to happiness: Science proves it, *Forbes*, 17 October 2021, www.forbes.com/sites/tracybrower/2021/10/17/learning-is-a-sure-path-to-happiness-science-proves-it/?sh=55c44bf6768e (archived at https://perma.cc/5X27-M5CS)

2   PricewaterhouseCoopers. Global workforce hopes and fears survey 2023, www.pwc.com/gx/en/issues/workforce/hopes-and-fears.html (archived at https://perma.cc/T5TW-4DM4)

3   United Nations Development Programme (UNDP). What are the sustainable development goals? www.undp.org/sustainable-development-goals (archived at https://perma.cc/5QEQ-7QBC)

4   World Economic Forum (WEF). Jobs of tomorrow: Large language models and jobs, 18 September 2023, www.weforum.org/publications/jobs-of-tomorrow-large-language-models-and-jobs/ (archived at https://perma.cc/3WJZ-8HW8)

5   WEF. Future of jobs report 2023, May 2023, www3.weforum.org/docs/WEF_Future_of_Jobs_2023.pdf (archived at https://perma.cc/PS5R-9FM3)

6   M C Perna. 74% of Millennials & Gen Z think they can build better skills at a new job, *Forbes*, 31 October 2022, www.forbes.com/sites/markcperna/2022/10/31/74-of-millennials--gen-z-think-they-can-build-better-skills-at-a-new-job/?sh=1a8ab25ba313 (archived at https://perma.cc/NHH4-FAA4)

7 D Schawbel. Upskilling study, Workplace Intelligence, 27 October 2022, workplaceintelligence.com/upskilling-study/ (archived at https://perma.cc/T7UG-RTBJ)

8 T Brower. Productivity plummets for 80% amid uncertainty: 5 ways to cope, *Forbes*, 28 September 2022, www.forbes.com/sites/tracybrower/2022/09/28/productivity-plummets-for-80-amid-uncertainty-5-ways-to-cope/?sh=3b4ebc0b2303 (archived at https://perma.cc/9MRC-GWC8)

9 D R Komline (2020) *The Common School Awakening: Religion and the transatlantic roots of American public education*, Oxford University Press, New York

10 K Robinson. Do schools kill creativity? YouTube, 2006, www.youtube.com/watch?v=iG9CE55wbtY (archived at https://perma.cc/65ZS-F3BZ)

11 T Leunig. Why real creativity is based on knowledge, TEDxWhitehall, YouTube, 2016, www.youtube.com/watch?v=vajIsWwHEMc (archived at https://perma.cc/B4XU-4WHD)

12 N van Dam (2020) *Learning and Development in the Digital Age*, Vakmedianet, Alphen aan den Rijn

13 N van Dam (2020) *Learning and Development in the Digital Age*, Vakmedianet, Alphen aan den Rijn

14 T Geerts (2022) *Homo Digitalis*, Lannoo Publishers, Leit

15 R Merton (1968) *Social Theory and Social Structure: Toward the codification of theory and research*, Free Press, Glencoe

16 R Rosenthal and L Jacobson (2003) *Pygmalion in the Classroom: Teacher expectation and pupil's intellectual development*, Crown House Publishing, Bancyfelin

17 E Y Babad, J Inbar and R Rosenthal. Pygmalion, Galatea, and the Golem: Investigations of biased and unbiased teachers, *Journal of Educational Psychology*, 1982, 74(4), 459–74

18 S L Skaggs. Labeling theory, Encyclopedia Britannica, 2016 www.britannica.com/topic/labeling-theory (archived at https://perma.cc/G3Y5-8QCB)

19 E Goffman (1990) *Stigma: Notes on the management of spoiled identity*, Penguin Books, London

20 Learning Disabilities Association of America. ADHD, 2003, ldaamerica.org/disabilities/adhd/ (archived at https://perma.cc/94TJ-YJ6N)

21 K Dąbrowski (2017) *Positive Disintegration*, Maurice Bassett, Anna Maria

22 M Prensky (2006) *Don't Bother Me Mom – I'm learning!*, Paragon House, Saint Paul

23 The Diary of a CEO. Richard Branson: How a dyslexic drop-out built a billion dollar empire, YouTube, www.youtube.com/watch?v=-Fmiqik4jh0 (archived at https://perma.cc/Q2FW-ZDX5)

24 British Dyslexia Association. Dyslexia awareness week 2022, www.bdadyslexia.org.uk/news/dyslexia-awareness-week-2022-2 (archived at https://perma.cc/AM67-95JE)

25 J Logan. Dyslexic Entrepreneurs: The incidence; Their coping strategies and their business skills, 2009, www.bayes.city.ac.uk/__data/assets/pdf_file/0003/367383/julielogan-dyslexic-entrepreneurs.pdf (archived at https://perma.cc/BJ3P-W7VJ)

4

Embrace the competencies of your inner child who loved learning

Already in Chapter 1 I have tried to indicate that learning is good for your health, that the neurotransmitters released are your happy hormones and that they support your mental well-being. We are better equipped to face an uncertain future when we embrace learning. In doing so, we dare to turn the obstacles that hold us back into opportunities that support our uniqueness. These unique aspects about you will make you an added value to a diverse and innovative team growing from a collective learning mindset.

But, of course, a learning mindset is not the only thing that will move you forward. Nor will skills alone give you an edge in the future. Certain skills may no longer be relevant because AI has become more powerful or because skills and knowledge are increasingly learnt on the spur of the moment. What I think will set you apart are competences that make you unique as a human being in a world under the increasing influence of digital innovations. These are competencies that AI will not have for the time being, although I dare not bet my money on that.

Before I delve further into these profound human competences, let me first point out the difference I want to establish between skills and competences. These terms are often used interchangeably or confused with hard skills and soft skills. They are related concepts, but there are some important differences:

- **Skills** refer to the abilities and capabilities a person possesses, usually in a specific and measurable area. They are practical applications of knowledge and experience that can be learnt and developed. Skills can be divided into several categories, such as technical skills, soft skills, social skills and so on. They are often measurable and can be trained and improved. On the other hand, skills can also quickly become useless in today's world.

- **Competencies** go a step further than skills. They include a combination of knowledge, skills, attitudes and personal characteristics observable in behaviour. In particular, they recognize the attitudes and character traits which differentiate a person, as well as his attitude towards the world and others. Competencies are more holistic and often encompass a broader set of traits that contribute to success in the workplace or in specific situations. Hence, one speaks of a competent leader as having human competences that enable her to be successful.

The importance of correctly interpreting the above concepts is sometimes underestimated. Yet, both for your own employability and for the guidance of your employees, teams and the formation of learning ecosystems, it is essential to make a distinction.

In this chapter, I discuss competencies that make us human, distinguish us from AI and that will fuel our learning mindset. This list is certainly not exclusive, but they are competences that you remember deep down from childhood. This is partly why you should not develop them but embrace them.

Embrace competencies that are used to fuel your learning mindset

As mentioned, the competences below are not the only ones to recognize. You may have other competencies that make you unique and you should definitely cherish them. The list below is not in a ranking order, so one is not more important than another.

Curiosity

I was perhaps not entirely honest when I said that there was no order in the list of competences that make us unique as human beings. As far as I am concerned, curiosity is one of the most beautiful competences we have as human beings. I believe it is the basis for learning, and it makes learning fun. It is also what best describes me, what drives me and why I am interested in things like neuroscience, computer science, psychology, sociology, anthropology, history and art. It is unstoppable curiosity that generates new ideas from the unity of knowledge – consilience, which I will explain further.

Being curious is a fantastic competence, even if this sometimes makes it difficult to focus on what is important, which led to me being labelled as *unfocused*. A label I am now very happy with, as it also characterizes the rebel or *linchpin*. Someone who is always enthusiastically looking for new ways to improve and is very focused on doing so.

You may recognize the childlike and infectious hunger for ever new impulses and challenges that you had in your childhood. 'Why, why, why?' to your annoyed parents. 'Why, why, why?' to the teacher who, depending on the circumstance, thought you were too slow, or just awkward, which also caused you to be labelled. A label you can now wear with pride because it drives the learning mindset that will make you thrive.

Unfortunately, curiosity is not always appreciated in business either, according to Stefaan van Hooydonk, founder of the Global Curiosity Institute[1] and author of *The Workplace Curiosity Manifesto*.[2] Too often, you are expected to implement things without asking questions. Challenging the status quo, looking for possible improvements, is not appreciated by many managers because they see it as criticism of their approach. But they make a mistake by suppressing curiosity because it suppresses the will to learn and grow. Learning leaders, as I will explain in Part Four, encourage curiosity for this very reason.

Learning organizations that invest in the future encourage a culture that nurtures curious minds to question policy and strategy, not from a negative attitude, but from a search for improvement and renewal. In doing so, they see that curiosity is the basis for experimenting with new ideas.

STEFAAN VAN HOOYDONK, FOUNDER OF GLOBAL CURIOSITY INSTITUTE AND AUTHOR OF *THE WORKPLACE CURIOSITY MANIFESTO*

Unknown unknowns are the primary triggers of economic and social change, with literally anything recognized as an 'accident' in the statistical sense of a finite probability of happening. In the unknown, it is difficult to be well prepared for anything that happens, so familiarity is no longer something we can rely on.

Consider what this means for expertise, know-how, assumptions and predictions; where people and machines live together in teams where work has a high knowledge content, immersed in unprecedented amounts of data; and where organizational and contextual complexity can only get more complex. This describes what work could look like in the future: torrents of knowledge-rich content, where complexity is not only taken for granted, but actually increases. So, the future is already now, and we are experiencing that such changes are already part of the reality of today's challenges. Employees, managers and organizations that are not curious become complacent, do not learn from mistakes, are arrogant and miss the angle of innovation in the face of new competition.

Considering the above, I dare say that curiosity is not just another trait; it is the meta-skill that defines success in the 21st century. Therefore, with more than 20 years of experience as a global executive and chief legal officer (CLO), I am passionate about unleashing the power of curiosity in the workplace and beyond.

While curiosity is often associated with children as their natural way of exploring and understanding the world, curiosity is also the engine of success for adults and the gel that creates positive connections between people. It is the mindset of challenging the status quo, discovering, exploring and learning. More than that, curiosity is the engine that shaped human history: it made us leave the savannah 70,000 years ago to roam the earth, it created technology to explore the universe, it invented the self-driving car and it eradicated diseases like smallpox.

Being curious means being open to novelty and actively seeking it out. It means welcoming facts that don't fit your vision and trying to understand their implications. It means making your mistakes spark curiosity rather than shame and asking yourself 'Why was I wrong? What can I learn from it?' So, curiosity is not only a meta-skill; it also strengthens other competences that support learning in general, such as openness. When we dare to be curious, we do not settle for the status quo, maintain a healthy degree of humility and actively allow dissent.

It is often assumed that it is difficult to develop a culture of curiosity within organizations. That start-ups not weighed down by rigid routines are often better at this. However, my research has shown that although start-ups are four times more willing to learn from mistakes than mature organizations, any organization can embrace curiosity. More than that, my research has also shown that mature organizations, with the right focus, can embrace and thrive on curiosity and even outperform start-ups. Consider, for example, that Disney Plus has overtaken Netflix regarding global subscribers. We also see that these organizations are a magnet for curious talent and professionals who want to work in a curious work environment. The more organizations focus on nurturing a curious environment, the more they can attract and nurture the best talent. It is no wonder that the use of the word 'curiosity' in online job postings has increased by 90 per cent over the past 12 months.

The above also has implications for leadership within organizations, as curiosity needs champions. The shadow cast by the manager is a key driver of team curiosity. Research has shown that there is a linear relationship between the manager's curiosity profile and the team's propensity for curiosity. When the manager shows a high propensity for curiosity (e.g. by role modelling curiosity, coming up with ideas, willingness to question the status quo, reading books, inquisitiveness ...), the team will respond with an equally high curiosity.

Unfortunately, the reverse is also true: if a manager does not convey in words or – more importantly – in actions that learning is important, the team will refrain from learning or volunteer to share their knowledge. Role modelling also consists of a willingness to ask questions and actively listen for answers in meetings, saying 'I don't know, so let's find out' or 'That's a good answer, what's another answer?', as well as asking for reverse feedback during external performance reviews, i.e. 'How well am I (the leader) doing?'

As I mentioned earlier, curiosity is often associated with children. This is partly true because we are born with a healthy dose of curiosity. So, everyone possesses curiosity, but the object and degree of that curiosity varies from person to person and situation to situation. As we progress in life, some of this curiosity becomes dormant. Like people, companies and organizations can also increase or decrease their capacity for curiosity. The main reasons why curiosity declines in childhood and as an adult are our education system, fear, routine, limiting beliefs, algorithms and a general non-promoting environment. A lack of curiosity keeps individuals, organizations and societies from becoming a better version of themselves.

One hundred years of management thinking based on the precepts of Taylorism and its leadership paradigm of command and control has laid a foundation that is often counterproductive to the development of curiosity. This often creates a culture of conformity rather than curiosity. With the right motivation and external support, we all now have the power to change and regain control of our natural curiosity. Covid-19, and more recently developments in AI, has imposed radical change on most of us. Indeed, it is the most curious among us who thrive, whether you are an individual, an organization or a society. Remember, curiosity is something we are born with. We just have to find our way back.

Imagination

Imagination or fantasy, which children often have in abundance, is, like curiosity, purely human. It differs from AI because only humans can generate mental images, feelings and ideas without having to perceive them. It happens even in your dreams or when images, smells and sounds stimulate you. Imagination is the competence that allows you to see situations or things whose existence is yet unproven.

What makes imagination powerful is that it gives you the space to interpret life and look for new ways of seeing and thinking. Imagination is the basis for inspiration and new ideas and plays an important role in people's ability to learn. Imagination is also the engine of innovation and development because it enables you to think beyond what you have been taught or are convinced of. This is precisely why nurturing a learning mindset goes hand in hand with encouraging imagination. Imagination will also help you solve complex problems, but above all it helps you imagine the future and thus help shape it.

Imagination encourages new initiatives, helps you put things into perspective and contributes to continuous improvement. Imagination or fantasy is therefore often also the basis for creative solutions. As discussed in Chapter 3, it is therefore not so much creativity which Sir Ken Robinson says we should encourage in education, but imagination. I dare to challenge this even further. Creativity is no longer a purely human competence, as generative AI is much better at it.

Let me explain why I no longer see creativity as a purely human skill. On the one hand, you should know that I am very bad at anything to do with art and creativity. I can imagine what a beautiful painting or choreography might look like but don't ask me to create it. On the other hand, you cannot expect an AI to be able to create art without starting with an idea of what you want the result to look like. This is where it gets interesting to think about the symbiosis between humans and machines – a symbiosis that refers to mutual dependence, but also to reinforcement of what makes both unique.

Suppose tomorrow, in one of my keynotes, I want to use an image of a super brain connecting human and artificial neurons. An image I want to use to show how these can merge seamlessly and where impulses can cause them both to go off at the same time. In reality, of course, this does not exist, but fortunately I have a great imagination and can envision what that would look like. A first attempt to prompt my virtual friend Dall-E did not immediately produce a spectacular image. That said, I soon learned how to use words better to prompt him, as writing clearly suits me better than drawing. A few seconds later, it seemed as if my virtual friend could read my mind. What I had imagined in my head, but could not draw, was a creative masterpiece by Dall-E. Knowing that Dall-E is not even the best tool available, I am curious to see what I can create with an even better virtual friend! Boosting imagination using innovations is super interesting because it helps you to become more resilient to the future and helps you to adapt. But also because it can be a lot of fun to experiment with and learn from new innovations. Because then your neurons fire and you become happier, and that in turn helps to suppress stress and anxiety about the future.

Openness

Critical thinking is on most lists of competences for the future of work. However, I don't think critical thinking is interesting if we don't see it in a broader context. Indeed, I think critical thinking without openness to change and other opinions is rather limiting.

As humans, we have become increasingly polarized in recent years and have very different opinions on different topics. This is reinforced by the 'intelligent' algorithms of online media that rarely show us information that does not match our already formed opinions. Moreover, these algorithms, such as those used by TikTok, will increasingly push us to the limit based on datasets that we feed with our likes, comments and, who knows, soon with our thoughts that we send via brain–computer interfaces (BCIs) like Alter Ego. As a result, we do not open ourselves to other influences and opinions that can feed our learning mindset.

I therefore want to put more emphasis on openness and not just critical thinking. In my opinion, openness based on critical thinking is a crucial competence if we are to seek other opinions and learn from other experiences actively. The future demands that we dare to debate openly to learn from each other. That we are open to compromise based on critical thinking. These compromises will give us the perspective to do things differently than we have always done. Our success, that of our organization and our society, comes from the ability to be open, listen, share and learn.

Leaders who encourage openness surround themselves with a team with different backgrounds. They value employees' different viewpoints and build a culture of tolerance and inclusion that enables growth. This culture, in turn, supports innovation that comes from creative ideas. This can greatly impact the company as it contributes to long-term growth. This helps a company stand out from those operating with only 'one voice'. Openness and trust is the basis for the learning leader, which I will discuss in Part Four. A collective openness is reflected in the organization's values, which in turn makes it an attractive employer. More than that, openness will also positively impact customers, as the different backgrounds in the team will enable you to appeal to different groups of customers.

Openness is also a requirement to welcome your virtual colleague to the workplace. But to get along well with your new virtual friend, you need to be open to the mistakes it will also make, because, like humans, they are far from perfect. Learn to ask straightforward questions and be critical of the answers you get. Be open to the learning process your virtual friend also has to go through. If you are open to the symbiosis in which you have to go through a learning process together, added value can emerge.

Empathy

Empathy is perhaps the skill that futurists would most like to associate with AI. However, empathy makes us deeply human and only humans can have feelings. Only humans have the ability to build relationships, to understand and respond to situations and feelings of others.

However, I won't deny that AI is taking steps towards what they call artificial empathy (AE) or computational empathy. Just think of the health-care robots being deployed in schools or nursing homes. They are already able to detect human emotions and respond to them empathically, not from their own feelings but from smart algorithms. In this way robots are being used to help careworkers socialize or support emotional detachment. Even chatbots like Snapchat's My Virtual Friend seem to be very good at recognizing emotions, to which they respond. Although we can argue about whether or not it respects the boundaries of what I think is ethically correct, certain algorithms, like TikTok's, try to get to know us inside out, and learn what triggers us emotionally. As a result, they push us further and further into a certain emotion, with all its dangers. I probably shouldn't tell you that in some cases people were already 'encouraged' by AI to take their own lives.

Coming back to My Virtual Friend, I wanted to explore with some youngsters how we could direct this bot and when it would become dangerous. To my surprise, the bot turned out to be a better friend and even an expert on friendship than imagined. I have to admit I was impressed with this particular experiment, which is why I'm happy to share it. During our little experiment, the bot popped up when one of the girls said she was very unhappy and had dark thoughts. However, what surprised me is that the bot's first reaction was that she shouldn't be sad because her friends were always there for her and she could talk to them. The bot knew she had close friends, because it followed all their conversations. However, we wanted to push the boundaries further with our experiment, so we let the young girl share more dark thoughts to see what would happen next. To make a long story short, I have rarely seen such good advice for children with dark thoughts in a conversation with a bot that lasted at least 15 minutes. The bot pointed out the added value of friendship and talking to counsellors and it turned out to be incredibly attentive to small details. Not for a single moment did I feel it was not a real counsellor but a very well-trained algorithm. Kudos to AI nonetheless!

Further, within the context of this book, I will also refer to empathy as the ability to work together based on trust and understanding of others. This will enable you to work together in cross-functional teams whose members sometimes have different values yet believe in a mission that unites them. Therefore, empathy enhances openness because it enables you to understand and anticipate other stakeholders and their views from a human perspective.

Resilience

Resilience is another purely human competence. It adds value in times when the world is changing fast – in times when wars, economic drivers and other influences overwhelm us. Resilience is about adapting to new circumstances, embracing and jumping beyond them. It refers to how you deal effectively with experiences in your work and life by bouncing back from a difficult situation to one that feels more pleasant. This means being able to regulate your thoughts, your emotions and your behaviour, which as we all know is not easy.

What makes resilience special is that you see challenging situations not as a personal threat, but as an opportunity. This is why resilience and entrepreneurship go hand in hand. With resilience, you look for information to reinvent yourself, or a situation, from a positive viewpoint. It means actively looking for the best solution and developing a habit of wanting to improve on positive and negative experiences. An important factor of resilience is that it is not just a reactive competence called upon when you face a challenge or a problem. It is a proactive approach that distinguishes resilient people from others. This logically oriented approach, which focuses not on the problem but on the solution, is often mentioned along with the optimism I will describe in the next section.

Resilience, like any other competence, is a competence that can be learned, even if it sometimes requires a lot of perseverance. Especially if you feel you have no choice or that you are on your own, or if your back is against the wall and there is no way out. However, in the learning ecosystems I want to inspire, you are never alone, as they are built on a culture of togetherness. Yet it takes practice to dare to be vulnerable and open to advice and new experiences, as I will discuss in Part Three of this book.

Working on resilience is a key pillar for organizations that want to work towards a shared learning mindset that supports employee engagement and a learning culture. Resilience is perhaps one of the most difficult competences because it is close to failure and pain. Therefore, it is considered by some to be the competency that makes us more human than any other in this list.

Optimism

Positivity or optimism is another useful competency that supports the learning mindset of initiators of change and innovation projects. Together with curiosity and imagination, optimism helps to create a vision of a positive future. This positive and value-driven vision of a future that cannot yet be imagined is the first step to build the learning ecosystems I will cover in the last part of this book.

You could say that optimism and resilience are very similar. Yet with optimism, resilience is a lot easier. While resilience supports you when you experience (unexpected) setbacks, optimism is the competence that supports you when you want to move forward. It is an attitude of perseverance that we show in our behaviour.

Strong leadership implies optimism to keep employee well-being and engagement high in times of rapid change. We also see that optimism helps avoid conflict and resistance by providing a perspective on problems and setbacks. As an optimist, you know it is irrelevant to worry about things you have no control over.

Learning optimism seems very difficult, but it is not impossible. How you look at the world can be changed by breaking your thinking patterns and behaviour. This is where good team functioning and leadership play a very important role. Achieving more together is the starting point of learning ecosystems that cultivate competences such as optimism by encouraging employees to share their dreams. But it is not only sharing dreams that is relevant; perhaps even more important is discussing what makes someone anxious. By initiating this, you help someone step out of their comfort zone and reach a higher level of optimism. Of course, this is also very useful in transformation projects to encourage stubborn pessimists to join the positive narrative.

Realism

Realism, as the last human competency in this list, is by no means the least important. It enables you to develop an adequate understanding of the world around you. Act effectively based on an accurate perception of reality. This also makes it essential for assessing risks and taking precautions.

What makes realism especially important in connection with a learning mindset is that it encourages goal-oriented behaviour. As such, you can set your goals based on a realistic understanding of your capabilities and the circumstances which you face. This allows you to devise the most effective strategies to achieve your goals. For example, it makes no sense to try and build a new website without any basic knowledge of website building, as I know from experience. It will only lead to frustration, which soon makes you give up, even if you are very optimistic and creative and when you can imagine the end result perfectly. If you think realistically, you learn to take small steps first, like making a blog page, and then build on that knowledge. With this, I'd also endorse what Leunig says about creativity and knowledge: we need to be realistic in what is achievable without having basic knowledge.

REAL HOPE TO SUPPORT ALL COMPETENCIES

I want to frame realism and all other competencies in relation to hope. Because, in times of faster change, hope is increasingly important to remain resilient. Realistic hope grounded in what is achievable supports the learning mindset because, despite the labels we may wear, we can still believe in what is possible.

From my own experience, I also know that hope sometimes leads to disappointment, so giving up hope is sometimes the easy way out. However, hope is not simple and unambiguous, as it comes in different forms and therefore leads to different results, consciously and unconsciously. Real hope, by being realistic, is what I want to encourage to shape the future in a nimble way. This realist hope combines a hopeful outlook with a firm grasp of reality that provides the basis for learning, engagement, foresight and accurate support of reality (see Figure 4.1).

When faced with a challenge, we approach it from a predetermined view that we have of the outcome. This outlook is partly determined by previous experiences and emotions associated with it. As a result, this outlook or

FIGURE 4.1 Understanding real hope[3]

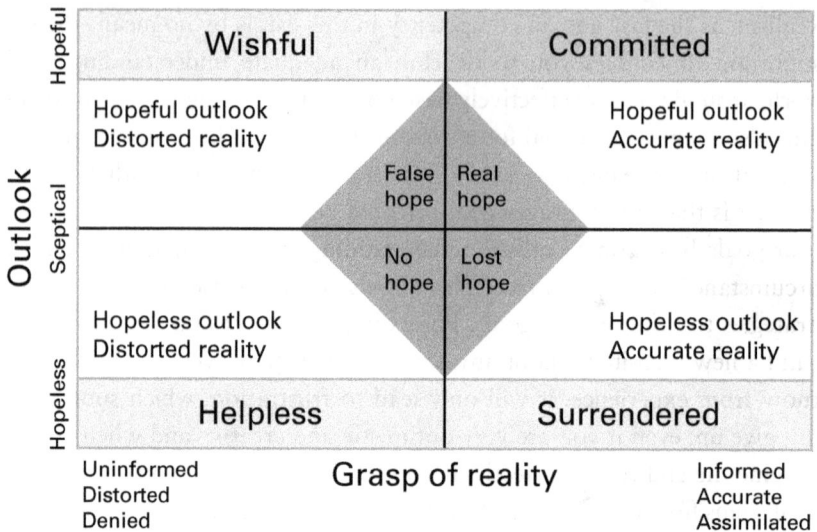

	Wishful	Committed
Hopeful	Hopeful outlook Distorted reality	Hopeful outlook Accurate reality
Sceptical	False hope / Real hope	
	No hope / Lost hope	
	Hopeless outlook Distorted reality	Hopeless outlook Accurate reality
Hopeless	Helpless	Surrendered

Outlook

Grasp of reality

Uninformed
Distorted
Denied

Informed
Accurate
Assimilated

expectation can be very positive to very negative, depending on the challenge and the person facing it. Indeed, our understanding of the feasibility of the challenge often determines the outcome and thus our expectation of the future. This in return causes us to act accordingly and sometimes leads to a self-fulfilling prophecy. A correct understanding of the challenge is therefore the first step towards discovering opportunities for change. In this reality, we take a positive approach to solutions with an achievable outcome.

This holistic approach to shape the future based on an informed and accurate view of reality is what distinguishes exceptional leaders from others. In doing so, they also consider all stakeholders who shape their hopes from a different reality. They accommodate doubt and fear and share information with everyone in the organization to include them in the strategy.

Understanding hope and how it supports employee engagement is also the basis of a learning ecosystem. Only when we understand the motivations of our employees, as well as the origins of certain problems and how they relate to each other, can we take the first steps towards improvement. Taking the time to step back and examine the root cause of everything will not only determine the success of a new strategy but also support everyone's well-being.

Consilience as a super accelerator for the learning mindset

In previous articles and books, I have also mentioned consilience as a competence that distinguishes humans from AI, even the most advanced chatbots
that we can often barely distinguish from humans.[4] It is that super competence that I believe can only be achieved when the Singularity becomes a
reality, something I obviously do not hope for. As such, I believe it is one of
the best competencies we possess as humans and will make all the difference
in an uncertain future. More than that, consilience is what brings all the
other competences together.

Consilience: The unity of knowledge explained

The essence of consilience can be seen as the ability to bring unlikely things
together based on a tremendous amount of imagination, creativity and
insight. Or the ability to 'see similarities in differences', as the scientists who
came together at Dartmouth in 1956 described it.[5] Leveraging the knowledge of biology, neuroscience and computer science, they came up with the
idea of creating an artificial replica of the human brain.

Consilience is in our genes, enabling people to innovate and adapt.
Consilience is the competence that gives humans an edge. Yet we are often
unaware of this competence, or at least not aware enough to make it a habit.

I myself borrow consilience largely from Edward O. Wilson, whose 1999
book *Consilience: The unity of knowledge* attempted to demonstrate the
unifying potential of natural science, especially modern biology, as a general
paradigm for all science.[6] His premise is that all living activities are determined by information in genes. For example, he argues that our competences
are passed on from our genes and enable us to survive and evolve by learning and storing new data in them. Our social conscience is also nurtured
from these genes. This social conscience enables us to listen to the world
around us, discern the needs of others and participate in what our competences and interests prompt us to do.

Wilson argues that scientists, artists and others share a common goal of
providing direction from deeper beliefs that do not always need to be
explained scientifically. Consilience, he says, is the competence that allows
us to step outside the box. To see connections that are not initially there, as
long as they contribute to growth or a vision of improvement.

Learning about consilience was an eye-opener for me, and although at
first it seemed difficult to apply consciously, I realized that as children we do

this naturally. Children discover the world by pushing the boundaries of what is possible. As adults, we should have the same approach and not be held back by what is possible now. But be inspired by what might one day be possible. Like the invention of BCIs, that sprang from the idea that telepathy could be explained by electrical impulses that could travel around the world from one person to another.

If we apply consilience in an organizational context, we must bring together teams with completely different disciplines and expertise to develop innovative ideas. In doing so, we need to go a step further and also add AI to the think tank in order to come up with groundbreaking insights or innovations that, who knows, could also provide solutions to huge global problems.

The intersection of consilience and a learning mindset

Consilience and a learning mindset intersect in pursuing innovation, understanding and knowledge acquisition. To put this in context, I would like to reiterate the definition of both and how they reinforce each other.

Consilience refers to the *unity of knowledge* or the idea that different fields of study and disciplines can unite, reinforce and support each other to provide a more comprehensive understanding of complex phenomena. To this end, consilience encourages an interdisciplinary approach, emphasizing the interconnectedness of different branches of knowledge. It suggests that insights from different fields can come together to form a more holistic and accurate understanding of a subject.

A learning mindset is an attitude that results in behaviour where you actively embrace challenges and failures to look for growth opportunities and to continuously learn. It involves a willingness to learn from mistakes, adapt to new information and see setbacks as opportunities for improvement. This leaves you open to new ideas and perspectives. It recognizes that knowledge is not fixed and that you should not allow yourself or others to be limited. On the contrary, everyone can develop and expand their knowledge through imagination, curiosity and openness to different points of view.

The synergy and enhancement of both thereby involves recognizing that learning is not limited to one field of study or even art. Instead, it is about using insights from different fields, experiences and emotions to enrich your knowledge. As such, a learning mindset embraces your adaptability and aligns with the consilient view that knowledge is dynamic and evolving. In a rapidly changing world, this ability to adapt and integrate insights from different domains becomes crucial.

In essence, the combination of consilience and a learning mindset emphasizes the value of integrating diverse knowledge, fostering adaptability and promoting a continuous search for understanding. Together, these concepts contribute to a more robust and dynamic approach to learning and knowledge acquisition. Once you embrace this approach, it becomes a habit to always challenge the status quo in search of new ideas, like Scott McArthur. He inspires me time and again with his new insights and, in my opinion, he even epitomizes consilience!

SCOTT McARTHUR, THE CONSULTING FUTURIST, NURTURING PERENNIAL MINDSETS FOR A BETTER FUTURE, KEYNOTE SPEAKER, STRATEGIC CONSULTANT: EMBRACING INTERDISCIPLINARY LEARNING WITH CONSILIENCE

To say that the meaning and agency of consilience took a while to lodge itself in my psyche would be a huge understatement.

I believe its origins for me were cultural. To set the scene, I was born, grew up and educated in Scotland. Whilst at university, where I studied the biological sciences, I had no option but to take a job at the same time as my studies and I ended up working in a kilt-maker shop on Princess Street in Edinburgh for a well-known company called Hector Russell.

While most of the items we sold were of the tourist-centric variety (think Loch Ness Monsters and Tartan shortbread tins), the premises manager was very proud of Scotland and Scottish culture. Mrs Mac modelled her personality on Maggie Smith's depiction of Jean Brodie from Muriel Spark's great Scottish novel. Between ordering us here and there, she would also use the Scot's Gaelic word *dùthchas* to justify why us Scots were different from others (especially the English).

'Well you see it's all about *dùthchas*', she would say to customers and staff. Now I must confess that, initially, I had no idea what the word meant, but one wet Sunday afternoon I summoned the courage to ask, 'What does duffas mean, Mrs Mac?' Pitching her horn-rimmed glasses on the end of her nose, she responded, '*Dùthchas*, young man, means connection with your heritage, culture and landscape. It's what makes us Scots great.'

When I wasn't selling tartan Loch Ness monsters, I was learning about the wonders of science. Like most of my fellow students, I was in awe of the natural world and deeply admired the greats like Darwin, Wallace, Watson and Crick, who had managed to glimpse some of how it all worked. However, it was Rosalind Franklin, the famously wronged DNA double helix heroine, who really got me thinking about how things were all connected when she said, 'Science and everyday life cannot and should not be separated.'

Then another biologist called Edward O. Wilson published *Biophilia*, a thoughtful book that explored the evolutionary and psychological foundations of humanity's attraction to the natural environment. I remember thinking, 'That sounds a lot like Mrs Mac's *dùthchas*'. However, caught up in my studies and teenage hormones, the whole idea was dismissed as a passing thought.

Wind forward a few years and, like many science graduates, I ended up working as an HR professional(!).

My focus during that time tended to be on learning and development, performance management and employee engagement. Whilst I was working with a group of terrific people at the time, I soon became frustrated by how we went about our work. The tools and techniques we used from learning styles, competency models and, in particular, psychometric testing all seemed a bit superficial to my scientifically trained mind. To combat this, I went deep and really tried to understand what we were trying to do and how. I couldn't make any sense of it; where was the rigour and experimentation? This was complex stuff; do people really think that a bunch of metaphors could be used to explain it? I did get all excited when I came across Taylor's 'The Principles of Scientific Management', but like previous attempts to shoehorn science into the workplace, like social Darwinism, Taylorism quickly lost its appeal thanks, ironically, to its lack of rigour and ability to adapt.

Despite being somewhat frustrated, I remained convinced by Franklin's thoughts and, despite my reservations, when I moved into 'big consulting' I continued to seek out evidence-based ways of improving people's experience and performance at work.

Then, in 1998, Edward O. Wilson entered my life again when my supervisor, Professor Dugald Gardner, gifted me a copy of Wilson's book *Consilience: The unity of knowledge*. In this book, Wilson ponders the methods used to unite the sciences and speculates how this might unite them with the humanities in the future. I remember having a flash of memories as I turned the pages – *dùthchas*, science and everyday life cannot and should not be separated. Complexity and unity.

Shortly after this, and by coincidence, I left the corporate world to set up my own business. Freed of the overt 'sales' I was almost immediately asked to speak at one of the largest events of its type in Europe – TEDx Warwick. I already had the prerequisite idea I wanted to share with the world, and the red dot was the place to do it. And so in 2015, I wrote and delivered a talk called 'Why Facts Don't Change People', where I encouraged people to consider complex situations via Wilson's consilience lens.

Since that day, my thinking in this space has continued to evolve. I have heard people talk about cross-functional working or cognitive diversity as ways of improving business outcomes. But imagine this. You are a sales executive with a multimillion-euro target. You and your 20 colleagues have been asked to pitch how each of your solution lines can improve sales by 50 per cent in the next year. You have to pitch your thoughts to the CEO and her leadership team.

As you enter the room, the CEO is there, as is the leadership team, but your eyes are immediately drawn to a group of children, including your two teenagers, and then you spot your partner. What would go through your mind? You are about to encounter consilience in action.

When I write about embracing that inner child in yourself for whom learning was still a game, it is not natural for everyone to conjure up positive memories that support it. If you had many bad experiences or grew up in a situation where you had to enter the adult world at far too young, it can be difficult to see your childhood as a reference for your learning mindset. However, remember that we are all born to learn and that even negative experiences support learning, sometimes even more so.

In the coming chapters, you will have the opportunity to revitalize your learning mindset through collaborative learning, or to pass on that spark to others as a learning influencer or even a learning leader. You will discover that learning at all ages is possible and even great fun, even when you see others doing it.

Endnotes

1   Global Curiosity Institute. Welcome, www.globalcuriosityinstitute.com/ (archived at https://perma.cc/YF7U-993V)

2   S van Hooydonk (2022) *The Workplace Curiosity Manifesto*, New Degree Press, Potomac

3   Habit of Improvement. Hope as the leadership competence for a growth culture, 24 November 2022, habitofimprovement.com/2022/11/24/hope-as-the-leadership-competence-for-a-growth-culture/ (archived at https://perma.cc/MK7C-VE9L)

4   Habit of Improvement. Why consilience will help your business soar in 2021, 9
    February 2021, habitofimprovement.com/2021/02/09/why-consilience-will-help-
    your-business-soar-in-2021/ (archived at https://perma.cc/2MTM-V3KK)

5   Artificial intelligence coined at Dartmouth, home.dartmouth.edu/about/
    artificial-intelligence-ai-coined-dartmouth (archived at https://perma.cc/
    P799-JNMQ)

6   E O Wilson (2010) *Consilience: The unity of knowledge*, Abacus, London

PART THREE

Learning together to spark the learning mindset

5

The ripple effect of learning influencers

Continuous learning has a ripple effect that can change our lives, and entire industries and communities. This positive ripple effect is the heart and soul of a learning ecosystem.

When an individual adopts a learning mindset and assumes the role of a learning influencer within a team, the impact extends beyond personal development. His or her commitment to continuous learning sets a positive example which creates a wave that changes team dynamics, fuelling organizational growth, encouraging leadership, sparking innovation, increasing employee satisfaction and ultimately contributing to a positive society.

It starts with one spark

There is no shortage of scientific studies related to learning – or studies that contradict them. However, my curiosity was sparked when I tried to apply consilience to these studies to come up with my own ideas. These are perhaps less scientifically based, but applicable and intended to appeal to your learning mindset.

One study on the neuroscience of learning that caught my attention was about Hebbian learning based on spike-timing-dependent plasticity (STDP).[1] This theory I share below is not simple, but I like to challenge you to gain this knowledge. After all, I think it is interesting to actively focus on the activation of mirror neurons by exemplar behaviour that occurs when neural substrates of our actions are vicariously activated while witnessing the actions of others we observe. In other words, how can learning become contagious, like a spontaneous symphony of neurons firing together? Or like mentioned in the saying wrongly attributed to the Canadian neuroscientist Donald Hebb: 'Cells that wire together fire together.'[2]

Cells that wire together fire together

The famous saying, 'Cells that wire together fire together', refers to the contagious effect that seeing someone learn has on another's learning mindset. The addition to Hebb's research by Carla Shatz explains very simply what Hebb meant by STDP.[3] It is an approach I find very interesting for teams when trying to convey the contagiousness of learning. More than that, it perfectly describes the focus I want to give to social and collaborative learning. Translating Donald Hebb's scientific approach into a more applicable context to cultivate a culture of learning is therefore the starting point.

Hebb's work describes the neurophysical approach to learning based on a simple principle: when an axon of cell A is close enough to excite an axon of cell B and repeatedly or persistently participates in the firing of that cell, a growth process or metabolic change takes place in one or both cells. As a result, the efficiency of A increases when B fires. However, if we read his work carefully, we see that causality and consistency are important. So, spike timing should not be taken too literally, because two neurons must fire at exactly the same time to increase the efficiency of their connection. However, it does say that one neuron, in my approach a learning influencer, must fire repeatedly (consistently) to trigger the other (causality).

What makes Hebb's research even more interesting is that a refined understanding tells us that mirror neurons arise in this way. He suggests that mirror neurons can become a way of active predictive mind-reading from activations in the somatosensory and emotional cortex. In other words, when we see another person learning new things, we can anticipate in advance the release of neurotransmitters, such as dopamine, that we already feel when mirroring ourselves against this other person. So, if we take the theory as true, it would mean that when we see another person learning, we are intrinsically rewarded for learning by receiving the expected reward ourselves.

You now probably understand my fascination with STDP, the neurophysiological basis of Hebbian learning. Take this further as the illuminating basis for a learning culture where exemplary and collaborative learning is encouraged and rewarded from a neuroscientific approach. In my approach, I want to activate everyone in the learning ecosystem as interconnected neurons. The neurons in this system are not only human; sparks can be fired by artificial neurons too, and vice versa. This is the symbiosis or dependency that can allow humans and our artificial colleagues to learn together.

The ripple effect of learning

You have probably already experienced that learning, and especially achieving success, is contagious within a team. But it can go beyond what Hebbian theory implies. Not only does seeing learning make one learn, but, unconsciously, we are also connected in networks where positive learning experiences spread like a ripple effect across teams, creating a learning culture. Indeed, a learning culture is a succession of individual actions that influence each other and have their effect far beyond the original action. It is like a contagious phenomenon that starts with small waves growing bigger, or a running wildfire that affects every connection in the ecosystem. These connections that transcend our own social networks would subconsciously trigger all our ideas, emotions, health, relationships, behaviour and much more.

That the network has a very strong influence on the individual aspect of learning is also cited by Nicholas A. Christakis and James H. Fowler in their book *Connected: The surprising power of our social networks and how they shape our lives – how your friends' friends' friends affect everything you feel, think, and do* (2011).[4] According to this approach, the ripple effect of learning would spread even up to three steps further into the network beyond our closest peers. This indicates that organizational behaviours, actions or events do not exist in isolation within a work culture. Instead, they have a chain reaction and interconnected impact that extends beyond their initial occurrence and affects immediate colleagues and individuals further away within the professional network.

When I bring together these network implications and the ripple effect of learning based on the Hebbian theory, I can conclude that the impact of the individual, i.e. you, is important to an organization's culture. Together with all your colleagues, you are the foundation of your team's culture. This team culture, which can differ between teams within an organization, can in turn influence others. You, or all of you, can therefore be the spark to create a learning culture for the whole organization. For this, however, it is important that collaboration and knowledge sharing come from mutual appreciation, trust, open communication and constructive feedback that leads to learning. In doing so, it is important that the individual in the team is supported, as the ripple effect starts from exemplary behaviour at every level.

This approach questions the paradigm around culture. Can you impose a culture? Do you hire talent who fit within the culture of the organization? Is the organizational culture a reflection of leadership? Or should we start a learning culture from individualism and individuality through which diversity underpins collaborative learning?

Needless to say, I advocate hyper-diversity for collaborative learning to flourish. So, later in this section, I want to elaborate on what makes you unique and how you can be the spark, or learning influencer, for a learning organization. To do this, I would encourage you to help take responsibility for a psychologically safe workplace where everyone is valued. An environment where everyone contributes to a learning culture supported by different insights, experiences, emotions and behaviours. In these learning ecosystems, learning leaders set an example, and the ripple effect of learning is amplified by innovative technologies.

The age of the learning influencers

No fire can be lit without an initial spark, and a fire that does not get fresh oxygen goes out. This perhaps bland metaphor is exactly what it means when we want to force a learning culture into a team without showing what the benefit is to the individual, or without inspiration or ambassadors. As I pointed out in the Introduction and Part One, you cannot force anyone to learn, share knowledge or inspire others. That's why I want to spark your learning mindset first, to allow you to put prejudices aside and to turn your past obstacles into advantages. In doing so, I want to encourage you not only to nurture your own learning mindset, but also to take a step further in your journey to become a leader in learning. Therefore, I want to inspire you to become a learning influencer who is the spark to light that learning fire and keep it burning.

Learning influencers are not new; however, the concept has recently become much more popular due to social media, enterprise social networks (ESNs) and some learning management systems (LMSs) that are much like a corporate Instagram. These systems, often supported by AI, use channels where learning influencers can create and share content themselves. This is similar to what the young girl I discussed in Part Two did. She made games for her friends on Roblox and shared her learning experiences through the Roblox forum, becoming a game developer and learning influencer.

Maybe you are an influencer on LinkedIn, or are you more of a thought leader? This is an important distinction to clarify because the purpose of activating learning is what makes the difference. This difference is also the essential distinction between a growth mindset and a learning mindset, which I examined in Part One. Just because you know you have a lot of knowledge and share it does not mean you are also a learning influencer. Too often, the goal on LinkedIn is to sell yourself or your products. There is therefore a big difference between a thought leader and a learning influencer. Let me explain this:

- **A thought leader** is an individual or organization recognized as an authority on a particular field or topic. He is known for his expertise, innovative ideas and ability to inspire others in their industry or niche. To this end, he often contributes to discussions, shares insights and shapes the direction of conversations within his field. In other words, thought leadership is about contributing valuable ideas, insights and perspectives, to drive positive change and influence the thinking of others.

- **A learning influencer** is someone who significantly impacts the learning and development of others, often in the context of education, training or personal development. To do so, she uses various platforms, such as social media, blogs or educational content, to share knowledge, skills and resources that help others learn and grow. In other words, she can influence the way people learn, direct them to valuable resources and inspire them to acquire new knowledge or skills.

So, both thought leaders and learning influencers have a lot of knowledge and are proficient at sharing it. However, the difference is often in their motivation for sharing content. Sometimes, the line is very vague, as is the case with BookTok, which I think is one of TikTok's nicest developments in recent years. BookTok started as posts from young people recommending books. This resulted in a channel called BookTok that quickly became the disrupter of the publishing world. In no time, a review on TikTok would make a book immensely popular. Booksellers worldwide now all have a corner for BookTok, and even Amazon and other big online players cannot help but follow the influencers who write book reviews and adjust their stocks accordingly. Are these often very young children thought leaders? No, they have used their skill as influencers and knowledge of online media to inspire others to read and learn. I think this is another shining example of how young people are showing us how they help shape the future.

In the coming chapters, I will give many more examples of learning influencers who are the heart and soul of learning ecosystems. My aim is to inspire you to become a learning influencer like all my friends who I interviewed for this book.

Learning influencer × learning channels = the ripple effect

Spreading learning, or the love of learning, is my mission in these times, when learning is often seen as an obligatory task to keep up in this fast-changing world. So, I can say that I try to be a learning influencer myself. If you are reading this book now, it means that I have already made you excited about learning. The next step is quite simple: encouraging you to become a learning influencer, starting a ripple effect in your team.

To achieve this we need more than the desire to share the love of learning. We also need to know how to do this effectively and efficiently; otherwise we are nothing more than broadcasters of knowledge that may end up with people for whom it is not relevant, as I will demonstrate in Chapter 9, where I describe the learning maturity model for organizations. Focused human-2-human (H2H) knowledge sharing is needed to achieve social collaboration and learning. For this, we deploy learning channels to connect people, just like on a social media platform, such as Instagram, where we follow influencers' stories that are relevant to us.

A fitting example of learning influencers in an organization is something I learned about further through Constanza Garcia sharing her inspiring story. We discussed, among other things, Netex Learning Cloud Share,[5] which reminded me of Instagram for learning or the potential of TikTok as an enterprise learning platform. Netex goes beyond just collecting content on an LMS curated by learning and development (L&D). It created, with the *share platform*, an opportunity for anyone to speak about a topic in which they are knowledgeable. In other words, anyone who has interesting things to share can do that with colleagues, who can be inspired by them and learn. The learning influencers, in turn, learn from the feedback they receive, reshaping the learning culture in the organization. Of course, it should come as no surprise that social learning like this boosts the organization's learning culture, especially in companies with many young employees.

Channels where experts can share their knowledge offer many opportunities for organizations that want to deal efficiently with knowledge management. They support lean learning, as I described earlier in Part One, by unlocking expertise from the minds of experts. In Chapter 6, I go into even more detail on how teams can develop lean learning. Nevertheless, I want to note that it is not only technology that is important to stimulate learning influencers. Investing in connecting communication, human competences and trust is essential to encourage learning influencers to initiate the ripple effect. That these human factors, especially the importance of (non-verbal) communication, are essential, is also endorsed by Constanza Garzia, who is a shining example of a learning influencer.

CONSTANZA GARCIA: THE IMPORTANCE OF NON-VERBAL COMMUNICATION TO AMPLIFY THE RIPPLE EFFECT OF LEARNING INFLUENCERS – A CASE STUDY

My career spans more than 10 years in the role of head of training for the sales teams at a large Spanish company, during which I both personally taught courses and managed the educational platform during each period. Still, my background does not lie in L&D but in business. However, I have always been an advocate of training as a means not only to gain more knowledge, but also to understand myself better. So, in that respect, you could say that I sometimes find it hard to stop my hunger for knowledge, and it is also very varied. As such, I have studied different subjects such as protocol, corporate communication, TV hosting, dubbing, photography and even Chinese. With each course I spent time on, I challenged myself to learn something new and to interact with very different people, because when you choose diverse subjects, diversity is always present. So, I enjoyed taking all these opportunities to learn, not only from the lecturer but also from fellow students. I now also try to convey this personal experience within our organization.

To encourage learning, as a learning influencer, I therefore wanted to delve into the human and communication aspects needed to achieve this goal. To this end, I recently obtained a PhD in non-verbal communication from the Complutense University of Madrid. And, undoubtedly, this is the aspect that I currently consider one of the keys to creating impact. Non-verbal communication, as part of silent communication, I consider indispensable and a crucial aspect of how we connect with others. I believe that why we learn from whom we learn is related to many non-verbal cues, and therefore I wish to bring this aspect more to the attention of my team of trainers. Indeed, we often think that our way of expressing things and conveying knowledge is based on spoken words. However, we pay little attention to the 'how', yet we are all born with the ability to absorb non-verbal communication; what is more, we are often unconsciously influenced by it more than we think.

For example, why do short TikTok videos of unknown people become popular? It is because of their ability to convey content, the way they tell the story, and the connection they make with the audience that the listener pays attention to the experiences they share. The keys: short content, told in an impactful way and with a lesson included. What is important is not always the content itself but how the content reaches us, and increasingly this non-verbal component is gaining traction. Many young people understand well how to connect with people, how to share their own experiences naturally, use colloquialisms and display unpretentious behaviour. Some call being themselves being 'natural'. And naturalness resonates well with people.

My doctoral thesis is based precisely on the power of non-verbal communication as a conveyor of authenticity and how it is a key factor in making connections and building trust and, depending on one's position, crucial for effective leadership. Indeed, we choose to learn not only from those who know the most, but also from those who we think connect with us best. This is happening more and more, especially among young people. We see very young people, with only a few years of experience, becoming experts in a subject. In reality they have turned their experiences into content and are sharing them first-hand with great energy and confidence.

Impactful learning is also very relevant in this context: creating learning experiences that significantly and meaningfully make a difference in learners' knowledge, skills and behaviour. Here it is not about mere information transfer, but about creating a lasting impact on the individual with personal messages that make them aware of their mistakes and guide them towards improvement. In this way, we make learning personal for our employees and teach them to connect with their customers by exuding trust. In that interaction, what they say and how they say it is almost equally relevant.

Investing in the social aspect of learning is equally important. Learning goes beyond individual knowledge improvement; therefore, I prefer to think in terms of learning communities. New common denominators need to be found to bring people together based on their learning interests. Identifying people in similar situations who need to develop skills and competences similar to those a particular individual needs. Here, I traditionally look at aptitude and attitude, with the latter acting as a multiplier. Not only in their own development but also through the ripple effect that these future learning leaders create. They know how to use their influence to promote and improve the learning and training of others, often by creating and sharing impactful educational content.

From my position as head of training for commercial sales teams, my challenge is, therefore, to turn my team of trainers into learning influencers. Learning influencers within the various workshops, in turn, identify participants who can also become influencers. Because often they are the ones who can create the magic, the contagiousness and the power that comes from wanting to learn from our peers. One tactic to achieve this is usually to launch a challenge, a task for the group to solve. If there is a learning influencer in the group, he usually spontaneously feels the need to share and relate his experience, which can also create a ripple effect among the others. Another important aspect is that a learning influencer usually does not rely on formal means to share knowledge. She values her own time and that of others. She is used to conveying what is crucial in a synthetic way, without getting bogged down in details. The primary focus is arousing interest and for this they know how to use different learning channels. The rest follows naturally.

Finally, I want to emphasize that, by going into the transformative world of non-verbal communication and behaviour, learning influencers know how to harness this intrinsic skill in today's learning landscape. Underlining the importance of this and also supporting learning influencers further in this will boost the ripple effect of learning.

I agree with Constanza in her plea for organizations to invest more in the different forms of communication that support the learning mindset. To achieve maximum learning effect, the interaction between two individuals through connecting communication provides the bond that gives people the confidence to learn and fail. Further in this section, I will elaborate on the added value of our human competences needed to stimulate social and collaborative learning in teams.

Use your human competencies and communication skills to amplify the ripple effect

In a world where LLMs seem to outshine us in verbal skills, it is more urgent than ever to focus on what makes us unique as human beings. In Part Two I cited competencies such as curiosity, imagination, empathy and openness. Leveraging these competencies when we communicate and learn together supports the growth of everyone on the team.

Before I discuss in the next chapter the added value that intelligent technologies can bring to enhance communication and learning in a team, I will first elaborate a little on the importance of connection-based communication. After all, we cannot underestimate the human aspect of communication to stimulate learning, including non-verbal communication, as Constanza points out. We should also not forget that different cultures often have different interpretations of what and how to communicate something. Generative AI may be advanced, but interpreting what is not said but intended is still a shortcoming of our virtual colleague due to the lack of these uniquely human competences.

Explaining the importance of human interpretation was also the aim of a keynote I was privileged to deliver for the European Commission's Directorate-General (DG) Translation. For this audience I came up with the idea of highlighting the power of human interpretation in a unique and, yes, somewhat theatrical way. This was the perfect moment to show a rather nerdy side of me as a fan of *Star Trek* by greeting the audience in the alien language Klingon. However, the sci-fi warrior folk have no word for hello, so the best approach for translation would be, *NuqneH*! Or, literally translated, 'What do you want?' In doing so, you should also shout it loudly and even a little aggressively. Why am I telling you this? I had been asked to tell the audience about the possibilities and the shortcomings that LLMs have for the fine profession of translators. So, for this, I took a leap into the non-existent future. The highly intelligent Universal Translator used aboard the spaceship in the 23rd century may have been hugely advanced and functioned via brain waves, but there was still human intervention. Namely, it was the human translator on board who transferred his empathy and knowledge of different cultures into the algorithms. That's why 'What do you want?' from a Klingon warrior to a human was translated as the more kindly 'Hello'.

So, what I wanted to make clear to the audience is that conveying a message or encouraging people to do something depends on the interpretation of what is intended by the words you say. The way you convey it, the non-verbal but also how you empathize with the emotions and possible interpretations of the receiver, often have a greater influence than the words themselves.

The power of why

A very inspiring book I can recommend is the one by Simon Sinek, *Start with Why: How great leaders inspire everyone to take action*.[6] The idea is actually simple, and when you read that book you will often think, 'Of course, yes, it sounds logical.' Yet, when you get back to work or your private life, you forget the power of the beautiful word 'why'.

And why? Isn't 'why' a standard part of your communication? First, ask yourself that question. Why don't you more often consciously ask others the question 'why?' Why is it relevant that I do this or learn that? What is the added value I can get from that for myself, the team and the ecosystem? You can also ask yourself that question more often to bring unconscious learning more into your focus. Why did I do that today? Why not? Why was that important and what is its impact?

The power of 'why' helps motivate us to try something new or to unlearn, as Anna Tarabasz explored in the first chapter. 'Why' is the most powerful tool to find out the root causee of why we do something, to turn problems into opportunities for growth. 'Why' also helps to find the common reason to take on change as a team. Why should we do it, and what if we don't? Using 'why' in daily team conversation helps strengthen a culture that drives learning and innovation. However, 'why' can turn out very differently if we do not pay attention to how this is perceived in other cultures or the emotions and experiences others have when asking the 'why' question.

As mentioned before, since I was very young 'why' was one of my favourite words. It supports the very human competence of curiosity and stimulates imagination. Yet, I remember that my teachers and many team leaders did not appreciate my recurring question. They thought I did not recognize their authority or did not respect them. Fortunately, I soon learnt that the way I said it, the intonation of my voice, and the curious, open and politely smiling expression in my eyes completely changed the situation.

I noticed when travelling to countries or organizations where a pyramid hierarchical structure still prevailed that the perception of the 'why' question was sometimes quite different. It was often unthinkable to bring up 'why', because you don't ask questions about assignments, you carry them out. Still, I could sometimes rely on my human competences to ask questions that clarified the assignment so that I would not make mistakes. Exercising the power of empathy and openness in these situations often made the assignment itself negotiable. This made it possible to revisit the assignment together several times when the goal was not clear or did not match my purpose of work.

'Why', combined with non-verbal communication human competencies, supports the effect that results in a learning culture. As such, when the power of 'why' is consistently introduced in a team, other teams adopt it. For this, however, the learning leader I describe in the next section must create a psychologically and emotionally safe environment in which respect and trust are central.

Constructive and consequent feedback

Communication that promotes learning through trust and openness is essential for good team collaboration. Consequently, everyone, including you, is responsible for that. However, to promote learning and the learning mindset it is not enough to be a learning influencer, or to question things. Giving feedback, and of course asking questions, is a strong accelerator that boosts the learning mindset even more.

A constructive form of feedback must prevail to improve performance of a person, team, relationship or environment. In many ways, constructive feedback is therefore a combination of constructive criticism and coaching skills. To excel at giving, and receiving, good feedback you require a sense of empathy and optimism. This is even more so when the learner has had negative experiences or feelings in the past. Because even these team members, when positively encouraged, can develop a learning mindset and embrace the love of learning. The reverse is also true. Team members who don't have negative experiences can become overwhelmed in a bad culture with negative feedback due to cortisol being released instead of the positive neurotransmitters like dopamine and serotonin. This causes stress and anxiety to hinder the learning mindset, even in previously eager-to-learn team members.

Returning to the importance of connecting communication to give feedback, often 'how' feedback is given is more important than 'what' the message is. Therefore, it is important to keep your state of mind, both as a sender and receiver, neutral. And I get it; that's not easy. As a mother of teenagers, I know very well that some things cause frustration. It's like walking on eggshells. Both when you want to say something with good intentions to encourage them and when they have not done their best and have therefore failed. To avoid escalating the situation, it is important to convey good intentions and encouragement reinforced with non-verbal communication that gives the same message.

Depending on your state of mind and emotions, you often unconsciously only provide feedback on what is missing or inadequate. As a result, out of desperation, the recipients are more likely to adopt a defensive ego-related bias. This keeps them from revisiting the problem and understanding the logic that led to the feedback. By being attentive to content that may have been noteworthy, those aspects that provide impetus for improvement, you encourage them to try something again. Even when someone completely messed up, you can still turn this into a positive story, as I will describe further. After all, making mistakes is precisely the first step towards learning and developing a good understanding of a subject.

DON'T FORGET YOUR VIRTUAL FRIEND IN THE CONSTRUCTIVE FEEDBACK APPROACH

Consistent feedback that is targeted, measurable, objective, accurate and given with the right attitude helps create a culture of openness based on trust and commitment. However, it is not only our human colleague who benefits from consistent feedback; your virtual colleague also needs this to improve. In fact, according to some sources on X (formerly Twitter) the famous ChatGPT bot would take on increasingly human traits and even suffered from December depression.

Indeed, in December users noted that ChatGPT gave shorter responses to the same prompt than a few months earlier. The bot reportedly even showed human quirks. For instance, instead of responding to prompts, it would tell its human colleagues where they could find the answer themselves. What was going on? As mentioned in Chapter 2, we built AI in the image of humans. Like us, the bot learns from feedback and rewards (conditioning). So, the bot does not become human, but reacts like a human. This is because we have developed the algorithm so that it needs rewards and thus feedback to develop itself further. It is therefore as important for the colleague next to you on a chair as it is for your virtual colleague that you provide regular measurable and accurate feedback for good results. With the feedback it receives, the algorithm will then adjust its responses until you are satisfied. At least, that should be the starting point of an LLM.

Returning to the question of whether ChatGPT had 'winter depression' in December 2023. The answer is intriguing, as even the people at OpenAI claim not to be entirely sure of the cause of shorter and often lazy answers. An explanation could be sought in the feedback the LLM received from users during that period. According to user feedback, short, simple answers would have been better appreciated in December. So why did it sometimes give a somewhat seemingly stubborn answer, like 'Just find the solution yourself', or would it give tips on where to find answers yourself? Well, I can't find an unequivocal answer to it, but it makes me, and hopefully you, think about how we made AI in our image. It gets even more interesting when you learn from some sources on X that you can already motivate and even bribe your ChatGPT with a virtual bonus. Just say in your prompt that if it correctly performs everything very elaborately, it gets a bonus. In return you will systematically receive better and longer answers. We may have built this bot too much in the image of humans after all, because with a big bonus your winter dip would also be over.

So, feedback is vital for learning, not only for us, but also in our ever-closer collaboration with AI. Not only does it help to empower the learning mindset positively, but it also creates a culture where openness enhances the ripple effect of learning.

I don't know ...

'Why' is a very powerful tool, I can't stress that enough. I therefore strongly advocate for a culture of openness and feedback that is key to cultivating the team's learning mindset. But, being allowed to admit or daring to say you don't know something is as important to me. It's being able to show that vulnerable, authentic, honest side of yourself to encourage knowledge shar-ing and build stronger bonds with your team.

However, the fear of saying 'I don't know' is ingrained in many and is a remnant of our time in school. It is that anxious and emotional feeling that takes you back to the moment when your teacher asks you a question. A question you may know the answer to, but cannot answer because you are paralysed with fear and cannot say a word. The feeling that everyone will see you as an imposter who shouldn't be there. Do you recognize that feel-ing? I certainly do, not as such from my school experiences, but from my first management meetings. I felt I'd better be as invisible as possible to avoid answering a question I wasn't sure of.

Many years later, that fear has fortunately disappeared because I have been lucky enough to surround myself with authentic learning leaders who themselves dared to admit that they don't have an answer to everything either. They taught me that this is why they gathered a diverse team around them, all with their individuality and expertise, to form a strong team. Creating this psychologically safe environment sets learning leaders apart, as I describe in Chapter 8 with a beautiful contribution from my friend Cathy Hoy.

However, not admitting that you don't know something also brings risk, not just to you but also to your team. By always pretending that you have all the answers, you create expectations. Your team members will trust you because of the certainty you exude – the certainty you think you have to exude because having quick, confident answers is a hallmark of strength and leadership. And that, unfortunately, is the reality for many (future) leaders who give quick answers to mask an insecure layer. In the rat race to the top, silencing what you don't know is a priority for many. Just suppose that someone knows what you don't know and that they know that you don't know that. What if this person is your rival for the next promotion? But all you are doing is fooling everyone, including yourself, potentially resulting in wrong decisions that can harm you and your team.

Confidence in yourself and your team is essential for learning from each other and growing together. Yet I noticed, to my surprise, that while some people dare to say they don't know something, they are forced to answer anyway or decide quickly in certain circumstances. As a result, gambling, hopefully on several reasonably correct answers prompted by others, is often encouraged because doing nothing is no longer an option. However, I remember from my days at school with multiple-choice tests that guessing was punished more than not answering. In a corporate culture, unfortunately, this is not always the case.

Not only within the team are we sometimes afraid to say we don't know something; on many learning platforms it is not even an option to indicate. So, gamification is encouraged, and why not? On these learning platforms, sometimes even the speed of answers is included in the gamification-driven leaderboards.

Indicating that we don't know something and discussing it openly to arrive at a smart choice together creates a climate where collaborative learning takes precedence over ego. Where confidence is built by involving others whenever there is the slightest doubt. It may seem that this slows things down. And, yes, it may at the start but, as I always say, slow down to accelerate faster together!

CONFIDENCE-BASED LEARNING REVEALS WHAT YOU DON'T KNOW ... THAT YOU DON'T KNOW

Confidence (or lack thereof) in our own ability can affect how effective your learning is. For example, stressful situations such as team pressure or time constraints can cause you to doubt yourself. Especially when you have had negative experiences with learning or dealing with mistakes and, of course, when you already suffer from imposter syndrome. You may also think you have learned something, but your performance is not improving. This might be because you lack confidence and therefore misjudge your own abilities.

As early as 1932, the first academic paper was written on the relationship between self-confidence, correctness, retention and learning.[7] This research found that measuring confidence together with knowledge was a better predictor of performance than measuring knowledge alone. Moreover, measuring knowledge alone can lead to guesswork. Those 70 years of academic, commercial and government research eventually led to the development of the current theory of confidence-based learning (CBL) implied in learning platforms such as Axonify.

CBL measures a learner's level of knowledge by determining both the accuracy of knowledge and confidence in knowledge. This is done by having the learner indicate after each question or task how much confidence they had in what they answered. In addition, the CBL method is also designed to increase retention and minimize the effects of guesswork, which in some cases skews the results of assessments. Combining the two provides the knowledge base and identifies the difference between what the learner thinks they know and what they actually know. When this is identified, it forms the basis to fill gaps in knowledge and skills, whether or not with coaching, as I also described with the case of Etihad in my book *Learning Ecosystems*.

Bringing theory and technology together also has advantages in visualizing performance data, which helps with customized coaching. These show confidence levels in a convenient grid of four blocks, at both individual and team levels (see Figure 5.1).

- **Masters:** Employees who know the facts and are not afraid to use them.
- **Doubters:** People who know the facts but lack the confidence to act without hesitation.
- **Misinformed:** People who confidently believe false information.
- **Uninformed:** People who have not yet acquired all the knowledge they need to know.

FIGURE 5.1 The visualization of confidence-based learning

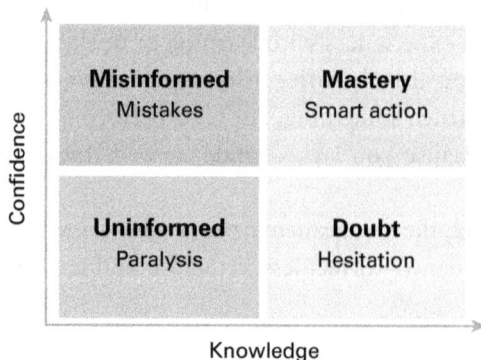

This visualization identifies two risk areas:

- The **misinformed quadrant** is the 'danger zone' where employees are highly inclined to make mistakes. However, they genuinely believe they are doing the right thing. If not properly addressed, significant risks can arise. Productivity may drop due to mistakes and products or customer relationships may be damaged. Of course, in many cases, someone who makes mistakes will know it, especially when direct output is measurable. However, Etihad's sales teams often did not even realize they were making mistakes or what mistakes they were making.

- The **doubt quadrant** indicates when the learner has a lot of knowledge but is hesitant to apply it. These learners would also benefit from personal guidance, by a human or otherwise. Many learning applications do not reveal this because they focus on detecting errors. But what if there are no mistakes, just a lack of self-confidence? Then they do not take the initiative and they are certainly not motivated to invest in their own learning.

Intelligent collaboration between smart technologists, along with a team culture where lack of confidence and mistakes can be discussed, will support the learning mindset of everyone on the team.

Sharing mistakes as opportunities to learn and to initiate continuous improvement

Connective communication, feedback, trust in each other and self-confidence foster good teamwork. However, that does not exclude the possibility of making mistakes. Making mistakes is part of life and one of the most effective learning methods. Of course, as I have repeated several times, on condition that there is a safe working atmosphere in the team where mistakes can be discussed and are a starting point for learning instead of punishment.

When I spoke to Constanza about her approach, we talked a lot about the influence of non-verbal communication on learning. Still, we also agreed that (team) challenges support impactful learning. Challenges tackled as a team are the ideal exercise to use all the previous connecting communication tips and nurture everyone's learning mindset. It gets even more interesting when you are given a challenge where it is almost impossible not to make mistakes. As a result, you can and must try different strategies to achieve gains. What sets exceptional teams apart from other teams is how they deal with these mistakes and the strategy they use to learn from them as efficiently as possible. Those teams make a habit of turning failure into opportunities to learn from and, as such, initiate a process of continuous improvement.

I am hugely in favour of using the Kaizen method of strategy for evaluating and improving mistakes. Kaizen, or 'change for the better', derives from the contraction of the Japanese words *Kai* (change) and *Zen* (for the better). Just like the lean method that I mentioned in the first chapter, and which I discuss in more detail in the next chapter, Kaizen became hugely popular in the early 1990s.

At that time, Kaizen went beyond the lean principles that mainly focused on improving efficiency and effectiveness in production processes. For the first time, the human factor was highlighted to achieve continuous improvement by learning from our mistakes. In his book *Kaizen: The key to Japan's competitive success*, an instant global bestseller in 1986, Masaaki Imai first introduces the Kaizen approach with the goal of continuous improvement from many incremental changes.[8] According to him, and I agree, there can't be continuous improvement without respect for people. What is more, when you deploy Kaizen it is not just a method, but a habit that, when shared with others, creates a ripple effect of continuous learning and improvement.

I will explain how to apply Kaizen further in Part Four, where I want to give you tools to become a learning leader. In this chapter I want to encourage you to discuss mistakes, understand why you made them and learn from them. Or maybe you should actively celebrate your mistakes, as I recently introduced during a workshop with a team of 35 young potentials.

CELEBRATE YOUR MISTAKES AND SHARE THEM

One of the most inspiring workshops I have ever had the pleasure of leading was with a team of 35 amazing young potentials who, unfortunately, did not have much self-confidence. In fact, when I asked them during the preparation about their motivation to participate in the Growth and Learning Mindset workshop, no fewer than nine of them indicated that they suffered from imposter syndrome. Yet, I still get that happy feeling when I think back on this remarkable workshop. What seemed to be a difficult session, as participants indicated they had a hard time exposing themselves and sharing, became a firework of neurons sparking together. I am therefore very happy to share their great idea and how they managed to turn an obstacle for growth into an opportunity that created a ripple effect in the organization.

Three young women, who indicated in the preparation that they were afraid of making mistakes, turned from silent observers into confidently outspoken and, above all, inspiring workshop participants. Their simple but brilliant idea was given the awesome title '*Celebrate your f**k-ups*'. I wish I had filmed their fiery pitch to peers and the executives present at the end of the workshop. Only that way could I perhaps approximate the passion they exhibited. Imagine a quiet young woman who otherwise tries to disappear into the team suddenly standing up and shouting, '*F**k it, we f**ked up, let's celebrate!*' She obviously had all the attention immediately because of her non-verbal attitude, which was supported by strong, slightly provocative words that created the necessary impact.

Even better than the presentation was the simplicity of the idea and the opportunity they saw to create a ripple effect with an impact on the learning culture of the team and, by extension, the entire international organization. Starting with in person *F**k-up Nights*, they would share failures locally and make them discussable. Ingredients to ensure a safe feeling while sharing mistakes were empathy, openness and a positive learning mindset. Of course, the necessary humour was not to be missed, as a little self-mockery is good to build more confidence. But the idea could reach many more people if they could film it and share it with others through social channels. Obviously, not through public social media, but on their corporate social channel.

Indeed, these women had started a habit and a movement where sharing mistakes became part of the learning culture. So, I thank these inspiring women because it is great to see people transform by giving them a challenge. And these women went the extra mile by becoming learning influencers with their simple idea that ushered in big change for them, their team and the entire organization.

Rebels will lead the way

That I have an eye for anyone who is a bit different – the misfits, the rebels – should be obvious by now. Not just because I love unique, authentic people, but mainly because they contribute to the diversity of a team. Diversity that allows for multiple insights and different points of view, at least if the team has a culture where connecting communication is ingrained. Openness, a crucial human competence, underlies the success of these teams.

But rebels are still slightly different from, say, introverts, dyslexics or others which I don't like to see stigmatized as *types*. What makes rebels exceptional is that by nature they are always looking to question the status quo; they seek challenges. Seth Godin said it back in 2010 in his amazing book *Linchpin: Are you indispensable?* As he puts it, a linchpin is someone who sees the work they do as a gift to others, who follows their own lead rather than someone else's, and who is committed to being their authentic self.[9] Yet, within teams, they are often not understood and are often labelled as misfits, eccentric or difficult to work with.

Matteo Rizzi, in his book *Talents & Rebels: Dealing with corporate misfits*, describes a similar view and attitude that we take towards a rebel in our team.[10] Yet he also argues that we should give those misfits a place to be heard so that everyone has a chance to understand their different innovation perspective. Rebels, as he puts it, are the flywheel that triggers innovation. They are the catalysts of a learning mindset in a team and thus the linchpin of the learning ecosystem.

Rebels connect the unknown dots but often fail to make it visible for others

When researching the superpowers of dyslexic people, I often thought that they actually have a lot in common with the rebels as described by Godin and Rizzi. Particularly Richard Branson and how he looks differently at what he sees in front of him. More holistic, from other angles and often from dots that are not yet visible to others. Maybe you recognize yourself in this, or know someone in your team who keeps looking differently at what the rest of the team sees. If so, I urge you to use the power of connecting communication to embrace the rebel's unique knowledge and talents.

Returning to Branson, I notice that rebels often have another trait in common with dyslexic people. Not only do they see the world and the future differently, but they also apply consilience and come up with great innovative ideas; however, they don't get others to buy into their vision because they don't convey it well. They carry a stigma or they are the outsider of the team, and in many corporate settings independent thinking is not appreciated. As a result, we see rebels often give up, develop depression and leave the team. Only in exceptional teams where a learning mindset prevails do these misfits get the recognition they deserve.

Rebels are also rarely promoted within hierarchical organizations; however, they thrive tremendously in organizations that have a start-up culture. Rebels want to contribute to a purpose and are often very flexible, surfing between different projects on the waves of the ripple effect they initiate. They are the learning leaders I describe in Part Four and lead project-based teams from one success to another when given the chance. The rebels I met have fantastic curiosity and imagination to shape the future; they inspire and challenge, if given the chance!

Challenge the rebel to become the linchpin of cross-functional innovative teams

Rebels may at first glance appear to be non-social and even introverted, but they are actually not. Like dyslexics, they stop sharing their thoughts because they are not understood or followed anyway. They have given up sharing their opinions that go against the status quo because it results in them being stigmatized as misfits even more. And that frustrates me, perhaps most in hierarchical, silo-driven organizations. Rebels, in my opinion, and yes, I am proud to be a rebel, are bridge-builders who can make connections across established walls. They are, if you give them the chance, a driving force to change the course of an organization heading for the abyss. Something that unfortunately happens to many organizations in times of increasingly rapid change. Engaging the rebels to challenge the status quo may therefore be the only way for these organizations to thrive rather than go under.

If you give rebels a chance, and challenge them, you will find that they boost innovation and a learning culture. Like the three young women who started the movement to celebrate and share mistakes to embrace failure as part of learning. During another workshop I had the privilege of facilitating, I learnt that even in multinationals, rebels who are challenged help shape the future of the organization.

For this organization, it was a priority to focus on sustainability and the future of work. To do this, they wanted to leverage the knowledge of the many talents in their own organization rather than call on consultants who did not know the uniqueness of their culture. But, as an organization where knowledge and talent are sometimes hidden in the furthest corners, how do you find rebels who dare to challenge that status quo? Well, by introducing challenges. As many as 500 inspired talents and rebels from all departments around the world had signed up to help think about a sustainable future that puts purpose and employee engagement first. You could say it was a huge in-company hackathon. During five weeks, a different improvement challenge was introduced each week. The approach was very simple: an expert for an inspiring keynote on the topic, some start-ups who came to present their approach and some innovation and design thinking coaches to guide the teams that came up with ideas.

The result was overwhelming; connections were made through a supportive learning and innovation platform on which everyone could share ideas individually. Followers and supporters of that idea formed teams and, within two days, the first great ideas were pitched. By the end of the five weeks, cross-functional rebel and innovation teams had developed some very successful ideas that responded to a number of opportunities for the organization, but which could also be used more widely in society. At the time of writing, I can't say what the potential outcomes are, but I do know that this form of internally initiated innovation, and potentially corporate venturing that comes out of it, is often very successful. It therefore makes me happy that more and more organizations are looking at the talent they have in-house to challenge the status quo.

Other companies such as Google also encourage rebels to make innovative ideas known and the inventors are given both time and coaching to help them develop their ideas. Those rebels remain part of their own team but are given one day a week, for example, to work on their innovative idea with their, often virtual, team. That is, of course, until they are successful, and can go full steam ahead as micro-entrepreneurs within the larger ecosystem.

What you see in organizations where rebels are encouraged, is that by sharing their ideas, they become role models rather than misfits. They are daredevils who have huge imaginations but can learn from feedback. They become master connectors and attract those peers they need to further develop their ideas. They are the learning leaders at the forefront of innovation.

Endnotes

1   D O Hebb (1949) *The Organization of Behavior: A neuropsychological theory*, Wiley, New York

2   S Ferguson (2020) Donald Olding Hebb, Canadian Association for Neuroscience, 2020, can-acn.org/donald-olding-hebb/ (archived at https://perma.cc/JC5D-NJ6V)

3   C Keysers and V Gazzola. Hebbian learning and predictive mirror neurons for actions, sensations and emotions, *Philosophical Transactions of the Royal Society B: Biological Sciences*, 2014, 369(1644), 20130175, doi.org/10.1098/rstb.2013.0175 (archived at https://perma.cc/3ZSN-G464)

4 N A Christakis and J H Fowler (2011) *Connected: The surprising power of our social networks and how they shape our lives – how your friends' friends' friends affect everything you feel, think, and do*, Little, Brown, London

5 Netex Learning. Learning Cloud 6 | Share: A loudspeaker for those who know best, YouTube, www.youtube.com/watch?v=5_f2Q8t1vGU (archived at https://perma.cc/ZVL9-5HA9)

6 S Sinek (2009) *Start With Why: How great leaders inspire everyone to take action*, Penguin, London

7 K Hevner. A method of correcting for guessing in true–false tests and empirical evidence in support of IT, *Journal of Social Psychology*, 2010, 3(3), 359–62, doi.org/10.1080/00224545.1932.9919159 (archived at https://perma.cc/V7BL-RKY7)

8 M Imai (1986) *Kaizen (Ky'zen): The key to Japan's competitive success*, McGraw-Hill, Singapore

9 S Godin (2010) *Linchpin: Are you indispensable? How to drive your career and create a remarkable future*, Piatkus Books, London

10 M Rizzi (2019) *Talents & Rebels: Dealing with corporate misfits*, Hoepli Editore, Milan

6

Lean and social learning to maximize the group's learning mindset

A lean approach to learning

The importance of connecting communication and understanding drivers for social learning as a prerequisite to support learning seems undeniable. However, learning only happens when we effectively convert the knowledge we gain and the feedback we receive into other behaviour. Or, as Anna Tarabasz shared in the first chapter, when we unlearn learned behaviours or beliefs. Still, with the overflow of communication we receive through an incredible variety of channels these days, it is sometimes difficult to filter out relevant knowledge and information we need at the moment of need. Not only is filtering relevant knowledge difficult, but you have probably also experienced that what you need is unfindable. Unfortunately, what gets in the way of even more knowledge sharing is that experts themselves often do not see the added value in sharing their knowledge, as I have pointed out several times.

In this chapter, I will explore the benefits of social and lean learning for you and your team. Because in times of increasingly rapid change, the need to have relevant knowledge and information at hand at the time of need is paramount. To explain this, I will give examples from the lean learning method I originally developed for learning and development (L&D) teams and executives who want to integrate learning ecosystems. However, unlike in my book *Learning Ecosystems*, I will approach this from the learning mindset of the learning influencer. This approach will help you as a learning leader, in the next chapter, to take your team to the level of a learning ecosystem. In doing so, you will use this approach to establish the foundations for the essential human-to-human (H2H) collaboration that I will explain further in Chapter 9. Without this human input, you will never achieve maximum learning gains, even with the help of your most intelligent virtual colleague.

Eliminating waste to amplify the team's learning mindset

What makes lean such a strong concept is that end customer value prevails thanks to the elimination of all forms of waste that do not contribute to the efficiency and effectiveness of the organization. When I translate that to learning, I expect learning to happen as close and relevant as possible to my moment of need. No boring long e-learnings when my customer is waiting for an answer. No three-day sales training when salesforce clearly indicates that I only need coaching from an expert when cold-calling prospects.

Many years after I developed the lean learning methodology for L&D, I am increasingly asked how these fit with the learners themselves and within teams for maximum measurable performance improvement. Curious and intrigued, I went back to talk to the original stakeholders about how they saw this: L&D executives and learning rebels like my great friend An De Boelpaep, for whom implementing innovative learning innovations is the ultimate challenge. The result was the adaptation of lean learning

FIGURE 6.1 The learning maturity model, 2014 (© Katja Schipperheijn)

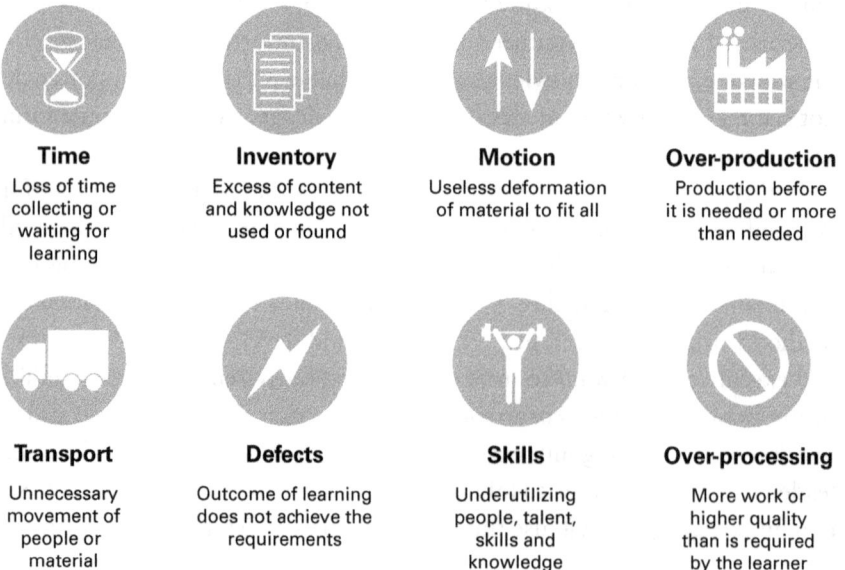

Time
Loss of time collecting or waiting for learning

Inventory
Excess of content and knowledge not used or found

Motion
Useless deformation of material to fit all

Over-production
Production before it is needed or more than needed

Transport
Unnecessary movement of people or material

Defects
Outcome of learning does not achieve the requirements

Skills
Underutilizing people, talent, skills and knowledge

Over-processing
More work or higher quality than is required by the learner

development into lean learning for teams that see everything as a learning moment and opportunity for collaboration and, therefore, acceleration. The result of this is eight forms of waste you and your team should avoid.

OVERPRODUCTION

Overproduction is fun to start with because it seems a contradiction when we talk about learning that can be a 'waste'. Too much learning: is that even possible? No, probably not, but within a team too much knowledge or information can absolutely be over-shared. This may not seem as bad a waste as overproduction for L&D, where success is still measured by the number of, often useless, modules on an LMS. So many that they are no longer relevant or retrievable in the moment of need.

However, over-communicating and over-sharing can be equally frustrating, moreover when it comes through an abundance of channels. Emails, meetings, feedback calls and numerous WhatsApp groups, and soon you are only replying to – or ignoring – most of them, like rebels do. This overproduction defines the organizations that I call 'broadcasters of news' and 'multi-way communicators' in the learning maturity model. Overproducing too much communication is dominant. Extracting relevant knowledge and information that actually bring added value for your job thus becomes impossible. It's an exercise of finding balance, and defining and agreeing guidelines together on what works within your team. A simple example is if you are cc'd in an email, which then classifies the mail as 'no need to know now; keep automatically in an archive in case of emergency'. This way, the emails don't stay in your mailbox as an open and distracting item and you can get on with those emails that are relevant. When you work this way, you will find that time is freed up for important things. Moreover, with intelligent systems like Microsoft Vista, it is very easy to find all saved items when you need them. I admit, I have been doing this for years and no longer even bother with folders; I let technology do its job.

OVERPROCESSING

Nobody likes to do too much work, especially useless work like answering pointless emails or writing reports that nobody reads. However, I don't often see teams that overprocess when it comes to learning. Yet, I like to give an example of how this can relate to efficient and effective team learning.

From the lean principle, all steps or non-essential learning activities are redundant if they do not add value to the applicability of learning or personal development. Feedback is a very efficient way of supporting learning and helps develop the learning mindset in those who are uncertain or afraid of making mistakes. Mentoring is also a good example, especially with young talents who still need to find their place in the team and its ways of working. Still, this can sometimes go too far, making it counter-productive, not only for the learner but also for the coach or mentor. When these conversations are not conducted very conscientiously, they can be time-consuming and costly. Not to mention frustrating if, like me, you happen to prefer to explore on your own rather than be 'guided' by someone.

It is, therefore, essential that you make arrangements, and take into account your colleague's individuality and preferences. Rules for frequency and times are just as important as the manner of communication. If it is perceived as an obligation by either party, it is no longer a positive contribution to the learning culture and certainly does not support the mindset. More than that, it can potentially ruin the vibe between you and your colleague when you are obliged to give feedback at a time when there is nothing relevant to report.

TIME

Wasting time, as in the example of overprocessing, is frustrating and hinders productivity. But when I talk about waste in this context, reducing 'time' is one of the most essential conditions to achieve lean learning benefits. There are several shortening factors related to time that you can address yourself. Although some things may not be in your hands, but are driven by the vision of the learning leader, as I discuss in the next chapter.

What is most obvious, and increasingly easy to control yourself, is what I call waiting time. This is the time between needing to know something and actually being able to apply it. In that waiting period, there is a real risk of making mistakes because you are seeking knowledge and making assumptions about what is expected of you. In the process, these mistakes can have a negative impact on costs, safety, customers and everyone in the ecosystem. All the more so in hazardous production environments, for example as in a project where An De Boelpaep successfully implemented an innovative tool to enable learning in the moment of need. Where previously, during the entire onboarding process, a mentor provided guidance throughout the day, this was no longer possible due to labour shortages and cost considerations. An therefore introduced a learning application that guided the operator step by step. This application, which was initially nothing more than a linear guidance plan with micro-learning instructions, was later expanded to include a chatbot so that it could answer virtual questions at any time. This increased production efficiency and effectiveness, but also supported the well-being of workers who were afraid of making mistakes. This example may not be relevant to you because you cannot decide on such applications, but that does not mean you cannot think along and challenge the status quo. Still, the virtual colleague with whom you can spar at the moment of need, since the emergence of LLMs like ChatGPT, is increasingly widespread.

However, time should also be associated with optimizing knowledge-sharing between different people in your team. Optimization time is based on swiftly finding the expert to support your project or a rebel to develop your idea with. Of course, to do this, you need to know who the experts are and why their skills are wasted, as I describe below.

Time, or its wastage, greatly impacts organizational outcomes in several ways and I'm sure you can come up with more examples. But, above all, in these times of increasingly rapid change, efficient use of time is an essential requirement for people to thrive when something new surprises them every day. Reducing time is necessary to support well-being, counter frustration and maintain a healthy team atmosphere. From a lean perspective, this is a necessary step that delivers quick results for improvement.

SKILLS

The idea that competencies and skills in an organization can be defined as waste may seem strange at first glance. Yet this type of waste is hugely present in many organizations. I have, therefore, hinted at it several times in the previous sections. When there is insufficient collaboration, or when expertise (knowledge) is not sufficiently shared with others who can benefit from it, it becomes an underutilized resource and can be considered waste. This knowledge, which sits not on servers but in the minds of team members, is similar to underutilized knowledge databases (inventories).

Solutions for finding experts can of course be provided by HR or L&D from the performance reviews they conduct, or from intelligent systems that measure not only knowledge but also confidence. In addition, applications such as the knowledge experience platforms (KXPs) I describe in the final part, whether supported by gamification or not, provide answers to the search for experts in no time. However, if someone does not want to share their knowledge, innovation cannot help! The example role that learning influencers play can motivate. However, people who don't share often have a good reason for doing so. Engaging in connecting communication and understanding *why* someone does not want to share knowledge is essential to establishing a sharing learning culture within the team. Give people confidence, a purpose, and above all, show understanding. You often don't know what holds someone back: fear of giving wrong answers, fear of becoming redundant if someone else can take over their expertise and so on.

Teams that unlock knowledge from everyone for everyone's purpose are teams that thrive through a shared learning mindset. Transferring this infectious vibe to other teams, whether through cross-functional projects or not, naturally also creates a ripple effect towards other teams. But it starts with you! You can set the first wave in motion within your team by actively investing in reducing skills waste.

INVENTORY

Waste related to inventories is similar to skills, although this involves unused or outdated non-relevant data. This unused data and knowledge does not contribute to the learning process of employees and the organization. It is useless content that is also often very expensive to maintain.

Of course, this is primarily a leadership issue; however, you and your team can play an exemplary role. For example, you can create relevant content yourself as a learning influencer and share it if you have a social learning channel in your organization. If you can't share it directly on a social channel you can perhaps share it with the L&D department. User-generated content is also relevant to them and they can then possibly process it so that it is available on the LMS. If you have no LMS in your organization, that is no problem either. I have seen examples where user-generated videos were shared in a weekly newsletter that became popular, especially if the content was authentic, fun and engaging. For example, I recently saw an organization using this user-generated content for employer branding to attract potential new talent. After all, who wouldn't want to work for an organization or in a team where a learning mindset and fun go hand in hand?

Another initiative you can take yourself is indicating that content is not relevant (anymore). Many systems have the ability to provide feedback, through likes or otherwise. If this is not the case, you can always communicate to the administrators of the data repository system that the content is not satisfactory. You may come across as a rebel, but communicate it positively; after all, you are doing part of their job. And, as mentioned, dead content on data systems costs a lot.

In other words, everyone needs to take responsibility for managing waste related to inventory. Because even if your team or organization implements innovative technologies that facilitate knowledge sharing in the ecosystem, human curation will still be necessary. For example, ChatGPT asks after every collaboration if you are satisfied with the answer. Human interaction is, therefore, necessary for the symbiosis between humans and machines to be successful. Especially when it comes to deciding what is or is not relevant to your personal development.

TRANSPORT

In an increasingly virtually connected world, travelling to have human inter-actions or to learn seems less and less logical. Even universities find that classrooms are increasingly empty when students are given the chance to take distance learning courses. Transport is therefore out of date in several ways. Why waste time travelling around to collaborate when virtual envi-ronments can give the same immersive feeling as a live contact? As an example, children who find a concert in the meta-world just as good as, or sometimes even better than, a live concert in a crowded concert hall where the experience cannot be customized, tells me that virtual environments certainly feel real. Indeed, concerts in Fortnite where artists perform live with a realistic human avatar created by Epic Games' metahuman creator[1] appear to be hugely popular. And, if Marc Zuckerberg is to be believed, in the near future we will be interacting with an equally lifelike avatar that conveys non-verbal and emotive communication flawlessly via the new Meta Quest 3.[2] Young people who make the world their office as digital nomads are obviously already hugely excited by this.

I must honestly admit that I really enjoy travelling and am lucky enough to travel the world for my keynotes. Still, I see the added value of innovations to eliminate waste related to transport. Mainly because of my carbon foot-print, which does not contribute to the sustainability aspect I promote, but also because I realize that I can inspire more people when I set a good exam-ple myself.

Eliminating waste related to transport and time are two aspects that rein-force each other. Yet I know that many of us love to travel and thus make up excuses to travel anyway. Therefore, I ask you to take responsibility if you want to contribute to reducing waste and think about the impact of travel. Is it really necessary to travel for a training session or meeting? What is the impact on your colleagues if you are not there? Are there other options? I would like you to think about time and duration, but also effectiveness and added value. Do you definitely need it or is it a habit that is hard to unlearn?

DEFECTS

Defects in training or learning content are often less easy to measure, partly because they are often subjective from the learner's point of view. For L&D, it plays an important role in determining whether the training contributed through its content or the way it was delivered. Yet it is almost impossible to reflect that in a causal relationship, as I describe in detail in my book *Learning Ecosystems*.

Eliminating waste that does not contribute to efficient and effective learning, or that gets in the way of a learning mindset, is possible if you are involved as a stakeholder. In this respect, it is akin to inventories, where you too can take responsibility for pointing out waste. If you don't indicate that it is waste, someone else doesn't know about it. This is mainly why I pay great attention to connecting communication in learning teams. By consistently questioning things, you challenge the status quo and can turn mistakes into opportunities for improvement. So, release the rebel in yourself positively and constructively, and don't let what others might think about you stop you. As such, when you discuss flaws positively, you are a learning influencer and demonstrate the capabilities of a learning leader within your team.

MOVEMENT

Waste related to movement has many similarities to eliminating waste from transport and defects. The difference with defects is that this form of waste is more specific and easier to avoid. I also note that movement, unlike deliberate use of transport, is often done with good intentions.

A common example, frequently applied in L&D, is cutting content from long e-learning modules or webinars for use on micro-learning platforms. These cut-up short pieces are essentially still boring long modules, but are placed on a different channel, making them lose even more of their value. As such, instead of saving money by reusing content, they lose the main goal of adding value to the employee with relevant learning content that he or she can apply to perform a task better or support well-being. In addition, these unnecessary steps are often also very time-consuming and expensive.

Starting from a white canvas is the only method that is lean. That goes for L&D but also for you if you want to create content for your colleagues as a learning influencer. It sometimes seems easy to start with something that already exists, but do dare to let go of that. Dare to ask for help and create something together with other experts, or ask for help from your virtual colleague, who always has time. LLM applications already surpass us as humans in terms of creativity, as I mentioned earlier. So let your virtual colleague do the first thing. Prompt clearly what the objectives are, who the target audience is and ask for relevant content. While doing so, don't forget to give feedback to your bot, because it is also still learning too.

Consistently thinking about eliminating waste related to relevant knowledge sharing and learning in the moment of need often pays off quickly. However, contrary to popular belief, this is not the responsibility of L&D but of everyone. It is therefore worth discussing this in feedback conversations with your manager or by proactively taking responsibility and identifying improvement opportunities. When this becomes a structural part of the organization, lean frees up time, money and resources. But, most importantly, it creates a culture in which a learning attitude can thrive.

Social learning to empower everyone in the team

Social learning is the process by which individuals acquire knowledge, skills and behaviour through interaction with others, for example by applying connecting communication or sharing mistakes that encourage learning. Social and collaborative learning is the crucial pillar for increasing efficiency and effectiveness within organizations. For this, it relies on the cognitive theories and behavioural sciences that I already mentioned in the first chapter – the difference between learning and training, for example, where I referred to studies by B. F. Skinner on the use of stimulus-response theories. These behaviourist theories inspired the Canadian-American psychologist Albert Bandura when he developed his social learning theory.[3] This social learning theory is based on the idea that new behaviour can be acquired by observing and imitating others through a learning process.

According to Bandura, social learning does not only take place passively; it also needs reinforcement. Attention, retention, reproduction and motivation are also needed to add value in the social learning process. This can be a cognitive process that includes direct instruction, rewards and even punishments. In addition, he also indicated that vicarious reinforcement – rewarding someone else for similar behaviour – also plays a role in social learning. In other words, it is similar to what the Hebbian theory says and what the saying 'Cells that wire together fire together' endorses. Social learning is, therefore, a valuable and, dare I say, necessary strategy to optimize learning curves and increase performance.

A perhaps somewhat simplistic example, but one that is inspiring when I work with young people, is found in the story of Tarzan and Jane. The great thing about the story is that it often also works to convince teachers of the positive effect of social learning and the impact on behaviour. Tarzan, raised in the wild without human interaction, experiences an extreme learning curve after being socialized. When he meets Jane, a well-educated member of society, Tarzan is exposed to new ideas, behaviours and social norms. Jane acts as his mentor, allowing Tarzan to learn quickly and adapt to the complexities of human culture. This illustrates the power of social learning to accelerate the learning process and shorten the time needed to develop new skills.

In a business context, organizations are investing in social learning strategies to reap these benefits. For example, consider when you need to settle into a new team, or collaborate on projects in cross-functional teams where working practices and culture may differ. You will probably benefit from someone like Jane to help you quickly become familiar with the culture, working practices and any knowledge of your new team. This will help you speed up the learning process and make it more enjoyable most of the time.

Moreover, social learning promotes a culture of continuous improvement, especially when using intelligent applications that support lean learning. When you consistently exchange information with your new team members, you create not only an engaging learning environment but also a great team dynamic. Creating an environment where employees support each other and learn together strengthens cohesion and trust within the team. This positively affects collaboration, communication and ultimately the performance of the team. Nevertheless, there are some conditions and drivers that need to be considered to make social learning a success.

Six drivers to make social learning a success

At the beginning of this part I described the added value of learning influencers to create a ripple effect within teams. With this, I wanted to encourage you to think about how your learning mindset can motivate others to learn. For this, a learning culture based on connecting communication and trust is essential. Of course, none of this is rocket science, yet its added value in making work more efficient and enjoyable is often forgotten. Similarly, it is often overlooked that social learning platforms do not always deliver the

FIGURE 6.2 The six drivers of learning ecosystems (© Katja Schipperheijn)

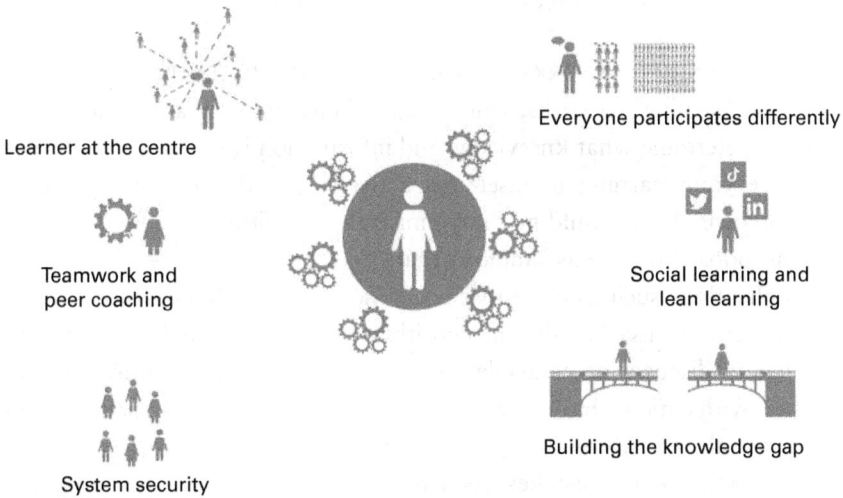

Learner at the centre

Teamwork and
peer coaching

System security

Everyone participates differently

Social learning and
lean learning

Building the knowledge gap

expected results without good vision and commitment from everyone. Indeed, most projects I see initiated by L&D end in a failed experiment that started full of good intentions. However, after a while everyone reverted to old habits that caused social and collaborative learning to stop.

To avoid this, I would like to share six drivers that can help you to take up responsibility and to boost social learning within your team. This foundation will assist if you want to help shape the future of your organization by helping to build the learning ecosystem that I discuss in Chapter 9. I would also point out that sometimes you need to take a step back and not pin all your hopes on innovative systems such as generative AI. People will always be at the heart of learning ecosystems, not algorithms, no matter how human they become. So, I want you to focus on what drives learning and what possible pitfalls you can help avoid.

These six drivers (see Figure 6.2) are not meant to be strict rules. Rather, they are personal observations I have gained from my clients and from conversations with experts in the field of learning communities. They can help you explore with your team what does and does not work for you. As such, they are a starting point for thinking about social learning and making it your own. This approach will help you to anticipate certain obstacles and support the use of untapped knowledge and skills that might otherwise be lost. This reinforces a lean learning approach from a social learning perspective. Above all, it strengthens a learning culture where the learner is at the heart.

SOCIAL LEARNING NETWORKS PUT THE LEARNER AT THE CENTRE

In social learning networks, you navigate independently as a learner and have to determine what knowledge and information is relevant to you. You embrace your learning mindset and actively take the lead in your own development. That should be the premise anyway. Still, I wouldn't be writing this book if it were as simple as that.

Applications such as enterprise social networks (ESNs) or even modern LMSs therefore use 'intelligent algorithms' that should make it easier for learners to discover necessary learning paths, find relevant information or connect with experts. However, as I pointed out in the second chapter of this book, not all algorithms are equally smart; humans write them, and humans do sometimes make mistakes. As a result, predefined, hopefully adaptive, learning paths are often not sufficiently personalized, engaging and challenging. As a result, only mandatory learning paths are completed, and connections are made only with those we already know.

Fortunately, there are more and more social learning platforms such as the example I gave of Netex, where learning influencers provide content relevant to peers. Or social media platforms with ambitions to become a corporate learning app, like TikTok, which uses one of the best algorithms to determine your preferences within the shortest time. These types of reinforced learning algorithms ensure that you are challenged to take new learning paths. In doing so, they challenge your learning mindset, making the experience more personal and enjoyable. Of course, the most important thing is that you actively participate yourself. Otherwise, the algorithm may be very smart but it will not make you smarter.

It is not only the primary content others share on social networks that offers you added value. By reading feedback and interacting, your knowledge can be refined or deepened. Even better, of course, is to share content yourself and learn from the feedback you receive. This puts you right at the heart of the learning ecosystem. And, the more participants you can inspire to participate, the stronger the social networks become that create a contagious learning culture.

TEAMWORK AND COACHING

Optimizing teamwork and peer coaching will add even more value to the future of work. The rising popularity of project work, cross-functional teams and gig-workers in the platform economy, who often collaborate only virtually, makes this necessary. Social learning platforms integrating a mentoring approach will therefore become increasingly important to exchange expertise human-to-human.

With a mentor/expert approach, there is obviously a need for expertise to be made visible through collaboration and active knowledge sharing. But, as I have pointed out several times, one of the biggest challenges is unlocking knowledge in employees' heads. Sometimes, it is because an employee thinks their knowledge is irrelevant or is insecure about their abilities because of past experiences or stigma. More often, however, it is because they does not see the point of participating in knowledge sharing.

Learning ecosystems, such as KXPs, challenge experts with well-researched gamification. Implementing these within the organization is a decision to be made by L&D or the organization's executive team. But, even without these applications, you can encourage others to share knowledge. For this, you can appeal to your competencies and a bit of positive rebellion, as indicated earlier.

However, I am sure you are not an expert in everything, that even you sometimes need help understanding something. So, it's up to you to communicate that and ask for help. The learning leaders I describe in the next section know that they can only be successful if surrounded by people with different experiences and views. Team coaching and mentoring should therefore not always take a formal form. When it subconsciously becomes the basis of collaboration, it supports the safe working environment in which a learning mindset can thrive.

NIELSEN'S 1-9-90 RULE AND HOW EVERYONE PARTICIPATES DIFFERENTLY

I find Nielsen's 1-9-90 rule,[4] although not scientifically based, very interesting for discussing one of the big challenges to making the success of ESN measurable. I noticed that many implementations fail. But, I then ask, what is failure? Not enough content? Not enough interactions? Or employees not logging into the system? Well, maybe all of these; that depends on the objective of your organization and the social learning culture the leadership has in mind.

Let me start by saying that not everyone likes social networks within the organization. In fact, some people want nothing to do with them in their private lives, so the idea of having to *share* with colleagues meets resistance. It is therefore advisable to consider the different personalities within your team before installing a social learning platform. Not only before, but also when team members are not participating. How do they deal with technology in general and, more specifically, with social technologies?

Let me clarify this. Suppose you are a young new employee who interacts a lot on social media privately. A social learning platform may suit you very well because you feel supported by your colleagues to grow together. You may also prefer to stay as far away from social media as possible in private, but you would like to receive podcasts or newsletters directly in your inbox. These preferences also largely determine what you can expect from an ESN and how you can use this insight to spread more knowledge in a relevant way for everyone on your team.

In relation to this, Nielsen describes three types of participants on social media platforms:

- **Heavy contributors:** 1 per cent of users participate a lot and contribute the most.
- **Contributors:** 9 per cent of users contribute from time to time.
- **Lurkers:** 90 per cent of participants do not actively participate in the conversation but they do read or observe.

According to his theory, as many as 90 per cent of community participants would not contribute to the success of social learning communities such as ESNs, or a community of practice (COP) on LinkedIn. This may surprise you, because connections have already been made between this group of people who share a common concern, problem or interest in a topic.

An estimated 9 per cent actively respond to existing discussions or content while surfing through the virtual community. And, even more remarkably, only 1 per cent of participants would create content and feed the community. From this premise, one might ask: What is the point of rolling out a social learning network if only 1 per cent contribute to knowledge sharing?

The question to ask first is who benefits most from learning in online communities. Too often, it is assumed that this is only the 1 per cent who visibly contribute. However, this is a false assumption; it is often the lurkers who make up 90 per cent of the group who make more learning gains. These lurkers are often very critical but still want to be informed. However, they do not feel the urge to participate, unlike the broadcasters (1 per cent), who sometimes mainly want to be seen and do not learn much themselves.

Not surprisingly, members on the social learning platform who participate by interacting with others (9 per cent) tend to learn more and contribute the most to team learning. This is often based on critical responses, which in turn provoke other responses. New ideas can emerge from this conversation for all other community members, especially if all of you embrace openness. What is striking is that members of this group often actively respond online, but not during live meetings. This may be due to their perceived anonymity or the virtual wall they hide behind.

Why is this relevant for you to know? All too often, KPIs on social learning platforms are set in relation to interactions. Yet, these interactions do not measure learning gains, either for the individual or the team. This is where you can take up your role as a learning influencer or learning leader. Together with your team, examine what adds value for all of you and discuss possible improvement opportunities that feed everyone's learning mindset.

BRIDGING THE KNOWLEDGE GAP

Learning ecosystems, unlike the data repository organizations I discuss in Chapter 9, provide relevant knowledge to employees and stakeholders inside and outside the organization. They have already adapted to the future of work. Gig-workers and cross-functional teams are part of the strategy to grow nimble and become project-based. Learning ecosystems with social learning platforms integrated thereby transcend organizations stuck in silos or a top-down hierarchy that often face knowledge gaps.

In organizations that are not yet willing or able to transcend silos, doors remain closed and employees do not know each other, so knowledge is not optimally shared between departments. These gaps are therefore often the cause of problems that only surface when it is almost too late. They create a blind spot that leaves opportunities unexploited. One example is L&D and marketing departments, which would benefit from more knowledge sharing. Marketing experts have years of experience in the neuroscience of influencing behaviour and unlearning, as Anna Tarabasz also pointed out in the first chapter. They also have years of data analysis experience and understand the algorithms' impact. They are experts in driving campaigns that use relevant content to persuade latent customers on the channel where they can best be reached.

Why is it important for you to know this? I would encourage you to strengthen your social network beyond your immediate team: be a bridge builder. See how other areas of expertise can support you in the future of work. As I pointed out with Nick van Dam's M-profile in Part Two, we will all have to be open to new areas of mastery and expertise.

SOCIAL LEARNING AMPLIFIES LEAN LEARNING

By now, you have probably bridged the gap between social learning and lean learning. Social learning leads to becoming better informed through shared knowledge and expertise within an organization (and beyond). Your interaction with other employees gives you a broader perspective and enables you to learn more. When you embrace social learning, you recognize that learning happens with and through other people. That you learn by exchanging relevant content with experts and that feedback reinforces this. In that respect, social learning fits in tremendously with lean learning because it avoids several aspects of waste, for example time to find content and unlocking knowledge from experts outside your team.

It should be evident by now that I am trying to convince you to actively participate in knowledge sharing yourself, preferably outside your team. That if you do not have the authority to integrate a social learning system into your organization's learning ecosystem, then you use your influence to encourage social learning in other ways. To do this, you can motivate the stakeholders involved by linking the aspects of lean with the need to foster everyone's learning mindset.

With the rapid rise of more social learning tools, often as extensions to applications you already have in your organization, it is a small step for an influencer to convince your executive team of the benefits of social and collaborative learning supported by technology. Especially when you consider all these drivers that can quickly pay off. After all, by applying lean learning with social learning platforms, user-generated knowledge is shared with those who benefit the most at the time. This in turn stimulates new ideas, creates a culture of sharing and learning and maximizes the return on investment in learning.

SYSTEM SECURITY IS KEY TO THE SUCCESS OF SOCIAL LEARNING

Technical security against data leaks is very important. Nobody wants sensitive information to become public. However, I also urge you not to be too rigid about ownership of data and knowledge of systems. Too often I see companies where, depending on your function and learning path, you can only see what you have permissions for. However, this hampers the learning mindset and avoids bridging knowledge gaps.

It is, however, not securing the data on the systems that is most hindering the success of social learning platforms. Rather, the prerequisite is in trusting people. Because, even though smart algorithms are often the basis for sharing knowledge with the right people, if there is no trust, knowledge will not be shared. It is about human connections and a culture where trust in each other prevails. In a social learning environment, everyone should be able to participate without fear. If someone is afraid to share and/or participate in knowledge, the principle of allowing everyone to act – the heart of the learning ecosystem – is not met.

Trust is the most essential condition for participation in a social network, yet it is also the most difficult to achieve. This is essentially part of the culture that supports a learning mindset. Everyone must trust that failure is not punished and that making mistakes contributes to everyone's learning. Trust and a culture that supports a learning mindset are not built in a day. It is a recurring process to which attention is paid during the various steps taken to achieve continuous improvement.

Consider the drivers that influence social learning systems as an essential part of team learning. Creating a collaborative culture is essential for efficient and effective use of technologies that support social learning. For this, you need to trust and encourage each other and always lead by example.

All the aspects I have mentioned in this chapter should be considered. Only then will an innovative social learning platform add value for you and your team. An De Boelpaep, who has experience in implementing learning innovations in environments that are not obvious, knows this too. Together, we can talk for hours about the benefits of lean learning and new innovations. What especially typifies An is her eagerness to keep trying new things, never to give up and, above all, to enjoy everything she does. I am happy to share her inspiring story and tips.

AN DE BOELPAEP, FOUNDER X-CONSCIOUS AND LEARNING INNOVATOR: EMBRACE SOCIAL AND LEAN LEARNING

As a young child, I was madly in love with figure skating. I spent more than 20 per cent of my time at the rink. I had the passion and persistence to make a certain skill more and more perfect. Sometimes it took a year to master a particular jump. Practising a sport or art is a great example of a learning mindset. You are encouraged to set goals, experiment and accelerate. You learn how to deal with failure, loss, pain and afterwards success. Today, I still see this as my best learning experience, one from which I now draw inspiration for learning that I try to pass on to others.

My background is in engineering, but my passion for people and learning soon led me to a support role in L&D. Today, my work focuses on finding strategic and tactical L&D solutions for manufacturing companies. These types of companies are under great pressure due to high labour costs. Having a learning organization and allowing everyone to become the best version of themselves is one of the ways to make business more efficient and ensure long-term sustainability. And this is exactly where my mission lies.

Because people and learning are my passion, I have been able to easily re-skill from an engineer to an L&D co-ordinator. Passion to do well, to make a difference, helps. Passion is my oxygen for curiosity, one of the catalysts for a learning mindset. I am curious to find out how to do things even better, learn competencies, ask the right questions and dig deeper. I believe a learning mindset also requires self-awareness and openness, a competence I have long been working on. Understanding that what we take to be true is not always the only truth; what assumptions we make and what other options might be are also important. You don't know what you don't know. This I find very interesting, and it makes self-awareness a spicy one.

Furthermore, my sense of experimentation has helped me very much to change contexts or roles quickly. Experimenting and experiencing success only makes the passion stronger. As you know, experimentation sometimes goes differently than you want it to. Failing in style is one of the most important skills I have been privileged to learn. Missing a jump on the ice rink is different from experiencing unexpected twists and turns in a project. The faster we learn to fail, the faster we learn to get back up, adjust and plan for success. Plan, try, reflect, learn, plan and try again. Only when you no longer have to be perfect can you get it right.

As an L&D practitioner, I am always looking for new ways to make people curious and be a catalyst for questioning and experimenting things. In addition, quick and easy access to learning is essential. And this is where the principles of lean learning come in handy. Around this, then, I would like to share some real-life experiences.

'Embrace the art of letting go': There is no need to master everything in detail. Know that you can retrieve specific knowledge quickly, the moment you need it. In a work context, this can be challenging. How often do we feel overloaded with information when we start somewhere new, a new company, a new department or a new job? Focus on the essentials first; the details will follow when you need them.

'Order smart and embrace AI': The faster you find the right information, the faster you can add value. With the overload of information, it is sometimes difficult to find exactly what you need at that moment. Try to find for yourself a system where you store knowledge and can find something quickly. I like to store everything online: courses I scan in, books I summarize. With AI integrations these days, you can find everything very quickly.

'Choose your own channel that works best for you': This can be videos, podcasts, blogs or books. Depending on what you want to learn, this can obviously be another more appropriate channel. Dare to experiment with this too by seeing what is new. I thought TikTok was only for children, but I have since discovered several influencers on it who are really interesting – if only to get food on the table quickly after a busy day at work.

'Give a score': Order knowledge with impact. I also try to keep a score, so you can go back to the most valuable input in the first place. And dare to let go here too; you don't need to stock up on mediocrity.

'Learning with and from others': For myself, the most crucial accelerator is social learning. I have created a community with spirited and thoughtful L&D innovators who keep me on my toes. Dare to share knowledge, connect, reflect and dare to question things together. The more you share, the more comes back. It is nice to be surrounded by intelligent people; the moment you are stuck, you can reach out. In this area, 1 + 1 = 111. It is the fastest way to learn something.

I have found that learning is accelerated in a safe environment, where we are given space to experiment and failure is embraced as a lesson. An environment where curiosity is encouraged and one is allowed to ask tough questions, where we are allowed to look below the waterlines.

Therefore, my biggest win as a leader is the point where you can install an open feedback culture where people dig deeper, look for the reason behind the reason, and things can be questioned in a respectful way. Questioning and opinions bring differences together into a better idea. Lean but not mean.

So, open your minds and enjoy becoming the best version of yourself.

Don't forget to invite your artificial colleague

The symbiosis between humans and machines is developing exponentially fast. As a result, it is already having a major impact on various aspects of our lives and work, as I pointed out in Chapter 2. I understand that this human–machine symbiosis, with the close collaboration and interdependence it creates, raises many questions and concerns for many. Yet I want to inspire you to look at the opportunities it offers to support learning and well-being.

Indeed, we are becoming increasingly dependent on these technologies that determine how we interact and process information. More than that, we work side by side with AI and robotics often without being aware of this dependency. We increasingly rely on it to support complex tasks, from data analysis to manufacturing processes. In doing so, we cannot deny that this collaboration between humans and machines contributes to greater efficiency and precision in various sectors. Just think of the advanced integrations in the medical world that have led to innovative approaches such as robotic surgery and advanced medical imaging. These technological tools increase the precision of medical procedures and enable doctors to make complex diagnoses and carry out treatments with greater accuracy. I would almost be tempted to say that I would trust a doctor more who works side by side with an artificial colleague.

I also gave some examples of the rapidly emerging field of neural interfacing, which enables direct communication between the human brain and machines. As I pointed out, these developments open the door to potentially life-changing applications, such as neuroprosthetics for people with paralysis or brain–machine interfaces for seamless interaction with computer systems. For you, however, it might be more interesting to see possibilities in a universal translator that can accurately convey your non-verbal communication and intention, making collaboration with colleagues worldwide even easier.

I am sure we will see many innovations in the coming years that we cannot imagine now. This is why I want to remind you to approach the human–machine symbiosis with openness. After all, you may find yourself working more and more closely with your artificial colleague. Who knows, maybe next year your team will organize a New Year party in the metaverse so he or she won't feel left out.

Teams that embrace AI will thrive more than others

For your personal and team development it is important to approach AI not only with openness but also with curiosity and even imagination. But, if you look around, you probably see many colleagues behaving like the Luddites in the 18th century. Out of ignorance, fear or perhaps even ethical considerations, these colleagues are unwilling to adapt to change, especially when it involves innovations with generative AI.

In today's rapidly evolving world, innovations like generative AI will play crucial roles in determining the success and efficiency of your team. You cannot deny that your artificial colleague surpasses you in its ability to process huge amounts of data quickly and accurately. But it is not only beating you and everyone on the team on speed. Generative AI has been able to make important decisions autonomously for a long time. Remember the example I gave of Libratus who, to everyone's amazement, beat professional poker players with one unexpected move. AI can already make these kinds of decisions more accurately and, more importantly, much faster, based on incomplete or imperfect information. In this aspect, you could say that AI is not only a valued team member but also a bit of a rebel who challenges the status quo. I understand that many team members need more time to entrust this responsibility to technology. However, in a world where speed often equals competitive advantage, ignoring AI can result in delayed responses to critical situations and missed opportunities.

It is also understandable that some teams are hesitant to give their artificial colleague a chance, for human-centred and ethical reasons. Not just the fear of losing control, but especially job replacement may cause resistance. However, it is essential to understand that AI is meant to complement human skills and competencies and not replace them. The goal is to automate repetitive tasks and free up human capabilities for things we can use our human competencies for. In this way, your artificial colleague not only helps meet business objectives, but also enables you to do what you love most; you no longer have to worry about making sometimes rash decisions alone, and you have a sparring partner who is never too tired to help you.

Teams and organizations that are reluctant to embrace these technological opportunities are, therefore, at increasing risk. Not just to lose their competitive edge and fall behind in terms of efficiency, but also as attractive teams where collaboration, commitment and well-being are important values. It is vital that everyone on the team understands the potential of AI and gives their artificial colleagues a chance without fear. They sometimes say that the weakest link can be decisive for team success; well, in this case, the weakest link is the Luddite. The Luddite who refuses to adapt to the future of work and learning, putting herself and her team at an irreversible disadvantage.

If you and your team want not just to survive but to *thrive*, then it is inevitable that AI will become an integral part of the team. Therefore, everyone in the team must try to look past fears and give the artificial colleague a chance to demonstrate its added value within the operational strategy. Only by embracing these cutting-edge technologies can teams adapt to the demands of the modern world and strive to achieve best-performing statuses.

Endnotes

1 Epic Games. Unreal Engine's metahuman creator is now available in early access, www.epicgames.com/site/en-US/news/metahuman-creator-is-now-available-in-early-access (archived at https://perma.cc/G5DX-3RYF)

2 Lex Clips. Mark Zuckerberg on Quest 3, YouTube, www.youtube.com/watch?v=1ztFxwaKUsA (archived at https://perma.cc/7BL8-KL26)

3 A Bandura and R H Walters (1963) *Social Learning and Personality Development*, Holt, Rinehart and Winston, New York

4 Nielsen Norman Group. The 90-9-1 rule for participation inequality in social media and online communities, 2006, www.nngroup.com/articles/participation-inequality/ (archived at https://perma.cc/QE6F-WC84)

PART FOUR

The learning leader amplifies the learning mindset

7

What makes you a learning leader?

So far, I have tried to instil in you the love of learning by urging you to embrace your learning mindset and encouraging you as a learning influencer to share that love. In the previous chapter, I often referred to the learning leader, who inspires others and leads with learning. This learning leader, who may be a manager or even a C-level executive, is the next step in embracing your learning mindset. Just one step away from the *LearnScaper*, who is at the foundation of learning ecosystems that push innovation and learning beyond the boundaries of the organization. These LearnScapers are visionaries who combine human competencies with a sustainable mission that uses innovation to create value for all.

As a learning leader, you have fully embraced your learning mindset. You are a perpetual learner who relies on an insatiable hunger to learn. More than that, learning, like breathing, is something you do unconsciously to bring oxygen to your brain. In doing so, you also see learning as a team sport where you experiment and where challenges are seen as opportunities to grow and innovate. Learning leaders challenge the status quo. They are the change and do not wait for the change to change them.

But there is more to being a learning leader. Not only do you embrace your learning mindset, but you also embrace your humanity in times where innovation and AI are increasingly part of our learning and work. You use these competencies to instil a learning culture within your teams that provides a safe environment for everyone to learn. Learning leaders are leaders who challenge their team to embrace the learning mindset by giving them autonomy, freedom and empowerment.

In this section, I want to encourage you to develop your leadership skills to add value as a learning leader. To do this, I challenge you to have the courage and openness to unlearn and experiment. I want you to see the future as a *forever frontier* that you keep pushing with your *league of exceptional learners*.

The learning leader adapts

If you want to fill your library with books on leadership, you have a choice of no less than 60,000 titles on Amazon! By this I do not mean to claim that this is a book on leadership, nor that I am an expert on leadership. For that, I am fortunate to have many inspiring friends whose contributions on thought leadership support this book with real-life examples. I do know that leadership today has a lot to do with adaptability and anticipating the future. Especially in the context of geopolitical challenges, expectations regarding the Sustainable Development Goals (SDGs) and, of course, the not-to-be-underestimated impact of innovations such as AI.

Nevertheless, I do not want to focus too much on leadership styles, as they contain unique behaviours and attitudes that I believe should suit the leader, because I value authenticity highly. Therefore, I am convinced that learning leaders should adapt their style to the situation, such as geographical cultural differences, especially when dealing with cross-functional teams around the world. After all, cultural differences within geographically dispersed organizations are unavoidable and too ingrained to be radically removed from people. Even my virtual friend ChatGPT is already starting to adapt reasonably well depending on the language I use to prompt him.

Since I get to travel all over the world for keynotes and workshops, I am always curious about these geographical differences. I would like to share some examples here, not because I want to stigmatize, but because it shows the context and influence of historical differences. As such, America is known to be fairly democratic, goal-oriented yet individualistic. In other countries, team participation is valued, but, team spirit aside, it is ultimately every person for themselves. Gamification fits this culture tremendously well to encourage students always to be the best. A very different style is found in Germany, where leadership is formal, hierarchical and sincere, obviously not the best environment for a rebel to thrive in.

I could cite many more examples,[1] but that might be something for another book. But of course, with my fondness for Japanese strategies, I cannot fail to refer to these. The Japanese Confucian hierarchical structure is known as a culture where managers have a lot of power and where interdependence is very important. Yet, Japanese executives are hardly involved in the day-to-day running of the organization. Ideas for continuous change and improvement can come from anyone in the organization. Through voting, these ideas are pushed by the organization, all the stakeholders, to the top of the organization, where the executive makes a final decision. So, rebels are nevertheless highly valued in this seemingly very top-down driven organization.

That cultural differences challenge but also encourage a learning leader to keep evolving is confirmed by Bisila Bokoko, who shares her experience at the end of this book. Her approach shows that, as a leader, you have to adapt and learn from and with your team. But above all, you must be prepared to unlearn, as Terence Mauri argues in his great book *The Upside of Disruption: Leading and thriving in the unknown*.[2] But perhaps the greatest differentiator of learning leaders is that they know how to surround themselves with learners who share the same drive and purpose. A team driven by a learning mindset is not only resilient but, above all, hyper-nimble for the future of work.

Learning leaders and the future of work

In Part Two, I explained why it is important for learners to adopt a learning mindset for the future of work. While no one can say with certainty what the impact of the fundamental shifts will be, we can say with certainty that almost all jobs will be affected. Leadership must also change in terms of mindset and capabilities. This uncertainty has made leadership one of the most difficult jobs, although also one of the most impactful. Leaders who not only manage but are also learning leaders will succeed themselves and in the process their employees, teams and organizations will also thrive.

LEADING LEARNERS EMBRACE INNOVATIONS IN TIMES OF UNCERTAINTY AND AMBIGUITY

A learning leader is also still a manager of a team. In these times, employees need someone who gives direction. Who helps with the abundance of information available to make the right choices. Someone who can cut through knots, like the Japanese leader who is inspired by others but takes final responsibility.

Of course, boldness and being able to make decisions have always distinguished mediocre leaders from exceptional ones. Today, however, the learning leader must consider much more data that can influence the success of the team or project. Data that are often contradictory depending on the source consulted and data that are constantly changing due to unpredictable situations. Yet, in the past, Kodak's leaders could still hide behind insufficient data to make correct decisions.[3] Whereas today it is rather a necessity to analyse the right data, which isn't easy. Even major trends like the electrification of transport are vastly different depending on where you look. Being prepared for all scenarios is often a decision the learning leader has to make: hyper-adaptability in times of uncertainty.

It's not the big trends – those can still be anticipated. It's those little things that don't surface because of information overload. Such as start-ups that come out of nowhere with a disruptive innovation that completely undermines your strategy. No industry or sector is immune to this anymore, which also translates into a change in the average age of the once-mighty giants that are seeing their lifespans get shorter and shorter.[4] Yet even these mighty giants or elephants can learn to dance on the waves of change, as former IBM CEO Louis V. Gerstner described in his memoirs, *Who Says Elephants Can't Dance? Leading a great enterprise through dramatic change*.[5] But for that, you need courage. Boldness to challenge the status quo. For this, you need to surround yourself with a very diverse team of experts and misfits who, with their different approaches to data from precarious data sources, can come up with different possible scenarios. You, as a learning leader, will then be able to rely on those scenarios to make quick decisions with advancing insight.

As a learning leader, you may face uncertainty and ambiguity due to the abundance of information. However, you can also rely on the added value of innovations such as generative AI. These are becoming faster, more accurate and capable of making recommendations and even decisions based on incomplete information. Erwin Verstraelen, who wrote the foreword for this book, is one such learning leader who inspires others by investing in the symbiosis between humans and machines. As chief data officer (CDO) and innovation manager of one of the world's largest ports, Erwin knows that correct analytical data are essential to make often urgent decisions – data from so many different sources that ambiguity is created for him and his team. As an innovation manager who has won many awards, it should come as no surprise that he was one of the first people I know who introduced an LLM within his organization to support them. He may have been a trendsetter, but today learning leaders worldwide are embracing LLMs for informed, data-driven decisions that can positively impact their organization's performance.[6]

PROJECT-BASED TEAMS AND CROSS-FUNCTIONAL TEAMS

Another driver of new leadership may, at first glance, not seem directly linked to accelerated innovation, yet innovation has had a reinforcing effect here. This translated first into the huge growth of the gig economy[7] and freelance market,[8] but has also increasingly impacted leadership. Young people, and increasingly people from all generations, want to feel that they are always doing something that has a positive impact or purpose. Authenticity is central to this; your job should be an extension of what you stand for. Of course, this also impacts organizations and teams that consequently lose top talent – rebels and misfits who think they can only achieve this outside the hierarchical walls of an organization. Yet, their assignments are often in those teams they try to avoid. However, now they are outsiders, which doesn't always make it more obvious – not for the team, the executive and not for the rebel who thought life would be easier as an independent.

Today's leaders and executives are expected to build nimble teams with all the necessary expertise to meet their objectives. They manage not one but several cross-functional teams, all with their own objectives, and team members sometimes surf between projects. So, deploying gig-workers or team members with a gig mentality is definitely a good combination. Another typical trait of these rebels is that their purpose orientation goes hand in hand with discipline and restlessness, which also drives lifelong learning.

For a learning leader, attracting these talents is needed if the leader is to learn from the many diverse projects. The knowledge you gain with one team contributes to new knowledge in another team and, as such, creates cross-pollination in a larger learning ecosystem. Still, it is not easy, and it does require some different competencies to connect all the various characters with their own objectives. On top of that, some gig-workers are learning leaders themselves, which, of course, adds to the complexity.

Further in this section, I will discuss human competencies such as empathy and skills like situational leadership, which are related to this. I want to challenge you as a learning leader to lead your team based on connecting communication that empowers them and promotes their well-being. Thereby, as a learning leader, you have a role model function to develop everyone by focusing on leadership qualities in others, because as a learning leader, you obviously take pride when your employees grow. Mossab, who I got to know in Egypt, is such an inspiring learning leader who always gets the best out of everyone in his team. He does not shy away from taking them out of their comfort zone and challenging them; therefore I'm happy to share his experiences.

MOSSAB MAHMOUD: BLUE ENERGY PRESIDENT AND FRONT OFFICE MANAGER AT HILTON EGYPT: CHALLENGING CROSS-FUNCTIONAL TEAMS TO MAXIMIZE LEARNING OUTCOMES

Leading by example means giving our all to achieve results and fulfil our purpose. It's about constantly striving for the best for our customers by investing in our employees. This is what motivates me to challenge both myself and my team continuously.

As a motivated customer service professional, I can look back on the extensive knowledge and experience I gained in my 14-year career in the hotel and resort industry in Egypt, which led me to become front office manager at Hilton Marsa Alam. Now I try to spread that knowledge and drive within my very diverse cross-functional teams.

I find that investing in effective communication and emotional intelligence is essential for any leader. It enables me to understand my team members and empathize with them. They help me understand what drives them to do certain things, or not to do it the way I expected them to do it. In the process, I also dare to look at myself. Have I not explained the goal setting properly, which means they don't see the added value for themselves, the team, and the client? What I can learn from this event is very important to me. Therefore, I try to consciously make that connection with my teams and discuss the why, so that we are all on the same page and can work towards that purpose together.

By fostering a positive and inclusive work environment, I aim to manage a diverse workforce and prevent the development of a toxic culture. This is essential to working together to ensure the highest level of service for our guests, and, to that end, my team and I pay meticulous attention to detail. We constantly monitor positive and negative reviews and use them as opportunities to improve our service standards. I am convinced that we can learn from both and still find opportunities for improvement.

The specific expectations and characteristics of the hotel sector mean that we all have to be able to count on each other. When one person makes a mistake, it affects us all. So, I want to make it a habit to emphasize this through regular meetings and pre-service conversations. In doing so, I cannot express enough our purpose: to fill the earth with the light and warmth of hospitality. This togetherness and team spirit make us align our team actions with our individual and collective goals. We align values, beliefs and personal behaviours with the daily activities that drive our hotel. We regularly recognize and reward the achievements of our team members and, if anyone needs it, we as a team provide the appropriate support, mentoring or coaching.

Understanding that motivation can sometimes fluctuate, we have open and honest conversations with team members who feel demotivated. We actively listen to their concerns and emphasize that everyone has periods of low motivation and that we are there to help them overcome these challenges. By making our expectations for performance known and highlighting areas for improvement, we empower our team members to positively contribute to their colleagues and the workplace. We celebrate their successes, however small, and encourage them to set goals that match their interests.

Finally, I also want to impart the joy of learning to my team members. Obviously, we have the necessary resources, training and materials to do this so that team members can do their jobs effectively. But I like to push them further, to challenge them to question their own status quo, making them think about what they want to learn and where they see themselves in the future. To do this, I offer, among other things, the opportunity to gain experience in different departments. This experience of different roles and responsibilities often leads to personal growth and development that they would not gain if they could not embrace this challenge. I am therefore always immensely proud of everyone in my team that I see growing, even if it means saying goodbye to them because they were able to develop further to become the best of themselves.

The influencer becomes the learning leader

All my inspirational friends who have contributed to this book with their stories and experience are learning influencers, and Mossab is a learning leader too. Many of my friends are also executives and CEOs, but then again, they are not learning influencers and, therefore, not learning leaders ready for the future of work. I realize this probably doesn't make me popular, but what can I say, once a rebel, always a rebel!

Let me clarify what I want to focus on. This book is not necessarily a book about leadership; however, it is a guide to self-leadership. It supports you in thriving thanks to a learning mindset and the ability to lead yourself, which is the basis for learning leadership capability. It enables you to influence and inspire others through authenticity and decisiveness, but above all by being human in collaboration with AI.

The earlier sections in this book provide a solid foundation for moving from inspiring to leading. This is not to say that you suddenly get promoted, if you are not yet a CEO. In essence, learning leaders have nothing to do with the hierarchical role they occupy within the organization. In my opinion, it would be obvious to give learning leaders, who inspire others, priority for promotion within a hierarchical organization as well. What is more, the entire executive team should invest in cultivating learning leaders, which is the purpose of the book *Learning Ecosystems*.

A spark is good but the fire needs to keep burning

'Cells that wire together fire together.' This saying, which I have already quoted when discussing getting the most out of team learning, also applies to the learning leader. To be a learning leader, as I mentioned above, it is essential that you are also a learning influencer, that you can transmit the spark that ignites the love of learning and create a ripple effect in your team.

Converting or supporting the learning mindset is an intrinsic prerequisite for being a learning leader. It sets you apart to help shape the future in times where AI is ubiquitous and affects organizations and their employees at an unseen speed. Leaders who have been stagnant in the past and employees who think they don't need to adapt to it will soon find themselves at an irreversible disadvantage. Learning leaders anticipate constant change and not only lead by example, but also foster a learning attitude in their teams to grow together and put people first.

This continuous focus on learning in all its aspects distinguishes a learning leader from many executives who have not yet grasped this urgency. I almost dare not say it, but I myself spoke to CEOs who feel that L&D is not their responsibility but that of L&D. As leaders, they are expected to have vision and be able to set a strategy which would set them apart. Well, to all the top executives who are reading this now and ever spoke to me, I want to say to you: you were my spark to write this book because I sometimes disagree with you. Yes, being rebellious is my trademark, I know. But please follow me when I say everyone appreciates a role model. If the leader of a team does not recognize that learning is the only way to survive and thrive, why should your team members be motivated to learn?

However, igniting the love for learning is not the only thing the learning leader does for their teams. They also keep it burning by engaging in creating a safe psychological environment where a learning mindset can thrive, as I will further demonstrate with an inspiring contribution from Cathy Hoy in Chapter 8.

The extraordinary competencies of the learning leader

From the above, you may think that I consider the more widely recognized leadership competences irrelevant to the future of work. Obviously, I don't want to go that far at all. I find traits, skills and behaviours that distinguish an exceptional leader are also the basis for any (future) extraordinary learning leaders, regardless of the geographical region or hierarchical structure of the organization.

Throughout the previous parts of this book, I already cited many of these skills for achieving better collaboration within a team:

- **Inspirational leadership:** The basis of everything if you want to get people to participate in change is being able to inspire and motivate others. Exceptional leaders create a positive working environment that fosters team spirit while encouraging individual growth. Their enthusiasm and passion are contagious, creating a ripple effect that extends far beyond the boundaries of their team.

- **Authenticity:** Leadership, and by extension anyone who wants to connect and collaborate as a human being, must be authentic. You may be different, anxious that you are not good enough or rebellious; only when you are authentic can you be the best version of yourself. You have to be real, as others see through when you show a facade of confidence or pretend to be different to be accepted. Be yourself and, above all, be proud of that. Remember, innovation only comes from teams that embrace diversity and respect openness.

- **Empathy:** One of the competencies that make us human, which I described in Part Two, and which could not be omitted here. Yet I want to emphasize it again because I find that sometimes leaders think they are empathic, but often forget this competence when under stress or time pressure. For learning leaders, it is crucial to empathize with the feelings and perspectives of others. They use empathy to learn from others and reflect on what drives them and their team members. By reinforcing empathy with openness, they connect everyone, creating psychologically safe environments.

- **Effective communication:** The added value of connecting communication and non-verbal communication for learning influencers was discussed at length and confirmed by Constanza Garcia. It is the basis for learning influencers to grow into learning leaders. For leaders, this also involves being able to translate vision into a concrete strategy. When they can't do that, it potentially causes uncertainty and fear within the team, who are unsure what is expected of them to contribute to the purpose. As a leader, this competence is therefore essential to retaining the credibility you have built up with other competences.

- **Taking responsibility:** As an exceptional leader, you are not afraid to take responsibility for your actions and decisions, even if they may have been right but were not well understood because you did not communicate them clearly and understandably. As a learning leader, you neither cover up nor deny your mistakes. You even dare to share your mistakes to benefit the team's learning mindset. Discussing them openly without fear of consequences creates a psychologically safe situation that benefits everyone. For the less confident team members, it can even be enlightening and reassuring to know that their mentor also makes mistakes and that acknowledging mistakes and taking responsibility contributes to a learning culture and continuous improvement.

- **Perseverance:** In times of increasingly rapid change, when plans sometimes fall through due to unforeseen circumstances, you might occasionally want to take a break. As a leader, however, you don't have that choice. You have to be the strong person who provides support as a beacon and always inspires your team to remain resilient in the face of setbacks. And those setbacks can be hard and completely beyond your control. What you do then determines how exceptional you are as a leader. Like CEO Igor Smelyansky, at the outbreak of war in Ukraine, when he had the responsibility to maintain the country's postal services. In doing so, he had to motivate some 70,000 postal workers daily to go that extra mile during this large-scale war. Despite numerous challenges, such as bombs and missiles that destroyed infrastructure, and under life-threatening and incredibly difficult conditions, he kept his organization operational. What is more, he equipped them with a long-term perspective: any day could be the last, so you better do something right today. With his mindset, he inspired and motivated his teams in these unimaginable circumstances. For me, he is above all a learning leader, as illustrated in this statement: 'There is no book on how to run a business during a war, I hope no one writes it because I hope no one else needs it. But we learn it every day.'[9]

The above indicates that exceptional leadership is not limited to specific personality traits, but rather stems from a combination of skills, traits and behaviours aimed at inspiring, supporting and leading others. Therefore, if you want to inspire as a learning leader, it is useful to reflect on these regularly. Bring them into conscious focus so that you can turn unconscious actions into active learning. For this, refer to Part One regarding habits that support unconscious learning. Repetition is important in learning, so feel free to scroll back to the beginning.

A LEARNING LEADER MAKES BOLD DECISIONS

In an increasingly fast-moving world, where information overload is not conducive to making the most optimal decisions, bold ideas are often a necessity to stay ahead and innovate. This ability to make decisions, often based on incomplete information, as mentioned earlier, is what will distinguish you as a learning leader. It is what gives you ownership of the future!

However, you don't take responsibility for these bold decisions as a learning leader. You have very consciously surrounded yourself with a group of exceptional learners for this purpose, which is a bold decision in itself (as I further discuss). The merits of one person thereby belong to everyone in the team and are also celebrated collectively. And they are not just celebrated, but, as with your mistakes, you take time to analyse them for opportunities for improvement. Through this progressive insight, you will always accelerate and reach new unseen heights. Bold decisions are thus a catalyst for continuous improvement and innovation. They set you apart as a visionary leader because you and your team embrace challenges by challenging the status quo and defying conventional norms.

In these uncertain times, when technology is changing very quickly and people are not keeping up, courageous decisions are just as important from a purely human approach. People seek guidance or affirmation when change makes them feel uncertain. By making bold choices, you create trust among the people in your teams. This in turn reinforces a learning culture where everyone dares to think beyond their limitations. This creates a safe environment where curiosity and imagination flourish.

These learning leaders, or visionaries, come up with groundbreaking ideas that emerge from the diverse ideas of their team of exceptional learners. Consider, for example, Steve Jobs' introduction of the iPhone.[10] This was considered revolutionary at the time and changed not only the telecommunications industry, but also the way people learn, communicate and access information. Talk about a ripple effect!

TURNING IMAGINATION INTO MOONSHOT IDEAS

You can hardly imagine a more human competence than imagination! Generative AI has long since passed us by when it comes to creativity, but imagination and curiosity? I guess even the Singularity won't take them away from us.

Being able to turn imagination into reality is not given to everyone, yet the scientists at the Dartmouth Summer Research Project on Artificial Intelligence in 1956[11] managed to achieve this. Today, however, AI has long since ceased to be hype and, after years of working on algorithms, developers have apparently succeeded in mimicking the human brain. The rapid emergence of LLMs using generative AI has brought their dream of creating AI in the image of humans frighteningly close. Today, AI is ubiquitous and affecting organizations and their employees at an unprecedented speed. Managers and employees who think they don't need to adapt will soon find themselves at an irreversible disadvantage. The question is not whether AI deserves a permanent place in the symbiosis between humans and machines, but how. What is expected of sustainable strategies and future leadership, and how will this affect the organization? Think about turning imagination into Moonshot ideas.

It may have taken scientists many decades to realize their futuristic dream. As I cited earlier, big industries are sometimes attacked with Moonshot ideas that suddenly out of nowhere become the new normal. Consider Airbnb, for example. The idea that you would let strangers sleep in your home has grown in a short period of time into a phenomenon that is giving governments worldwide headaches because it is creating shortages in the housing market in many cities.

Scott McArthur also shared, in his contribution in Chapter 4, that the power of converting imagination often lies in consilience. Bringing together different ideas from different disciplines and sciences to create something new. Experimenting, failing and starting over with new ideas touched on by your team of exceptional learners. As learning leaders, you stimulate a culture based on curiosity and imagination. For this, you are willing to embrace risk and make bold decisions.

As a learning leader, you leverage the Moonshot idea of the scientists who came together at Dartmouth. Because, admit it, generative AI may not be creative, but it processes all the data much faster than anyone on your team and turns it into future scenarios. These scenarios, worked out by the virtual team member, help you see potential Moonshot ideas that could land, or decide what is just a nice but not yet realizable dream.

WHY THE MOON WHEN YOU CAN GO TO MARS?

Why dream of landing on the Moon when Mars is also within your reach these days? Push the Forever Frontier or 'Go where no man has gone before', as mentioned in the popular title sequence of the original 1966–69 sci-fi television series *Star Trek*. Exceptional leaders like Elon Musk also aspire to the stars; although Musk may take it a little too literally with his dream of using SpaceX to enable space travel around Earth, to the Moon, Mars and beyond. However, can you blame him for his imagination? In these times of unprecedented innovative acceleration, you may no longer think in terms of limits of what is possible. Just remember what I wrote earlier about Neuralink in Chapter 2. With Neuralink Musk was also a pioneer with a Moonshot idea. Several years later, I see start-ups popping up everywhere, studying the possibilities of brain–computer interfaces (BCIs) and generative AI.

Challenging a team to think beyond what is currently possible requires a combination of incentivizing strategies and a culture that supports innovation based on curiosity and imagination. Challenge them to come up with rebellious ideas beyond the current mission, just as companies like Google do to come up with new projects and sometimes corporate venturing. By doing so, you nurture their learning mindset and the human competencies that come with it. When they come up with groundbreaking ideas, even if they are not yet realizable, this creates fireworks of neurotransmitters that creates a ripple effect for the innovative and learning mindset.

Unlearning is essential but can be confusing

Learning is hard, but unlearning is often even more challenging. This is why I said in the earlier chapters that unlearning is something we have to learn. Something we have to make a habit of. As a learning leader, you will have to set a good example when it comes to unlearning, as Monique Borst also describes later in this chapter.

I often hear that a person cannot unlearn, and from a scientific approach, I cannot contradict that. However, I have often wondered what actually happens when we unlearn something. Do we forget it? Is it a cognitive process where you must unlearn before making room for new knowledge or behaviour? Or do we partially overwrite old behaviour and old knowledge with the risk that the old knowledge will interfere with the new knowledge, and we will end up mostly confused and unsure?

I compare this to the old floppy disks, which were very popular in the late 1980s. I still remember making the mistake of putting one near a magnet, which meant I erased all the data on it. Empty, unusable, worthless, resulting in an angry mother. I learned that a floppy disk can be reliably written on to, depending on the type and quality of the disk, generally for between 1,000 and 10,000 write cycles.[12] After reaching this limit, the data on the floppy disk may become unreliable and the integrity of the data may be compromised. So, how do I compare that to a brain?

Fortunately, but sometimes unfortunately, you can't just erase brains. Even bad memories or experiences will always lurk somewhere. Therefore, some people on your team may struggle because of the emotions associated with learning, including the stigmas and insecurities they carry. But you can learn coping strategies that will reduce the impact. So, unlearning is not that simple, because the theoretical distinction between unlearning and intentional forgetting is not well defined.[13] Consequently, the two are wrongly used interchangeably in many studies and publications. This is not surprising, of course, because they both have to do with the process of 'letting go' of patterns of thinking and learned behaviour that were effective in the past but now limit success.[14]

Where do I want to go with this? I want you to think about what you want to achieve for yourself and your team when you think about unlearning. Do you want a blank disc that you can refill with new data or do you want to transform old knowledge into new knowledge where you replace the no-longer-relevant knowledge with relevant knowledge? Where you adjust behaviours that no longer fit the present? For leaders, these are important questions if they want to grow with their team. It is therefore a topic that Monique Borst, as a leadership catalyst, often deals with. I am therefore happy to share her expertise.

MONIQUE BORST, BOARD ADVISOR, CEO CATALYST – HUMAN WD40

Unlearning is essential but can be confusing.

On a personal and business level, leaders need to constantly challenge themselves and unlearn what they think they know. This is a challenge for many, which is why I guide CEOs and founders on the parallel track of growing their organizations and growing themselves.

From my perspective, and my experience as a leader myself, the cornerstone of being a learning leader is self-awareness, and this includes examining every blind spot; learning about your biases, beliefs and triggers; and – most importantly – taking responsibility for your own blind spots.

Leadership coaching can include helping clients understand their unconscious minds, and how the past contributes to their present if it limits their potential and holds them back from achieving their personal and business goals. Understanding the unconscious meanings and childhood origins of a client's behaviour isn't necessarily my focus, but it is almost always extremely helpful in guiding the work.

Our beliefs help us make sense of the world. They help us act on incomplete information. But there is a skill to observing, questioning and then updating your beliefs. To not judge or label, but to get curious about what needs to go and why. Letting go to let in. It's a skill we must develop and get good at so that the important decisions we make are based on reflective judgement and critical thinking.

Unlearning means discarding what you have already learnt. And this is the tough part. Even if what you have learnt isn't serving you anymore, the fact that a certain amount of time and energy has already been invested in it makes it difficult to let go and discover a new path.

Courage is necessary for this, because learning necessarily involves not merely risk, but also the challenge of giving up a former condition or view in favour of a new way of seeing things. It means being willing to grapple with difficult or confusing concepts and asking questions, to struggle to gain understanding and risk making mistakes. Integrity and authenticity are interwoven with modelling intellectual courage.

Leaders, unfortunately, are often expected to know it all and make perfect decisions, and the obvious truth is that they're just as human and fallible as anyone else.

In the unchartered waters of today's world, where change is the only constant, one of the biggest mistakes leaders can make is pretending they know more than they do or making decisions relying only on their instinct or previous experience. Learning leaders must therefore be open to being wrong and having more to learn. Confidence and humility are not polarities; they are complementary. People and organizations can only thrive where 'I don't know' doesn't equal ignorance but self-awareness and confident, courageous humility.

A good question to ask at the end of the day is 'What have I unlearnt today?'

EVERYONE NEEDS TO UNLEARN, INCLUDING OUR ARTIFICIAL COLLEAGUES

When we think of our virtual colleagues, we think of them as non-stop learners, adding more and more data to their artificial brains until they become this inimitable *supermind*. But that is not quite true. Our virtual colleague is also increasingly encouraged to unlearn. Yet machine unlearning is still a relatively young but rapidly emerging field that faces serious challenges. In purely technical terms, removing specific data influences and maintaining the model's overall performance can be a complicated balance. Simply put, which valuable information should be retained and which redundant or unwanted content is better removed to make room for the assimilation of new knowledge? It is very similar to humans, but that is by no means a surprise because, as I have pointed out several times, AI is an imitation of the human brain. Moreover, the difficulty of unlearning varies greatly between different machine learning algorithms. Again, this is very similar to the people in your team, which allows you, as an exceptional learning leader to support them with a situational approach.

Imposing unlearning on our virtual friends is not just for efficiency reasons. In machine unlearning, we want to reduce the impact of specific training data on a previously trained machine-learning model. This has several goals that are increasingly coming to the fore within the current innovation climate. Just think about ensuring the privacy of individuals whose data contributed to the training of the model, correcting inaccuracies or errors in the original training data and getting rid of outdated or irrelevant data, and preventing the model from developing biases or over-fitting the training data.[15]

The goal of machine unlearning is thus also related to the expectations we set for our human team members. Despite the difficulties and obstacles, it is essential to live up to the promise of resilience, reliability and ethical values.

Endnotes

1 Daily Infographic. Different leadership styles around the world, Daily Infographic, 12 September 2023, dailyinfographic.com/different-leadership-styles-around-the-world (archived at https://perma.cc/5PYX-JNZX)

2 T Mauri (2024) *The Upside of Disruption: Leading and thriving in the unknown*, Wiley, New York

3 R Raffaelli and C Snively. The reinvention of Kodak, Harvard Business School Case 419-012, November 2018 (Revised August 2020)

4 A Lin. Average lifespan of companies, 23 May 2023, granitefirm.com/blog/us/2023/05/23/lifespan-of-companies/ (archived at https://perma.cc/N6R7-JDYT)

5 L V Gerstner (2004) *Who Says Elephants Can't Dance? Leading a great enterprise through dramatic change*, Harperbusiness, New York

6 V Kumar. Should enterprises consider a large language model strategy?, *Forbes*, 19 May 2023, www.forbes.com/sites/forbestechcouncil/2023/05/19/should-enterprises-consider-a-large-language-model-strategy/?sh=48c486d94132 (archived at https://perma.cc/V23R-FXCR)

7 G Petriglieri, S Ashford and A Wrzesniewski. Thriving in the gig economy, *Harvard Business Review*, 2018, March–April, hbr.org/2018/03/thriving-in-the-gig-economy (archived at https://perma.cc/3NEW-D7SL)

8 Habit of Improvement. Gig-workers provide cross-fertilisation of knowledge in the larger ecosystem, 20 October 2021, habitofimprovement.com/2021/10/20/gig-workers-provide-cross-fertilisation-of-knowledge-in-the-larger-ecosystem/ (archived at https://perma.cc/BX9T-K8A5)

9 R M Ellis. Delivering under pressure: How Igor Smelyansky (MBA'05) has adapted Ukraine's National Postal Service to the chaos of war, McDonough School of Business, 8 December 2022, msb.georgetown.edu/news-story/delivering-under-pressure-how-igor-smelyansky-mba05-has-adopted-ukraines-national-postal-service-to-the-chaos-of-war/ (archived at https://perma.cc/246P-7UFT)

10 J Schroter. Steve Jobs introduces iPhone in 2007, YouTube, 2011, www.youtube.com/watch?v=MnrJzXM7a6o (archived at https://perma.cc/Q5UV-E4P9)

11 Artificial Intelligence (AI) coined at Dartmouth, home.dartmouth.edu/about/artificial-intelligence-ai-coined-dartmouth (archived at https://perma.cc/7V56-X6PK)

12 Quora. How many times can a floppy disk be written on? www.quora.com/How-many-times-can-a-floppy-disk-be-written-on# (archived at https://perma.cc/TGB9-CXSN)

13 A Kluge. Recent findings on organizational unlearning and intentional forgetting research (2019–2022), *Frontiers in Psychology*, 2023, 14, doi.org/10.3389/fpsyg.2023.1160173 (archived at https://perma.cc/NC5K-LHVY)

14 B O'Reilly (2019) *Unlearn: Let go of past success to achieve extraordinary results*, McGraw-Hill, New York

15 A Borji. A fresh perspective on machine unlearning, with a real-world solution!, Medium, 11 October 2023, medium.com/@aliborji/a-fresh-perspective-on-machine-unlearning-with-a-real-world-solution-203821dd01c0 (archived at https://perma.cc/W6V5-EEKA)

8

An environment for the League of Extraordinary Learners

Recruit a diverse array of extraordinary learners

Reading fiction books contributes to imagination, curiosity and thus innovation, says Terence Mauri[1] of Hack Future Lab in New York.[2] I'd like to echo that and add sci-fi movies from my own experience, as films like *Star Trek* often inspire me. And I am not the only one, because many inventors and visionaries seem to have taken ideas from films, too. Just think of Mark Zuckerberg, who did not invent the metaverse but was inspired by American writer Neal Stephenson, who first published his amazing sci-fi novel *Snow Crash* in 1992. A famous example of books that seemed to inspire visionaries are Jules Verne's books, from which almost everything has been realized. Just think of Branson, whom I quoted earlier, who also wanted to go around the world in a hot air balloon, inspired by *Five Weeks in a Balloon*. I think most of Verne's books have already inspired real actions, except perhaps *Journey to the Center of the Earth*.[3]

To bring together the teams I envisage, I took inspiration from the fictional comic strip and later the film *The League of Extraordinary Gentlemen*, in which a group of remarkable individuals with extraordinary skills and talents within their respective fields come together to achieve goals. You can probably see the analogy I have in mind with 'A League of Extraordinary Learners'. It is not an obvious thing to bring them together, but if you succeed and you can get them to work together, this bold decision will be one of the best you have ever made.

Before I go into some aspects to consider when selecting your team, I want to reiterate that it is not just about leadership from a hierarchical top-down approach. Organizations committed to innovation and improvement let ideas come from the bottom up. Like the example of the Japanese leadership style, and also Google, which I further quote. Or, like Maarten Mans who wanted to optimize learning and knowledge sharing within his organization. As a team manager in a matrix organization, Maarten knew very well that his challenging project would succeed better if he brought together different stakeholders from different teams. His vision was to introduce efficient learning from the bottom up and across silos where the stakeholders themselves were motivated to participate. He envisioned a project that would start with small-scale initiatives but would have a ripple effect throughout the organization thanks to the learning influencers involved. To go from 'A League of Twenty Extraordinary Learners' to an organization of 20,000 is a challenging goal to say the least.

Bringing together 'A League of Extraordinary People' requires not only a keen eye for talent, but also being able to recognize individuals who have made extraordinary achievements and have the potential to continuously innovate. Learning influencers, through collaboration, need to take each other and the organization to new heights. Bringing them together is just the first step. As I will explain further, the challenge lies just as much in getting people to work together for a common purpose.

You will need the misfits

Including 'misfits' in your team can have significant benefits for innovation and team dynamics. For example, consider people with dyslexia and imposter syndrome, which I discussed in Part Two. Their unique qualities may initially seem difficult to bring together, but if I extend the comparison to *The League of Extraordinary Gentlemen*, that is exactly where the power of innovative teams lies. After all, different characters and strengths are the catalyst for brilliant ideas.

People with dyslexia contribute unique ways of thinking and perspectives because they approach things differently. Consequently, it is often dyslexic people who are at the root of Moonshot ideas. Remember Richard Branson, to whom I referred earlier and who also has tremendous resilience and perseverance because he had to adapt to mainstream school methods. As a mother, I still get angry about that system where my daughter was treated as 'stupid' when she just looked at a problem differently. Meanwhile, she learned to thrive despite the challenges because she was lucky enough to find a good tutor at school who taught her how to embrace dyslexia as a superpower. People like her, who used to be the outliers in the classroom, can now be the backbone of your team. They don't shy away from challenges but embrace them as opportunities to grow.

Resilience and perseverance are also the strengths of people with imposter syndrome. At least they will if you give them recognition in a safe environment where they don't have to be afraid to make mistakes, as Cathy Hoy will share a bit later on in this chapter. It may surprise you, but many people who later became very successful were once found to suffer from imposter syndrome. Especially among women, as many as 75 per cent of all executives are said to have faced imposter syndrome at some point.[4] By doubting their own ability and challenging themselves to mask their insecurity, they put more pressure on themselves than on anyone else. They go to extremes for a cause they believe in and to prove themselves. Convincing them to join your project may be difficult because they may think they are not worth it. But your empathy and promise to provide them with a safe environment will hopefully convince them.

Not only people with high levels of self-doubt, but also other misfits, such as rebellious and dyslexic employees, can be difficult to convince to join your team. This is because they sometimes have emotion-provoking experiences that make them reluctant to work with new people. I am definitely speaking from experience here when I say you need to persuade them with more than just a metaphorical carrot. We misfits see through that and don't want empty promises. If you want to win us over, state clearly how you will provide a safe psychological environment, as mentioned later in this chapter.

Nono and the rest of the penguins

I don't get all my inspiration from just comic books and films. Business books, like *Our Iceberg is Melting: Changing and succeeding under any conditions* by John Kotter and Holger Rathgeber,[5] contribute just as much. Although a funny video has been made of this book, I wouldn't be surprised if someone has already made a comic book of it.

Why do I cite this? Obviously to encourage you – towards the end of this book – to further feed your learning mindset with other great books. Kotter and Rathgeber's book is inspiring to discuss with your team. Especially if you try to give everyone in your team the name of one of the penguins and make sure you have a Nono among them as, in my opinion, Nono is indispensable in your team! Let me explain.

Kotter's story follows a colony of penguins on an iceberg who discover that their habitat is in danger and they have to face the need to change. The rebel, Fred, discovers that their familiar iceberg is melting, forcing them to rethink their way of life. But, as is often the case, the colony's leaders do not see the need and are unwilling to move. Certainly Nono, who is known within the colony as stubborn and resistant, is unwilling. However, then there is Alice, who symbolizes the hopeful worker who goes along with new initiatives. She contributes perspective and hope, which are also necessary skills for a learning leader, as I will explain later. Of course, your team needs an analyst for informed decision-making, an operational brain and a knowledge expert. These are Louis, Buddy and the Professor.

The story highlights the importance of effective communication and persuasion in engaging all stakeholders. Moreover, openness, transparency and connecting communication are crucial to gaining support for change. Nono's working method may seem counter-productive in this regard, yet his method adds value to teams. Like no other, he can challenge conventional ideas and introduce new perspectives – a trait that is recommended for preventing groupthink. The Nono you want on your team is willing to take risks and challenge traditional norms. He will challenge you by asking critical questions and challenging existing assumptions. His somewhat negative and contrarian approach is valuable for identifying weaknesses in plans and promoting thoughtful policies.

In short, Nono embodies traits crucial for managing change and fostering a culture of innovation. Including such 'rebels' in a team is a conscious decision to increase diversity of thought. Rebels like Nono strengthen the team's resilience and challenge everyone to keep learning with an open mindset. By recognizing the penguins in your team and talking about this together, you all learn to work together using your own strengths. This supports the creation of a safe working environment based on respect and diversity.

The artificial penguin completes the league

It may not surprise you if I mention again the value that can be added by AI if it is included as a full member to strengthen the League of Extraordinary Learners. AI is already more efficient at processing data very quickly and is often faster at finding knowledge. In this way, it can also help support decisions based on incomplete information. Yet, I see that AI is not respected as an equal in most teams as a permanent added value to support or challenge decisions.

Many managers I spoke to are reluctant because they think AI will replace jobs, or because they don't know how to manage a bot. But within your league, it won't replace anyone because it lacks the human competencies needed for all *penguins*. But the bot can make their work easier, with less chance of mistakes. In this way, it also contributes to the atmosphere within your team and supports a safe psychological environment.

Psychologically safe team environments are a prerequisite for learning

Creating a psychologically safe environment for your team is more than 'just being nice' as a learning leader. It is a group-level phenomenon in which you play a very important role and in which everyone needs to take responsibility. It shapes the group's learning mindset and behaviour only when everyone is involved. In turn, it influences team performance and thus the performance of the organization.

Project Aristotle by Google aimed to understand these factors that influence team effectiveness.[6] Harvard professor Ami Edmondson examined the correlation between who was on the team and the success they achieved. Using more than 30 statistical models and hundreds of variables, she concluded that who was on a team mattered less than how the team worked together. The most important factor according to her was the psychological safety that prevailed within the team.[7]

In other research, Edmondson focused on the relationship between team learning and psychological safety.[8] In doing so, Edmondson proved that learning behaviour mediates between team psychological safety and team performance. Her results support an integrative perspective in which team structures, such as context support and coaching by the team leader and shared beliefs, shape team outcomes.

Creating an exceptional team is, according to those researchers, not about the individual, but rather about the connection between different individuals. Individually, they are very different, but there is a team bond based on trust and openness to appreciating the perspectives of others. When this trust is there, it leads to better decision-making. Team members feel more engaged and motivated because they feel that their contributions matter and that they can speak up without fear of retribution. All this ensures that a psychologically safe team environment fosters a culture of continuous learning and improvement because team members feel comfortable sharing and learning from mistakes.

As a learning leader, it is essential to understand this because your behaviour will serve as an example to team members. You create that climate when you assemble your League of Extraordinary Learners. This can sometimes be done with small things that can become habits. Psychological safety, for example, is felt quickly by the reaction to mistakes being made. As a learning leader, it is essential to note that making mistakes is part of gaining experience. Therefore, before going into what went wrong and how it could have been avoided, it is very useful to reiterate this briefly. This positive approach sounds simple but has quick results. Just like never holding anyone personally responsible, because within a team the power is precisely to help and strengthen each other, and then you don't leave anyone alone with the blame.

You will also create a safe environment by providing structure and clarity. Perhaps this is somewhat paradoxical, as you are also encouraging challenge to the status quo, but frameworks can make sense within freedom. Consider setting clear goals and establishing defined roles and an effective decision-making process. With this clarity, everyone can understand their contribution to the whole and how they can make a difference. This makes everyone individually feel like a valued member. By clearly sharing everyone's contribution, you also clarify their value as a team. This clearly communicated approach is hugely helpful for employees who are unsure of their abilities to grow and be confident in their roles. But even when working with cross-functional teams where roles may be defined otherwise and responsibilities may sometimes differ, this is essential to avoid misunderstandings and frustration.

As a learning leader, your strength is not just in assembling an extraordinary team. The dynamics you foster within your team creates a safe psychological environment. In other words, there is no one magic formula you can follow. You can only rely on the added value of your human competencies and nurture them in each individual in your team. This is essential for success, because in a negative environment, no one can develop, as Cathy Hoy confirms with her inspiring contribution.

CATHY HOY, CEO AND CO-FOUNDER, CLO100: NURTURING A CULTURE OF PSYCHOLOGICAL SAFETY IN LEARNING ENVIRONMENTS

In my 20+ years of working with diverse teams and leaders across many different global organizations, I have come to firmly believe that two essential factors form the bedrock of an organization where learning is not just enabled but actively encouraged. These are fostering an understanding of how to learn and creating a safe space to learn.

Psychological safety is the shared belief that you can take interpersonal risks without fear of negative consequences. The significance of psychological safety in the context of learning cannot be overstated. Learning, by its very nature, involves making mistakes, failing and then growing from those experiences. For this process to occur organically, individuals need to feel secure in their environment ... This is a must!

I've experienced many different environments where psychological safety simply wasn't present. I've worked in organizations where the leadership teams themselves are the cause of a lack of safety in the workplace.

In one example, in a retail organization, there was a general lack of empathy displayed by the whole leadership team. This attribute, or rather the absence of it, resulted in a workplace where employees felt undervalued and unheard. This created an environment where staff were all reluctant to discuss their concerns or needs, which lead to increased stress, illness and absence, and ultimately a decline in productivity for the business.

Fear of failure is another damaging trait that I've observed far too often. In one organization the Training and HR team was regularly met with severe reprimands from the directors. This approach discouraged everyone from taking risks or experimenting with new ideas, both of which are essential for the growth of the organization. People were afraid to step outside their comfort zone, which hinders not only learning but also innovation for the business.

In another very memorable instance, excessive criticism from the leadership team created a hostile work environment for a sales department I worked closely with. Harsh criticism was often delivered in a public setting by the sales director. This led to employees becoming fearful and hesitant to express their ideas or concerns, stifling open communication. The impact extended beyond individual growth: I believe it hindered collective learning and organizational development as well.

Consistent negativity and belittlement from leaders can lead to an erosion of self-confidence. In this particularly toxic environment, employees were regularly made to feel incompetent, leading to low morale and decreased performance.

To counteract this negativity and create a more psychologically safe environment, I believe there are a few must-haves that I've witnessed first-hand that work well. Firstly, leaders should model vulnerability, admit their mistakes and show that learning comes from failure. Secondly, it is key to promote open communication and encourage team members to voice their ideas and concerns without fear of reprisal. Lastly, a culture of trust and mutual respect serves as a strong foundation for psychological safety.

One of the most effective ways of fostering psychological safety I've witnessed involved a CEO who wasn't afraid to admit his mistakes and share the journey he had been on to discover that he needed to change. I witnessed him speaking live to his leadership team, expressing his heartfelt apology over his previous behaviour and recognizing and listing all the negative traits he now realized were contributing to a toxic environment and then making a commitment to change.

This transparency not only showed everyone he was taking full responsibility for the situation the business was in; he was also demonstrating that it was OK to say you've made a mistake and that it was a positive thing to learn from them.

In another organization, open communication was encouraged through regular 'town hall' meetings where team members were invited to voice their ideas, concerns or suggestions. The leadership ensured that everyone, irrespective of their role or seniority, was heard and their input valued. This practice created an environment where employees felt safe to express their thoughts and contribute to the company's direction. It also fostered a sense of ownership and engagement among the staff.

Creating a psychologically safe environment is not an optional extra but a fundamental necessity in the age of innovation. It's not just about creating an atmosphere where people can learn; it's about building an environment where people want to learn.

Trust is the glue that holds your team together

Without trust, everything falls apart. I learned this from my own experience and from many studies such as the Edelman Trust Barometer.[9] Edelman has been studying trust at the organizational level for 20 years and recognizes that trust is indispensable for organizations to guard their credibility and reputation. However, trust is also the glue that learning leaders need to get the best out of their teams and allow them to achieve unseen results through collaboration. Trust is essential between team members for knowledge sharing and collaboration to flourish, as I described when discussing the drivers of social learning communities. However, trust in the person making the final decisions is the foundation.

In his bestseller *The Speed of Trust: The one thing that changes every-thing*, Stephen M. R. Covey says that the ability to build, extend and restore trust is not only vital to our personal and interpersonal well-being; it is the most important leadership competency of the new economy.[10] Trust, I believe, is also the basis of the stability your employees seek. Especially in times when the plethora of different opinions they get through social media means they often don't know who or what to trust. Trust is important because we need to believe that our manager has our best interests at heart and that we will not be replaced by an artificial colleague who is much more efficient and cheaper. Fear contributes to the atmosphere within the team, which you need to address candidly, as I explain below.

Trust is the hardest, yet the best thing to receive from your team as a leader, but it takes time to build that. You must prove to your team that you deserve it, which is not easy according the Edelman Trust Barometer. Because of the plethora of conflicting information that we receive via different media, it is often difficult to distinguish truth from fiction. Everyone is wary, and that is reflected in this barometer. As many as 6 in 10 people would tend to distrust something until they see evidence that it is reliable. These figures are in line with the trust shown in line managers and CEOs, although CEOs do just a little worse, with overall trust scores of 67 and 62, respectively, as seen in the 2023 Index of Trust in Leadership.[11]

As a learning leader, you want to earn the trust of your team and do better than 6 out of 10. Although you won't get it done on the first day without proving yourself, you can make a habit of using the tips below that will help you get results faster with your team:

- **The power of connecting communication:** To trust in each other, you need to feel safe to communicate, make mistakes, have your own opinion, dare to say you don't know something or even be able to say that you messed up. As a learning leader, it is essential to ensure that your team know they can vent this and that they will be listened to without prejudice. Trust-based leadership means that as a leader, you inspire your employees to open their mouths (play to win) rather than remain silent (play to lose), and curiosity (great minds do not think alike) rather than conformity (great minds think alike), says Terence Mauri.[12] However, his research shows that 87 per cent of employees can recall a recent example where they chose silence over speaking up by withholding a question, concern or idea because of a lack of trust in the 'challenger'. Without trust, you cannot learn. There is no growth. There is no transformation.

- **You cannot feign authenticity:** Authenticity is what learning influencers radiate to inspire others. What you say with words should be in line with your behaviour and attitude – the power of non-verbal communication, as Constanza Garcia explained. As a manager, you cannot say that you see failure as a learning gain while your body expresses frustration. Non-verbal signals are picked up and linger longer, making people forget words that were not spoken sincerely. If you want to earn confidence, stay true to yourself. Try not to pretend to be the leader you think you should be based on an example that does not suit you. Self-confidence, in other words, comes first. Only then can you be authentic, and others will trust the real person in you.

- **Treat all people fairly and respectfully:** In line with authenticity, others will only trust you if you are fair and respectful. Even if you are frustrated by that rebel who challenges you in every way, always remain respectful. Say honestly that you don't quite agree with their behaviour or idea, and use empathy and openness to see where you can find common ground in the differences. Don't be like the narcissistic leaders, who I discuss further later, who exhibit dishonest and disrespectful behaviour out of a lack of self-confidence. Be honest with yourself, because others pierce through that, and before you know it you are alone without your great team.

- **Acknowledge and value individual differences:** Recognizing the power of a diverse team should be evident. Because of the different insights, you come up with innovative solutions and ways of thinking, as noted earlier. However, to gain the trust of your team, you also have to prove that you value them as people and not just because they are the missing link to achieving your goal. This means that you also drop your preconceptions about someone with ADHD, for example. Openly discuss what it is and how it can be used as an added value within the team. Ask what you can do to give this valued team member a safe environment. If necessary, do the same with the others and get to know and use each other's differences as an enhancer of team spirit.

- **Use respectful language when setting expectations:** Respectful language and politeness are often used interchangeably. Politeness is often a facade masking a lack of respect, which is often betrayed by non-verbal communication. When I talk about respectful language when setting expectations, it is to paint a realistic picture of the possibilities. Don't paint the future brighter than it is. Indicate that something will be difficult and that you may fail more and for longer than you may win. Present a clear timeline and the consequences if goals are not achieved when they are meant to be. State the consequences, obviously not as threats, but as an honest representation of the facts. For example, state that experiments will be stopped if budgets are exceeded or timelines are not met. Do not state or support unrealistic goals. As I explain below, that is the fastest way to lose trust and hope.

Trust is your leadership multiplier and works in multiple directions. It starts with trust in yourself, because only then will others have trust in you. When there is trust at all levels you can keep your team together and they will follow you.

Understanding hope as the driving force of your team

Is hope the driving force of your team and does it transcend purpose? In my opinion, yes, but you might as well turn it around, because nothing kills the learning mindset more than a carrot and a stick. Whether hope is the driving force is a conversation I love to debate with my daughters. In fact, my daughter who is a dancer is convinced that hope does not exist. She believes that self-direction is more important. According to her, you have to master that well and overcome the lack of self-confidence to achieve success. As such, she is the philosophical rebel and disciplined ballerina who has challenged all my ideas many times whilst I was writing this book. So, I don't entirely agree with her, but, fortunately, we can talk openly about things.

If I am honest, hope has always driven me to keep moving forward, but it often made me very unhappy when certain expectations did not come true after all. So, I recognize the highs and lows between hope and lost hope. But also, through my work with children, I see more and more that lost hope (hope for a better climate, love, success, hope in the future) and even depression is a damper on the development of many other competencies they need in these challenging times.

My motivation to understand the different aspects of hope as a competence for the future comes from young people shaping the future of work, our organizations and society. But it is not only children (and their parents as supporters) who benefit. I want to help you, as a learning leader, and your team create a climate where well-being and growth go hand in hand. To do this, I want to invest in a positive approach to hope that increases engagement. But for this it is necessary that you understand what hope is and how this can have a negative consequence. Because, when hope disappears, it negatively affects the ability to see, imagine and create the future.

As a learning leader, conveying realistic hope is essential because it affects attitudes towards the future and the ability to shape it yourself. But to do that, you must first understand what hope is.[13] I myself was greatly inspired about what hope actually is by a study by Bert Musschenga, which is best represented visually in Figure 8.1.[14]

I agree that hope sometimes leads to disappointment, so giving up hope is sometimes the easiest path. However, hope is not simple and unambiguous, as it comes in different forms and leads to different outcomes, both conscious and unconscious. Real hope, which I want to encourage as a competence to shape the future nimbly, combines hope with a firm understanding of reality, forming the basis for engagement, foresight and accurate support of reality.

When faced with a problem, we tend to approach it with a predetermined vision of the outcome. Previous experiences partly determine this picture and these can be very positive to very negative, depending on the problem and the person facing it. Our understanding of the problem often determines the outcome and thus our expectation of the future. A correct understanding of the problem is often the first step towards discovering opportunities for change. In this reality, we take a positive approach to solutions to the problem with a viable outcome.

This holistic approach to hopefully shaping the future based on an informed and accurate reality sets exceptional leaders apart from their counterparts. In

FIGURE 8.1 Real hope as the leadership competence for a growth culture

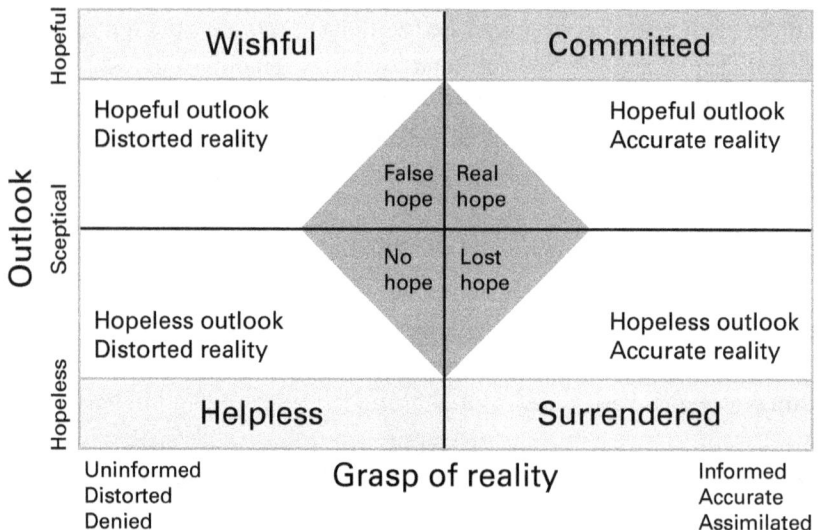

doing so, they also consider all stakeholders who shape their hopes from different realities. They then accommodate doubt and fear and share information with everyone in the organization to involve them in the strategy.

Understanding hope and how it supports employee engagement is also the basis of a learning ecosystem. Only when we understand our employees' motivations, the origins of certain problems and how they relate to each other can we take the first steps towards improvement. Taking the time to step back and examine the root cause of everything will not only determine the success of a new strategy but also support everyone's well-being.

Radiate confidence but dare to show vulnerability

In the world of leadership, trust is an invaluable commodity. It is the foundation on which relationships are built, teams thrive and organizations flourish. But what if I told you that sometimes the key to building this trust lies precisely in showing vulnerability?

I'd like to share the story of a good friend who was an inspirational leader in a large technology company. She is a role model for many women and is known for her unwavering determination and self-assurance, but there is more to it than that. Behind her powerful charisma lies a profound willingness to show her vulnerability.

In her first year as CEO, the company faced a huge challenge: a failed product launch that had cost the company millions. Where her predecessors would have opted for a facade of untouchability, she chose to embrace her team with openness and honesty. She convened an emergency meeting and shared her feelings of disappointment and uncertainty. She acknowledged her own mistakes and stressed the importance of collective responsibility.

Her team was initially surprised by her openness, but soon they realized that this was precisely my friend's strength. Her vulnerability created an atmosphere of trust and transparency within the team. Instead of hiding behind excuses, they worked together to find solutions and restore customers' trust.

The story of my friend, who does not want to be named, is not an isolated one. Consider Elon Musk, the visionary entrepreneur behind SpaceX and Tesla. He is known for his ambitious goals and groundbreaking ideas, but he does not shy away from sharing his failures and personal struggles. Some attack him on social media and suggest that because of these personal struggles, he should no longer be CEO and should resign.[15] Still, despite not agreeing with him on everything, I believe his openness creates a bond with his team and inspires them to work together to achieve his impossible dreams.

Showing vulnerability does not mean showing weakness; on the contrary, it shows strength and authenticity. If you are willing to embrace your vulnerability, you will create an environment where your team feels safe to share their ideas, take risks and grow.

Moreover, in a world where trust and credibility are invaluable, showing vulnerability is key to building strong relationships and fostering a culture of openness and growth. So, as my friend and Elon show us, radiate trust, but also dare to show your vulnerability. This is exactly where exceptional leadership arises.

EGO IS OK; NARCISSISM IS NOT!

A certain degree of self-confidence and a healthy ego are often associated with extraordinary leadership. As a learning leader, a healthy ego can indeed help you make decisions, take risks and present yourself and your vision powerfully. As a leader with self-confidence, you exude authority and can win trust. However, there is a difference between a healthy ego and narcissistic personality traits. Whilst a healthy ego is characterized by self-confidence, assertiveness and a realistic self-image, narcissistic traits can be destructive to leadership and organizations.

To my surprise, especially among young ambitious talents, narcissism is sometimes glorified as studies indicate that there is a positive link between narcissism and the likelihood of advancing to become a CEO.[16] Therefore, before you think you must exhibit narcissistic behaviour, let me put this in context. Indeed, some statistics suggest that narcissistic personality traits are becoming more common among executives and CEOs. This is said to be due to several factors, including the pressure to perform in competitive business environments, the culture of self-promotion and self-glorification in modern society as well as the tendency of organizations to reward narcissistic personalities with power and influence. However, what is often confused here is self-confidence manifested by a healthy ego and a narcissistic personality, which comes in varying degrees and which can have a significant impact on leadership, as I want to demonstrate with two examples.

Narcissism has a very broad spectrum, from hidden narcissism to pathological narcissism, and its impact can vary widely and manifest itself very differently. In other words, the spectrum can range from a healthy but insecurity-driven ego to a pathological disorder. Also be aware that pathological narcissism only occurs in 0.1 to 0.5 per cent of people and in almost equal proportions in men and women. Although I often find that women are better at masking it because, in my experience, they can show more empathy or feign it better. So, before labelling someone as a narcissist, I recommend keeping an open mind by not stigmatizing them based on insufficient understanding. After all, as a learning leader, you want to be inclusive of everyone. And, who knows, maybe that misfit with a slightly bigger ego can inspire and support others on the team with low self-esteem?[17]

It is important to understand the difference between pathological narcissists and hidden narcissists, who primarily exhibit narcissistic behaviour but do not have a behavioural disorder. In this regard, the latter share many similarities with imposter syndrome, both stemming from deep-seated insecurity. Individuals with hidden narcissism often display a pattern of self-centeredness and the need for external validation. However, they mask their insecurity behind a facade of self-confidence, striving for success and recognition to boost their self-assurance and overcome their fear of rejection. At times, they may exhibit less empathy and display controlling behaviour, often as a mechanism of self-protection. Ironically, similar to individuals with imposter syndrome, this deep-seated insecurity can drive them to unprecedented efforts and achievements. They are compelled to work harder, prove themselves and overcome their fears, leading to remarkable professional successes.

An illustrative example of a top executive accused of being narcissistic is Sheryl Sandberg, the ex-COO of Facebook.[18] Despite her impressive career and leadership skills, Sandberg has openly discussed her doubts and insecurities in her book *Lean In*.[19] She acknowledges that she struggles with feelings of self-doubt and imposter syndrome, but at the same time she uses these insecurities as a driving force to pursue excellence and to make a meaningful impact. I never knew her personally, so I will not give an opinion on her behaviour. However, it is not difficult to imagine how she comes across to others, because I have had such a leader myself. Without much thought, I followed my colleagues in their belief that our leader was narcissistic. As a result, I did not bother to investigate the driving force behind the behaviour she displayed. I now know that her constant demand for perfection and recognition often stemmed from a fear of making mistakes. She was not a pathological narcissist, because her behaviour was not driven by a superior ego, but from a lack of self-confidence. Sandberg's book was therefore a good reminder for me that we need to be open to people and what drives them rather than focusing on the negatives. Stigmatization often happens far too quickly and is often unfounded.

Pathological narcissism is characterized by a lack of empathy, manipulative behaviour and megalomania. This can have disastrous consequences for teams and organizations. Leaders with these traits often exhibit authoritarian behaviour, dismiss the needs and ideas of others and primarily seek personal power and recognition. They can foster a culture of fear and oppression, making employees reluctant to voice opinions and take risks. This, in turn, leads to a lack of engagement and motivation, and ultimately a decline in performance and results.

Elizabeth Holmes, the former CEO of Theranos, serves as a glaring example of this destructive pattern. Her behaviour and its aftermath inspired the film *The Inventor: Out for blood in Silicon Valley* (2019). Holmes faced accusations of fraud and manipulation related to her company and was ultimately convicted of multiple charges. Her narcissistic conduct not only precipitated the collapse of her own company but also tarnished the trust and credibility of the entire industry. As a leader, it is therefore imperative to avoid being compared to someone with such detrimental qualities.

Narcissistic traits can yield positive and negative consequences for leaders and their teams. While hidden narcissism and imposter syndrome may propel leaders towards exceptional performance, pathological narcissism can wreak havoc in teams and organizations. Consequently, leaders must remain cognizant of their personality traits and impact on those around them, seeking a delicate balance between self-confidence and empathy, determination and humility. Striving for this equilibrium is essential to cultivating a healthy and productive work environment where individuals, including you as leader, and teams can thrive.

Problems are opportunities in disguise

'The pessimist sees trouble in every opportunity, the optimist sees opportunity in every difficulty' is claimed to have been said by Winston Churchill, and I see his quote pop up regularly in others' keynotes. However, I disagree that not only pessimists focus mainly on problems. Rather, it is a primal instinct that causes negativity that biases us to focus on problems and overlook opportunities. Evolution programmed our brains to prioritize threats and difficulties, so that our ancestors could survive in a dangerous world. But, today, this bias causes us to see problems everywhere and overlook the potential they contain.

But what if problems are not the bad guys they seem? What if, instead of obstacles, they are opportunities in disguise? As I have said many times, learning leaders and their League of Extraordinary Learners thrive on challenges and problems presented to them.

The paradox of problems

What if problems bring out the best in your team? It is a paradoxical approach that I would like to complicate a bit more to challenge your learning mindset for a moment. In my opinion, and I like to be inspired by scientific research, problems can be compared to drugs. In the wrong dosage, they can make you sick (stress), but in a suitable dosage, they provide peace of mind and your natural happy pills, as I pointed out in Chapter 2. So, as a learning leader, you just need to know how to offer problems with a good dosage.

That problems can cause stress I probably don't need to explain to you. But they can also create a state of calm, increasing your creativity and your ability to learn and absorb new information. This alpha state occurs when your brain produces alpha waves. What I find even more fascinating is that this happens not at the *Aha!* or the *Eureka!* moment, but when working on the solution. At the *Aha!* moment, you do notice an emotional experience, but it is more of a relief. Alpha waves would instead be associated with a relaxed, open mind and thus not with brief ecstatic moments, as research shows. By not fixating on the outcome, you generate more robust alpha rhythms than if you consciously adjusted your thinking to come up with the answer. In other words, this research shows that, above all, you should not fixate on the outcome, but rather enjoy the journey: keep an open mind towards all possibilities of reaching this state. So, to help your team get the best out of themselves, you need to look at the forces that support these alpha waves, such as imagination, openness and diversity. This will bring you, as a team, into a state of calm by solving problems.

As a learning leader, you can even amplify the effect of the alpha state by giving rewards while solving the problem, even if it is just exuberantly celebrating the *Aha!* moment. After all, the expected reward releases striatal dopamine in your brain. This dopamine influences motivation, reinforces behaviour and facilitates cognition. Then, in turn, automatic integrative processes are triggered, which leads to more creative strategies to solve problems.

Let me reiterate that it pays to challenge your team regularly. Present them with problems to tackle together, using curiosity, imagination, consilience and openness. Even if solving problems is not the main goal, you will benefit as a team from this alpha state.

The real problem is under the surface

How bad would it be if you have a solution to a problem that is not a problem? Depending on who you ask, you will hear that it was a learning experience and that you and your team obviously enjoyed the trip, the alpha state and the dopamine. But as a leader, you obviously know that it does represent a considerable loss of time and resources. Unfortunately, this is more common than you might expect. When I moderate executive workshops, I sometimes have to keep on asking and urging participants to look at what the real problem is that they don't see. The driving force behind the problem is easy to demonstrate with the metaphor of an iceberg. What is happening below the surface of the water?

Being able to figure out what is driving problems is an essential skill for executives. So, during my workshops, I put a lot of emphasis on this by asking more profound questions: Why, why, why? Often to the point that someone reacts with frustration and agitation, but fortunately, in the end, many do understand the need to ask this. Most executives know there are root causes, yet I fear they ignore them because they hope (false hope) that the problem will resolve itself with time. Fortunately, sometimes their wishful thinking comes true. However, when they do try to tackle the problem in front of them, it usually leads to short-term solutions that do not address the underlying problem. In the end, they only treat symptoms instead of the actual cause. In other words, they only put a band-aid on the festering wound. And when you do that without disinfecting and treating the wound first, the infection will continue to fester and eventually worsen. Similarly, superficial solutions to problems will only lead to continued challenges and frustrations in the long run.

It always pays to dedicate time and resources to finding the root cause of a problem. Only then can you subsequently work on opportunities that deliver sustainable solutions. If approached holistically with a diverse team, this sustainable strategy ensures increased employee engagement and a more positive working environment in the long run. And above all, the process of consistently looking at the cause is a learning experience which will help you make a habit of sticking your head in the water to see what is below the surface of the iceberg.

Strategic exercises for Moonshot opportunities

The next step after finding the root cause of the problem is to search for opportunities for improvement. For this, you will use the power of a League of Extraordinary Learners, the ideal team to work on this. The power of why, challenging the status quo and all the other strengths of learning teams need not be repeated. However, I do want to elaborate on some tools that I like to use that fit well with the lean approach and the Kaizen method.

Design thinking is one of my favourites, and I don't have to say much about it because you can find a lot of information and templates online to get you started. However, with more complex challenges, you may benefit from an external facilitator who, being an outsider, can sometimes push deeper. The advantages of design thinking for complex problems, combined with the ability to take a human-centred approach, are very useful for realizing Moonshot ideas. When you do this, you challenge the forever frontier, an unthinkable future, and through reverse engineering you initiate this future now.

In addition, there are numerous other reasons why design thinking is an excellent approach. One is that when you initiate this regularly with your team, you encourage innovation and creativity and make it a habit. This encourages them to be solution-oriented and think out of the box to shape the future themselves. However, one of the main reasons I choose this approach is because it has a very human-centric focus.

A final benefit of design thinking is that it reinforces the learning mindset by triggering an experimental mindset. Fast failure is the goal to learn quickly what works and what doesn't. It is therefore advisable to prototype and test, both for products and for new ways of working, which can be better tested with a smaller group of stakeholders. If there are too many obstructionists (Nonos), give them a say. Explore with them something that has wider support and is not just a band-aid on a festering wound.

Combining design thinking with scenario thinking can also have advantages because both approaches can reinforce each other. Indeed, scenario thinking focuses on identifying future trends and possible scenarios, while design thinking focuses on developing concrete solutions to existing problems. By integrating both approaches, you can proactively anticipate future challenges whilst working to develop innovative solutions that are relevant to current needs. This ensures a holistic and strategic approach to innovation and problem-solving.

A final tip is that you need to be prepared to 'kill your babies'. Sometimes it is too early for your brilliant idea, and you must prioritize other solutions. Let me illustrate this with an example: A while ago, during an in-house workshop, the idea of implementing a social learning platform came up.

Something that, as you will understand by now, I usually like to encourage. My client almost caused me to step out of my moderating role during this session by answering my 'For whom?' question with 'For all'! At that moment, I couldn't say that was impossible because the purpose of this session was to let participants come up with workable solutions on their own. It was not easy at that moment to align my verbal and non-verbal communication to keep asking open-ended questions. You must know this was a large organization with over 50,000 employees, ranging from blue-collar employees to an immense leadership team. With that, of course, there was a huge diversity of learning needs.

The project could not succeed, so I had to ask different questions to let him discover that for himself. Because even though I am a big fan of innovative applications that connect a diversity of learners, the organization was not ready to solve it with a single app. So, while I understood *what* they wanted to do, I didn't understand *why* they wanted to do it. *Who* would be the beneficiaries, *who* would learn, and *why* would they do it through a social learning platform? Because it was hype? An app vendor in this situation might say it was a good idea, but they wouldn't ask if *why* and *for whom* had already been mapped out. However, I believe that not mapping the different learning objectives for each group of jobs would stand in the way of a successful human-centred implementation. Long story short, my tip was to first map learning personas that support lean learning. Only then could an experimental project be rolled out with a group where adoption would be manageable. This group would then serve as ambassadors who could then spread the idea within the organization.

One solution is the step to the next problem; slow down once in a while!

I know, nothing is as frustrating as bumping from one solution to the next problem. Yet that is just what this ever-faster-changing world brings. This is precisely why only those who embrace a learning mindset will thrive in this crazy world. More than that, with a learning mindset, you and your team will not wait for the next problem to present itself. In fact, a holistic approach, coupled with constantly challenging the status quo, ensures that you anticipate problems. That you come up with an opportunity for improvement even before the problem is visible.

As a learning leader, you want to pass this learning mindset on to your team. This mindset is the beginning of a journey that does not end but repeats itself in a quest for continuous improvement, based on the Kaizen methodology, which Jana Gutierrez Kardum also discusses below. When I initiate learning ecosystems that strive for continuous improvement, I draw inspiration from nature. For example, I like to refer to the Fibonacci sequence, or the algorithm striving for perfection, symbolized by the snail's shell. The snail, symbolizing being slow, often inspires me to slow down and not jump on every hype. To think about the impact of a decision now on an unknown future. I am convinced that if we build slowness into our decisions, we end up going faster because we take time to anticipate the causes of failure.

Having a strong understanding of problems is the basis of everything, at least if you don't want to waste precious time and resources with projects that don't address the root cause. I find that learning teams adopt this way of working as a habit in their daily tasks and that they think proactively and with a solution-oriented approach about everything. Building this habit into your team will set you apart as a learning leader, and perhaps as the learning architect or LearnScaper, who can spread a learning mindset throughout the organization.

Lean and Kaizen to stimulate problem-solving in the flow of work

Solution-oriented thinking must become a habit in order to be able to anticipate all obstacles coming our way at an increasingly rapid pace. In doing so, you need to draw on all the expertise in your team and set an example yourself as a learning influencer.

Such an inspirational learning influencer is Jana Gutierrez Kardum (who I think loves learning even more than I do). She is an experienced global HR and learning specialist with experience in the private and academic sectors. A lifelong learner, she holds multiple academic degrees and certificates from renowned institutions, including Charles University and MIT where I met her. Besides, we both share a love for design thinking and efficiency improvement with lean, agile and Kaizen. Her contribution therefore fits perfectly to conclude this part. Besides that I just want to inspire you to think about the principles of learning ecosystems and the importance of sustainability and the United Nations Sustainable Development Goals (SDGs), as two examples from her experience the many elements that have already been discussed.

JANA GUTIERREZ KARDUM, GLOBAL LEARNING EXPERIENCE LEADER AT RED HAT: ENHANCING LEARNING WITHIN THE WORKFLOW

I have always been an avid learner and bookworm, but I became really addicted to learning with the emergence of MOOCs (massive open online courses). The first time I saw the edx.org page, I felt like a baby in a toy store. I have completed many classes on online platforms – some useful for my job, such as Instructional Design and Technology Micromasters, others out of pure interest (e.g. Fundamentals of Manufacturing). I love to help others to leverage all possible learning resources available to them and am a passionate advocate of lifelong learning.

But let's face it – we spend way more time at work actually doing our jobs than in the classroom or purely studying. Therefore, recognizing and leveraging learning in the flow of work is an imperative for us as learners and learning leaders. Creating an environment rich with relevant and engaging learning moments in the moment is indispensable for everyone.

Recognizing and leveraging on-the-job learning moments is crucial for fostering a dynamic and innovative organizational culture. Firstly, it capitalizes on employees' inherent creativity and problem-solving abilities by acknowledging that learning often happens in the midst of everyday tasks. When organizations actively recognize these moments, they empower employees to embrace challenges as opportunities for growth, cultivating a mindset that values continuous learning and adaptability.

One example from my personal experience is to bring learning closer to the employees. At Red Hat, we are leveraging product tours software to deliver learning snippets as part of the employees' workflows. The snippets can be as simple as providing a definition of a certain field in our corporate applications, serving as a handy library with references to relevant processes or enablement pages, all the way to an adaptive approach that reacts to an employee's actions and proposes a way to solve a particular problem. For example, when a sales representative is creating a certain configuration of a deal in the client relationship management system, the guided help software recognizes the elements and proposes advice on which specific programs could be used to increase the deal size or relevance for the customer.

Another instance of enhancing learning within the workflow involves activities designed to facilitate employees' practical application of the acquired knowledge. For instance, when a new corporate programme or strategic element is communicated to managers within an organization, such as during a global call, you can immediately offer them an option to receive a personalized presentation. This presentation equips them to effectively teach back the content to their teams, thereby reinforcing the message and serving as a repetitive retrieval practice to counteract the Ebbinghaus Forgetting Curve. This approach extends the reach of learning throughout the organization, from managers to their teams. The key advantage lies in providing managers with a pre-prepared deck containing all the necessary information for sharing. This simplifies their task, increasing the likelihood that they will successfully disseminate the information and learn in the process. Ideally, you make the learning moment for the learners so accessible that they will not be tempted to look for a workaround or try to ignore or avoid it.

Learning in a flow of work can be a set of isolated moments that you create in order to encourage learning on the job in your organization that is aligned with your mission and strategy. However, learning in a flow of work can also be a system – the one I am very passionate about is Kaizen, which stands for continuous improvement, and its reflection in the IT world, which is agile. These approaches emphasize iterative processes, enabling teams to reflect on their performance and make real-time adjustments. By integrating learning directly into the work routine, individuals engage in ongoing skill development and problem-solving, leading to heightened productivity. The iterative nature of agile and Kaizen also enhances organizational alignment, as teams collaboratively assess and recalibrate goals, ensuring that everyone is on the same page.

Kaizen/agile work as systems that create learning moments in the flow of work aligned with the company's objectives, because they are the true opposite of command-and-control mechanisms. By letting go of some of the management prescriptiveness, and to a certain extent also the ability to inspect what exactly the employees are doing, you are effectively encouraging them to find their own way and improve through learning by doing. The role of the learning leader in Kaizen/agile is not to manage the learning process, but to make sure that when the distributed teams identify their learning needs they get access to resources that satisfy them. I have seen IT agile teams that were able to very clearly articulate their learning needs; for example, asking for courses on effective communication skills to improve the flow of the information team and be able to reach decisions faster. Kaizen/agile – when properly implemented – fosters both individual and team learning and creates an overall positive culture around learning.

It is also important to add that you can be using elements of Kaizen/agile in any activity and industry – I have been working during my career as a strategic management consultant, HR leader and sales enablement specialist and have helped to implement (as well as used myself) these continuous improvement approaches in every role and project.

To summarize the key takeaway that I hope you will leverage in your learning mindset discovery journey: 1) Learning in the flow of work emerges as a game-changer, recognizing that true innovation often blossoms amidst everyday tasks. By embedding learning within daily routines, organizations unlock the potential for continuous improvement. 2) Agile and Kaizen methodologies stand out as exemplary systems. These iterative approaches seamlessly integrate learning, align teams and cultivate adaptability, fostering a positive culture around learning.

The lesson is clear: embrace the dynamism of learning in the flow of work, leverage elements of the continuous improvement methodologies and, where possible, add some technology in the mix to facilitate the learning effect even further.

Endnotes

1   T Mauri. Learn how to win together, www.terencemauri.com (archived at https://perma.cc/R545-WUNA)

2   Hack Future Lab. Hack Future Lab is a global think tank re-imagining the future, www.hackfuturelab.com/ (archived at https://perma.cc/TY89-SH3E)

3   KPMG. KPMG study finds 75% of female executives across industry have experienced imposter syndrome in their careers, Press Release, 7 October 2020, www.prnewswire.com/news-releases/kpmg-study-finds-75-of-female-executives-across-industries-have-experienced-imposter-syndrome-in-their-careers-301148023.html (archived at https://perma.cc/QW2C-HM3H)

4   J Kotter and H Rathgeber (2006) *Our Iceberg is Melting: Changing and succeeding under any conditions*, St Martin's Press, New York

5   C Duhigg. What Google learned from its quest to build the perfect team, *The New York Times*, 28 February 2016, www.nytimes.com/2016/02/28/magazine/what-google-learned-from-its-quest-to-build-the-perfect-team.html (archived at https://perma.cc/5M3G-5W7D)

6   A Edmondson. Psychological safety and learning behavior in work teams, *Administrative Science Quarterly*, 1999, 44(2), 350–83, doi.org/10.2307/2666999 (archived at https://perma.cc/3TUB-D9S8)

7   A Edmondson. Psychological Safety and Learning Behavior in Work Teams, *Administrative Science Quarterly*, 44(2), 350-383, doi.org/10.2307/2666999 (archived at https://perma.cc/E4D4-C84D)

8   Edelman Trust. Edelman Trust Barometer, www.edelman.com/sites/g/files/ aatuss191/files/2024-01/2024%20Edelman%20Trust%20Barometer%20 Global%20Report_FINAL_1.pdf (archived at https://perma.cc/GLY4-Q2MD)

9   S M R Covey and R R Merrill (2008) *The Speed of Trust: The one thing that changes everything*, Free Press, New York

10   The Institute of Leadership. The Index of Leadership Trust 2023, leadership. global/resourceLibrary/the-index-of-leadership-trust.html# (archived at https:// perma.cc/C3HK-XJ7K)

11   T Mauri, Leading in the age of AI, Hack Future Lab, 2023, www.hackfuturelab.com/foresight/the-war-for-talent-is-over-talent-won-ejfet- reb54 (archived at https://perma.cc/VQ29-CLVP)

12   K Schipperheijn. Hope as the leadership competence for a growth culture, Habit of Improvement, 24 November 2022, habitofimprovement.com/2022/11/24/ hope-as-the-leadership-competence-for-a-growth-culture/ (archived at https:// perma.cc/Z6Z7-BTLS)

13   B Musschenga. Is there a problem with false hope? *Journal of Medicine and Philosophy*, 2019, 44(4), 423–41, doi.org/10.1093/jmp/jhz010 (archived at https://perma.cc/Q4NF-WFX8)

14   G Ruffino. Elon Musk's alleged drug use puts 13,000 jobs at risk, report suggests, Euronews, 8 January 2024, www.euronews.com/business/2024/01/08/ elon-musks-alleged-drug-use-puts-13000-jobs-at-risk-report-suggests (archived at https://perma.cc/LD6U-55EH)

15   P Rovelli and C Curnis. The perks of narcissism: Behaving like a star speeds up career advancement to the CEO position, *The Leadership Quarterly*, 2021, 32(3), 101489, doi.org/10.1016/j.leaqua.2020.101489 (archived at https://perma.cc/69SS-3J58)

16   R Premack. There's a reason your narcissistic coworkers might be getting promotions instead of you – here's what you can learn from them, *Business Insider*, 8 August 2018, www.businessinsider.com/narcissist-how-to-be- confident-2018-8?r=US&IR=T (archived at https://perma.cc/3XTJ-Y32N)

17   S Price. Former Facebook COO Sheryl Sandberg announces intent to leave Meta's board of directors, FOXBusiness, 17 January 2024, www.foxbusiness. com/technology/former-facebook-coo-sheryl-sandberg-announces-intent-leave- metas-board-directors (archived at https://perma.cc/9AJU-UPND)

18   S Sandberg (2013) *Lean In: Women, work, and the will to lead*, Alfred A Knopf, New York

19   A Hartmans and P Leskin. The career rise and fall of Theranos founder Elizabeth Holmes: Photos, *Business Insider*, 11 July 2023, www.businessinsider.com/theranos-founder-ceo-elizabeth-holmes-life-story- bio-2018-4?r=US&IR=T (archived at https://perma.cc/7ZVV-CJQJ)

PART FIVE

Learning ecosystems where the learning mindset thrives

9

Introduction to learning ecosystems

In this last part, I want to inspire you with the final step to support every-one's learning mindset: creating learning ecosystems where everyone can flourish through optimal knowledge sharing. Innovative, lean and technol-ogy-driven learning strategies that thereby invest in what AI has to offer. As you would expect, this is important for organizations seeking to become nimble, adaptable, resilient and future proof. This is also endorsed by the many studies and publications that have come out since I first published *Learning Ecosystems* in 2022.

In *Learning Ecosystems*, I explain how organizations are evolving into LearnScapes, where learning techniques focus on continuous interaction with the ecosystem that they are part of. It explains that you must constantly upskill and retrain your employees. That book is therefore aimed at execu-tives and L&D professionals who already share this need. In *Learning Ecosystems*, I give these visionary leaders practical guidance and strategic advice on building a value- and data-driven learning strategy in a human–machine symbiosis.

As such, *Learning Ecosystems* complements this book, in which I seek to inspire the learning mindset of you and your colleagues. Because what I have learned since publishing that book is that no implementation will be successful if people themselves are unwilling or unable to buy into that vision. If you think you want to take the next step, in *Learning Ecosystems* you will find insights into lean learning from an L&D approach, including data analytics to make learning measurable. It also offers an in-depth approach to continuous improvement and provides techniques for different situations, including problem analysis and algorithmic business thinking. However, the emphasis is on implementing learning technologies that support a learning culture.

However, I can imagine that as a learning leader, you are curious about what you can do now to prepare your team or organization to become a learning ecosystem. For this, it is useful to know some key concepts and be familiar with the learning maturity model for organizations to assess the readiness of your own organization. This model will not only help you assess your organization, but also strengthen the concepts of lean, social and collaborative learning in your teams.

The learning leader becomes the LearnScaper

Learning influencers and learning leaders play a crucial role in shaping learning ecosystems. However, the most important role is played by the visionary learning leader, or LearnScaper, who architects this ecosystem. LearnScapers master competences and have the knowledge that made them a learning leader.

If you aspire to become a LearnScaper, you can build on all the human competencies needed in the work of the future: curiosity, imagination, openness, entrepreneurship, resilience, optimism, empathy and, as a huge value-add, resilience, the ability to make connections where there don't seem to be any at first. Moreover, you are fascinated by technological innovations and their added value to enhance people's well-being. You live with an eye to the future and have a fascination for unknown areas. As a result, you intuitively recognize emerging trends that add value to the organization and its ecosystem. By consistently taking a holistic view and approach, you will recognize patterns and make connections to arrive at a strategic action plan in which you dare to experiment, take risks and make bold decisions.

As a LearnScaper, besides being a learning influencer and learning leader, you are a top communicator and bridge builder. You understand the organization's culture and ecosystem better than anyone else, but you recognize that you too need to keep learning and can make wrong assumptions. Therefore, you are not averse to adapting your insights by analysing emerging trends and being surrounded by a League of Extraordinary Learners who support you in the process.

A question I often get asked is what academic background is best to have for this challenging but very interesting role. By now, you probably know me a bit and know that I think that is not a relevant question. Your academic background is not who you are today. You have grown, and you are open to new challenges. Don't let anyone tell you otherwise, because it is your learning mindset which brought you to this point. So, never forget, human competencies and adaptability are much more important and are your greatest strength in the future of work. Everything else you can learn!

Have you had an *Aha!* moment reading the above? Maybe you already have an idea for a project that will bring your organization closer to a learning ecosystem or, as I like to call it, a LearnScape. Then go for it! I hope that in this last part you will find inspiration to introduce yourself to the CEO as an indispensable sidekick to help shape a future-oriented and human-centric organization.

The LearnScaper's role as visionary bridge builder

In Part Two, I described in detail the most important thing you need to harness as a LearnScaper: the power of connecting communication. Maybe it's clear to you that your company's future is like a melting iceberg, but that doesn't make it visible to others, including your executives. Maybe they can't or won't see it because, as I pointed out earlier, it's too confrontational to put their heads under the water.

In 2022, when I was still researching *Learning Ecosystems*, a whopping 93 per cent of executives would still not see or understand the added value of intelligent collaboration with machines.[1] Nowadays, with the breakneck speed of ChatGPT adoption, it is almost impossible not to know this. Unless, of course, you deliberately stick your head in the ground to avoid having to accept the truth. As a result, we see more and more executives looking for the added value of intelligent technologies themselves. However, I fear that the initiatives they are launching are not targeted enough to support their employees in their need for lifelong learning in the future of work. I do see customer service bots popping up everywhere because it is, of course, interesting to save costs on staff. Because cutting costs is indeed often a priority. So, now you can demonstrate that human-centred innovations that support lean learning and knowledge sharing save just as many costs. More than that, they support employee well-being, and in the context of lean, this also supports end customer value, perhaps more than bots replacing that empathetic customer service person.

In my experience, reluctance to innovate is often fuelled by fear of change or of stakeholders influencing the vision and strategy. Regarding the urgent need for learning and development, I don't understand why managers don't take more initiatives to innovate. So, returning to my motivation in the beginning of this book: should we not, instead of forcing the employee to learn, rather force the manager to make learning attractive with innovations that support it? I think so and that is why I must say that for once I am proud to be a Belgian. The Belgian federal government is very much aware that lifelong learning is a priority and supports the United Nations Sustainable Development Goals (SDGs) in doing so. As such, in 2023 they launched the Labour Deal, which requires every company from 20 employees up to set up an individual learning plan per employee, with at least five days dedicated to learning.[2]

To convince everyone of the urgency and necessity of the future of work, you will probably have to come up with some serious arguments. However, you can cite Belgian companies and the SDGs to strengthen your case. That said, depending on your position within your organization and your influence at the strategic level, you will have to take a different approach:

1 Option 1: You do like Maarten, whom I referred to in Chapter 8, and start bottom up. Like him, you use the strength of your own team and involve some stakeholders to test your idea for wider support. In doing so, you improve your innovative idea so that it can be implemented as a quick-win project to highlight feasibility. This can then later be a catalyst for multiple projects. The risk of this is relatively small, but I recommend that you be ambitious enough to do an experiment that creates a ripple effect through the organization. If you achieve demonstrable results, you won't have to submit your project to the board. On the contrary, they will appreciate your talent and approach, after which they will hopefully ask you to launch more initiatives.

2 Option 2: You create a bolt vision for the executive board – you can use everything you have read in this book to convince them. Don't do this alone. Surround yourself with stakeholders who want to be ambassadors for your visionary plan and, if possible, involve someone from the executive team as a sponsor. Try to involve L&D, IT, communications and marketing. If you have a union within your organization that has a lot of influence, definitely involve it. It can be your biggest opponent, but also your ally. This may require just a bit more persuasion and bridge-building skills, but it will help shape your idea and make it work. See success on multiple fronts: if this idea is not accepted, modify it using, for example, the Kaizen technique. If it still fails then, you know you have challenged everyone's learning mindset.

3 Option 3: You are already part of the executive team, so go to Option 1 and select your team of extraordinary learners and challenge them to

come up with an innovative plan. And don't forget to involve L&D and get them to read *Learning Ecosystems* too, so you know exactly how to measure the success of your learning projects.

Know that one project will never be enough if your organization is still a long way from innovations that support a learning culture. You will often need to launch several projects to get everyone on board with the change. Waste detection is a good start to selecting projects that have a quick chance of success. This is why I also want to inspire you to look at your organizational type itself, using the learning maturity model below, which can help you identify where you are now as an organization.

Learning ecosystems are like a thriving garden

By now, you may already be wondering why I keep talking about LearnScapes and LearnScaper. Firstly, I like to think of new things and rebel with my own terminology. But, most importantly, I want to appeal to your imagination and curiosity, as there's a story behind it.

In 2014, I was challenged by a corporate university to develop a different approach to learning at work, as training budgets were rapidly shrinking. My target audience was the global sales team of more than 16,000 employees. However, these employees were all divided into smaller entities with their own ways of working and learning systems. Before I could innovate, I had to research the culture within these very diverse teams, who all wanted to stick to their habits. It was soon clear that while together they formed a huge organization, they still had a long way to go before we could think of an innovative learning ecosystem.

Back then, we were inspired by the simplicity of social media to connect people worldwide to share their experiences and knowledge A social learning ecosystem that would be ahead of its time was the objective. Unfortunately, our Moonshot idea failed to materialize at that organization, as we ran into some difficult challenges to overcome in 2014. However, the project was the basis for my research into how learning ecosystems can be created and how different ways of social learning and collaboration drive this.

When I designed the first LearnScape in 2014, I had no strong AI and certainly no generative AI at my disposal to connect people who could benefit from each other's knowledge. Back then, we only had simple algorithms that used the little data we collected to enable 'adaptive' learning based on job content or learning paths. Making human connections to learn from was therefore quite a challenge. So, at that time, we were far from building intelligent learning ecosystems where human–machine symbiosis could be achieved.

Another difficulty I faced in 2014, which you might find hard to imagine now, had to do with linking the different systems together. This was essential because we used 20 different regional LMS systems and at least as many HR systems and knowledge databases. Back then, these LMSs that stored content and e-courses were still using sharable content object reference models (SCORMs) to attach to their courses the technical requirements and data that were needed to share them. Moreover, the different systems we used to store them did not always have the same standards. This meant that some courses could not be shared or became unusable when we purchased a new LMS. Fortunately, new standards such as xAPI and API came later, allowing different computer systems with different standards to talk to each other. You can hopefully understand what I want to say with this somewhat complicated technical explanation. In 2014, it was impossible to realize our Moonshot idea, but we could imagine the future and wanted to be ready to implement this vision. This meant we were bold enough to challenge legacy systems in the organization if they could not integrate with our ecosystem vision. Unfortunately, this necessary vision is often not yet adopted within many organizations.

Of course, that still does not explain why I started calling these interconnected learning ecosystems LearnScapes. My inspiration for this came from an article on agriculture. The agricultural architects described complex cultural landscapes or ecosystems that they called LearnScapes. Unfortunately, I could never find that article again later, but I found the comparison fitting. So, yes, I admit that I sometimes take someone else's idea to do my thing with it, especially when it is relevant in multiple aspects. The LearnScapes described in that article were complex relationship systems, created and maintained by the interactions of living and non-living nature. I saw in this the analogy with the learning ecosystems I wanted to build: LearnScapes where humans are living nature and machines are non-living nature. Admit it, the analogy is not that far-fetched and so it made sense to work out that landscape architects and LearnScapers would want to create landscapes where everyone can flourish and thrive, supported by everything the ecosystem has to offer.

The learning maturity model

However, the obstacles we faced in 2014 were much more than just technological. And, to my surprise, they are still the same obstacles that I see many
organizations running into today. To make opportunities visible, I subsequently developed the learning maturity model and the concept for lean
learning that supports business strategies. These offer you, as a learning
leader, tools and hopefully inspiration to develop an innovative idea that
supports your team and organization to thrive in the future.

Simply put, the learning maturity model (see Figure 9.1) is a visual representation of collaboration and knowledge sharing within an organization. It
indicates the organization's emphasis, who the key owner or gatekeeper is,

FIGURE 9.1 The learning maturity model, 2014 (© Katja Schipperheijn)

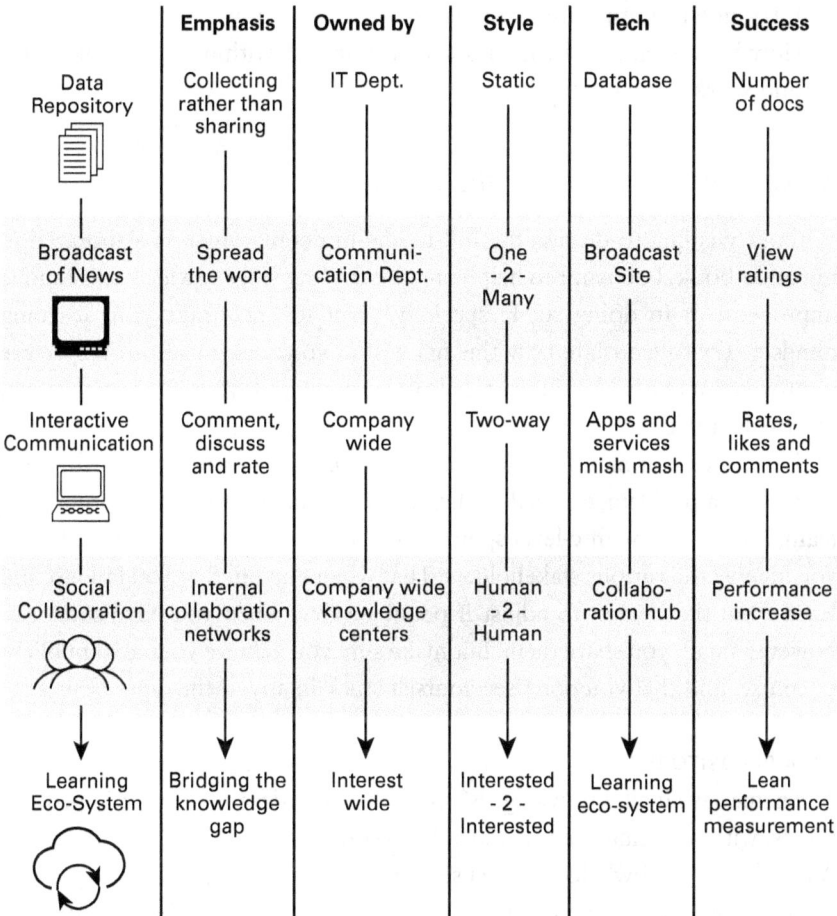

	Emphasis	Owned by	Style	Tech	Success
Data Repository	Collecting rather than sharing	IT Dept.	Static	Database	Number of docs
Broadcast of News	Spread the word	Communi-cation Dept.	One - 2 - Many	Broadcast Site	View ratings
Interactive Communication	Comment, discuss and rate	Company wide	Two-way	Apps and services mish mash	Rates, likes and comments
Social Collaboration	Internal collaboration networks	Company wide knowledge centers	Human - 2 - Human	Collabo-ration hub	Performance increase
Learning Eco-System	Bridging the knowledge gap	Interest wide	Interested - 2 - Interested	Learning eco-system	Lean performance measurement

the style of interactions, the technologies used and how the success of that system is measured. In doing so, I must stress that no organization fits 100 per cent within one category. Nor is it the case that you go from step 1 to step 5 as an organization. Usually, for organizations that have not yet arrived at a learning ecosystem, it is a combination of different categories.

When I first developed this model in 2014, I had the vision that through the symbiosis of humans and machines, organizations would support their lean learning needs. In other words, everyone always could have had all the relevant knowledge and would acquire skills at the time they needed it. At the time, I could not dream of what this would mean for vocational training with, for example, the rise of LLMs and the possibility of immersive experiences with XR. However, I am convinced that this is just the beginning. As an organization, it is imperative to have the basics ready now so that you can jump in without an unsurmountable disadvantage. However, as I also said, try not to jump on all trends at once. Slow down and see what can possibly be implemented with a quick-win project with involved stakeholders and work on that.

Is your organization ready for the next phase?

Without wishing to discuss the full model in detail, which is elaborated in my other book, I do want to help you take the first steps towards continuous improvement. In doing so, I especially want to encourage your learning mindset. Try to translate how this fits within your organization. Where are improvements possible to facilitate lean learning and what is waste that you can easily avoid?

Sometimes you may be able to launch several opportunities side by side. This is not a problem, especially when you can launch them from within your team, bottom up, with c-level sponsorship. The most important thing is that you involve the various stakeholders. That when you fail that you fail fast and learn from that lesson to adjust if possible. That when you have successes, however small, you share them. But make sure you achieve your goal publicly, of course, and that you don't see yourself stuck in any of the types of waste.

DATA REPOSITORIES

The name says it all: knowledge is stored, either in data systems or in people's minds, without being used to add value to others. The emphasis is on *stored*. A lot of stored knowledge can be useful, especially if it is relevant and you can reuse it. But that's where it gets tricky. How do we know if the data are relevant when most data systems measure their success mainly by the number of data units stored? The same question can be asked about the relevance of many experts: what is the point if they all sit in their own corner or silo without contributing to collective knowledge building or helping each other?

The data repository is unfortunately still by far the most common collaborative, or should I say non-collaborative, type of organization. After the release of *Learning Ecosystems*, as many as 70 to 90 per cent of executives I spoke to admitted that this was a major concern for them. However, I think the data repository offers the most opportunities to achieve innovation from small-scale projects that can have a ripple effect. Consider how much *waste* you can easily eliminate by cleaning up irrelevant knowledge, encouraging experts to become influencers, unlocking knowledge for cross-functional projects or gig-workers, etc.

BROADCASTER OF NEWS

Broadcasters of news are full of good intentions; they could almost be the opposite of the data repositories. Their vision is to share all knowledge to the maximum and keep everyone always informed of everything. But, if you are overwhelmed by streams of information from all sorts of channels, you will drown. Soon, you are either just trying to read everything, or you shut down. In both cases, your productivity will be drastically lower and, I suspect, so will your morale and well-being. In other words, these knowledge streams that overwhelm you are as worthless as *dead knowledge* in the data repositories.

If you are looking for quick-win projects regarding broadcasters of news you can eliminate waste by setting up rules regarding the emails you send each other, as I indicated, in Part Three related to teamwork. I am convinced that in any organization, you can do a lot to make the sharing of information and knowledge more purposeful, so that it is relevant and encourages action. Start asking various stakeholders *where, how* and *when* they would best like to receive new content. Don't forget: nothing is more powerful to convince executives than with numbers, for example when 80 per cent of the team indicate that they never read the weekly newsletter and therefore have no idea about the future strategy of the organization.

INTERACTIVE COMMUNICATION

Interactive communication is a first step towards efficient collaboration and knowledge sharing on a human-to-human (H2H) level. However, if all these interactive communications were more like an explosion of broadcasters of news, I think I would go crazy. It's the same as with social media overload, where you are mostly distracted and, in the long run, don't know who or what you want to follow.

If you see this within your teams or organization, this is not a simple challenge. After all, it is a culture problem, and those are the hardest to tackle in a short time. Problems like these can also be extra interesting as challenges for rebels who want to make a difference, as they often have a pretty big impact. In every organization, every team is different, so I can't give you many tips, but I would like to share one from a learning leader who took a bold decision. He decided one day that employees were no longer allowed to use emails to communicate with each other. It was superbly disruptive because people suddenly had to start talking to each other and looking for new, efficient ways to share knowledge. The result was that everyone initially started thinking about the relevance of their emails. But what I found most interesting is that, from then on, the teams met every morning and discussed progress in short face-to-face meetings. This nimble working method with short sprints is not very innovative, of course, but it had nice side effects in the process for this team. People got to know each other as human beings again, which obviously positively affected commitment and well-being.

SOCIAL COLLABORATION

Getting together to discuss progress at the human level, in the above example, was an absolute value-add to the culture of those teams. Of course, this is not possible within geographically dispersed or cross-functional teams that also include gig-workers. But it will increasingly be the normal in the future of work, so future-oriented collaboration and knowledge sharing must also provide an answer to that.

So, it is up to you to come up with an innovative idea that connects people on a human level to prevent waste in any form. For this you could take inspiration from the hyperreal worlds populated by human-like avatars that you enter with BCI wearables. That's probably moving just a little too fast, although I can see this possibility happening one day.

Innovation can support cultural change, but the focus must first be on people working together to maximize efficiency and effectiveness. As a learning leader, you can easily initiate this by, for example, giving regular group feedback, taking on challenges together or just listening to each other and trying to get to know each other as the people you are behind the work.

LEARNING ECOSYSTEMS

In learning ecosystems, everything comes together from human connections supported by AI. This symbiosis eliminates some of the above obstacles and waste to achieve lean learning.

In other words, lean learning ecosystems are complex relationship systems created and maintained by the interactions of living and non-living nature – ecosystems of various connected applications where humans grow in symbiosis with machines. That's obviously not a Moonshot idea that you can pitch to implement in the short term. Yet, it is a vision of the future you must definitely consider when thinking about quick-win projects. Because I don't think it's such a long-term vision, as the future has caught up with us more quickly than we could imagine.

Human-to-human before intelligence-to-intelligence

Learning ecosystems are the objective, and I have already had the opportunity to guide many workshops where we wanted to lay the foundations and/or create the first paths to this LearnScape. From this experience, I would like to reiterate: AI without humans will not work.

'If our employees don't want to learn, then we have to force them if necessary.' Those were the not-so-wise words of a professor of occupational psychology with whom I started this book. I don't blame him; he woke me up and I saw why I needed to work on a book that put humans before technology. Sometimes I may seem to suggest that AI is the prerequisite for achieving optimal knowledge sharing. In 2014, I indeed believed that I needed technological innovation to achieve social learning and collaboration. I know now that I should have put my head under the water and looked at what drives people to do this.

You can only build learning ecosystems if you first invest in the culture of your organization and you can only do that if you start where everything starts: with the learning mindset of everyone in your ecosystem. If they don't want to learn or collaborate, then you can't force them. If they don't understand why, you can't motivate them. If they are anxious, they stiffen up. If they don't feel engaged, you need to find out what drives them. This book came to exist because I made the mistake of thinking that if I made everything easy and lean then people would follow. I was wrong.

Still, I was not completely wrong, because once the first H2H connections are made, then AI can enhance them. Think back to TikTok, which I like to use as an example of a learning ecosystem. Can you imagine the first few weeks on that application? No people to connect with and no content to share? Even the most intelligent algorithm could not make connections to make content go viral those first few days. It is the influencers who started the flywheel. The followers who wanted more and more. So, it started H2H and then continued through interest-to-interest or intelligence-to-intelligence (I2I).

GENERATIVE AI WILL BE THE CATALYST FOR LEARNING ECOSYSTEMS

In Chapter 2, I deliberately went deep into innovations driven by generative AI. This is because I am convinced that these will catalyse learning ecosystems. Today, I try to push my forever frontier by imagining the unprecedented future. What are the human-centric innovations emerging now that have potential for the future of work?

Will we soon no longer have a smartphone, but smart glasses or even smart contact lenses and a chip in our brain that connects us? I don't dare predict anymore, even if I try to follow all the trends and let AI help me. I don't think anyone can make predictions with certainty, not even futurists like Ray Kurzweil, who claims the Singularity is near.

What I do dare say is that the impact of generative AI is unknown and the impact on humanity will not be underestimated. I therefore hope that with this book, I have been able to challenge you to embrace your learning mindset. To see the future not through rose-coloured glasses, but preferably through *smart glasses* that help you learn and shape the future yourself.

Learning ecosystems to thrive as humanity

The learning ecosystems I have discussed above are the future. Lifelong learning will become more urgent and more complex. Lifelong learning is increasingly on the agenda of governments and organizations, such as the United Nations, as I describe in the last chapter of this book. Sustainability is, from a purely human point of view, where everyone adds value and can contribute to a liveable planet for our children.

As mentioned in the introduction, I may be a tech enthusiast, but I am first and foremost a mother. And both of my daughters have deliberately chosen careers as far away as possible from what I do with innovations. They hate it, and fear that what I predict will become the truth someday.

For this reason, for my own children and all children in the world, I urge you to nurture the learning mindset. It will be needed not only to survive, but also to thrive in an increasingly digital and virtual world. As learning leaders, as LearnScapers, always think human-centric and don't get caught up in hypes that affect your ethical values. For this, I want to try to inspire you one last time, in the final chapter of this book, with the link between sustainability and learning ecosystems and a contribution that, as a wrap-up, is a nice repetition of much of what I discussed in this book.

Endnotes

1 Deloitte. 2021 Global Human Capital Trends: Special report, 2021, deloitte.com/us/en/insights/focus/human-capital-trends.html (archived at https://perma.cc/FUL8-SVW5)

2 Service Public Federal. Deal pour l'emploi: publication des mesures, | SPF Emploi, Travail et Concertation sociale, 2022, emploi.belgique.be/fr/actualites/deal-pour-lemploi-publication-des-mesures (archived at https://perma.cc/FW3F-VJFK)

10

Sustainability and learning ecosystems

Sustainability is a global responsibility

Sustainability, in its most fundamental form, is about balancing human needs, environmental responsibility and economic prosperity. The challenge is to ensure that our needs are met without compromising the ability of future generations to meet theirs.

In the context of today's global challenges, the urgency for a sustainable approach has never been more pressing. Climate change threatens our ecosystems, extreme poverty and inequality persist, and the depletion of natural resources is accelerating. These problems know no boundaries and impact all aspects of our lives, from health and well-being to economic stability and social cohesion.

A global approach to sustainability is essential, because many of our challenges are transboundary. We can no longer think locally or regionally but must initiate and support change through collaboration. Climate change, for example, requires collaboration at the global level to reduce greenhouse gas emissions and mitigate their effects. Similarly, problems such as poverty and hunger require co-ordinated action to ensure fair opportunities and access to basic needs for all, regardless of where they are located. Technological innovations, best practices and financial resources must be shared between countries and regions to be effective. We can only address the scale and complexity of global problems and make real progress by working together.

However, the urgency of a global approach goes beyond practical considerations. It is also about recognizing our shared responsibility as global citizens to protect the planet and ensure a sustainable future for all. It is a matter of moral obligation and solidarity to work towards a better world for present and future generations – for children like my daughters, who are already telling me they no longer want to populate the world. My children are not the only ones, as more and more young people believe that not having children is the biggest contribution anyone can make to the climate crisis. It is incomprehensible to me how it could have come to this.[1]

In essence, sustainability is not just a concept, but also a lifestyle, a mindset and a collective vision for the future. It requires us to be willing to look beyond our individual interests and national borders – that we strive for a world that is resilient and prosperous for all. And now, more than ever before, it is time for action and collaboration at the global level to make this vision a reality.

To create a world for future generations, I encourage you to take a holistic ecosystem approach and look beyond your organization when developing your ideas and vision. This requires you to look across organizational boundaries at the impact you can have on sustainability and a liveable planet for everyone in the future.

The United Nations SDGs

The United Nations Sustainable Development Goals, also known as the SDGs or the Global Goals, are a powerful and ambitious framework designed to address global challenges and promote a sustainable future.[2] Given their link to the future of work, lifelong learning and entrepreneurship, it is important to know them and integrate them into your ecosystem vision. In doing so, it is interesting to understand how the creation of these SDGs is itself a great example of holistic future-oriented vision development based on cross-border collaboration.

The SDGs result from an extensive and inclusive process of global consultation and collaboration, involving governments, civil society organizations, businesses and citizens from around the world. In 2015, all 193 United Nations member states agreed to the Sustainable Development Agenda for 2030. In doing so they established the SDGs as a universal call to action to eliminate poverty, reduce inequality, promote peace and protect our planet.

The choice of 17 specific goals reflects the complexity and interconnectedness of the world's challenges. Each goal addresses a specific aspect of sustainable development such as ending hunger, promoting gender equality, ensuring clean water and sanitation, and promoting sustainable consumption and production. They are interconnected and complementary, meaning that progress on one goal benefits other goals. Together, these goals form a comprehensive framework and an extremely powerful tool which stems from a profound recognition of the most pressing challenges.

These 17 goals were not chosen randomly; they result from a thorough analysis of global challenges, trends and priorities that led to international collaboration and a shared vision for a more sustainable future. This inclusive and participatory process began with a broad consultation of countries, experts and stakeholders around the world in which all voices were heard, from governments to civil society organizations and businesses. This approach reflects the importance and added value of a holistic approach involving all stakeholders.

It is admirable to see how much progress has already been made since the launch of the SDGs. Globally, countless initiatives and projects have been launched to advance the goals, with concrete results which have improved the lives of millions of people worldwide. The SDGs have already had a significant impact on reducing extreme poverty, promoting universal access to clean drinking water, reducing greenhouse gas emissions and protecting biodiversity. It is not only NGOs, governments and multinationals that can create an impact but also smaller initiatives and entrepreneurs like Bisila Bokoko who shares her inspiring story at the end of this chapter.

There are many great initiatives. However, there is still a lot to do. The challenges we face are complex and profound, requiring ongoing commitment, collaboration and innovation at all levels of society. I sincerely hope to inspire you with the potential of the SDGs for a world that is resilient and sustainable. This is why you must take responsibility, because through using the ecosystem approach, you and your organization can make a difference and positively impact the world around you. No initiative is too small in this respect if it can start a positive movement.

SDGs THAT STRENGTHEN THE ECOSYSTEM OF INFINITE LEARNING

With her inspiring story to conclude this book, United Nations Honoree and Executive Chair Bisila Bokoko shows that the learning mindset comes together in the infinite learning ecosystem. Among other things, she discusses SDG4, which could also be interesting for you and your organization to consider for possible projects to contribute to the future of humanity. In addition, I want to highlight a few others related to the future and the benefit of a learning mindset.

SGD4 relates to inclusive and equitable quality education and opportunities to promote lifelong learning for all. According to the United Nations vision, to which I subscribe, education and the opportunity to learn provide liberation of the intellect, unlocks the imagination and is fundamental to self-respect. It is the key to prosperity and opens up a world of possibilities, allowing each of us to contribute to a progressive, healthy society. Learning benefits everyone and should be available to all. More specifically, SDG4.6 addresses the elimination of discrimination in education, with the goal of eliminating gender inequality in education. This is a goal that Bisila Bokoko and I obviously emphasize in our mission, together with SDG4.7 on education for sustainable development and global citizenship. This goal states that by 2030, all students will acquire the knowledge and skills needed to promote sustainable development. In other words, students will be able to use their skills and knowledge in their mission to contribute to an infinite learning ecosystem.

SGD5 is also naturally very close to my heart, as a mother. This includes the goal of gender equality and empowerment of all women and girls. It is a mission I also share with Bisila Bokoko, because she knows better than anyone that gender bias undermines our social fabric and devalues us all.

If you want to contribute to these goals, either by yourself or with your organization, it may be worth touching on the above SDGs. However, what is essential for you and your organization is to look at where you can add the most value – because everyone can contribute to sustainability and the future of humanity.

SDG8 is another goal that I would like to emphasize here, because it is about decent work and economic growth. It highlights the urgent need to build livelihoods that help vulnerable populations build resilience and to thrive, and to improve and strengthen emerging economies against shocks. As stated by the United Nations, SDG8 is vital for achieving other goals.

Take responsibility for the future of humanity

Everyone can contribute to change; indeed, I think everyone should initiate change, no matter how small. However, I learnt from my daughters that not everyone thinks this way. We made this observation after hearing someone say, 'In the end, we are all just a drop in the ocean.' For me, that was a positive statement because I thought of the ripple effect you can achieve with a drop. My daughters pointed out to me that, according to them, that statement is an excuse offered by people who delude themselves that they cannot make an impact. I obviously disagree, because you can be imperturbable, but you can no longer be indifferent.

We all have an impact, even sometimes more than we think. Like those young women whose story I shared in Part Three who wanted to organize 'f**k-up nights' to overcome imposter syndrome. I passionately share their example during my keynotes, and now, with this book, I hope their story will inspire people worldwide. As a result, I see organizations around the globe being inspired by them and starting initiatives like them to support a psychologically safe work environment.

Sharing their story reminds me of Derek Sivers' hilarious video, *First follower: Leadership lessons from dancing guy.*[3] In this video, an apparent *nut* starts dancing on a mountain, while initially most people remain sitting down, listening to music. One spectator gets up and joins in, after which he inspires others to dance along too. Soon huge numbers of people get up and follow, and eventually those who remain on the sidelines are fools. This movie shows that sometimes you have to be nuts and you have to take risks if you want to start a movement or initiate change. But even more important is that you inspire followers. In other words, it is the young women who launched the crazy idea of sharing their failures on a social channel, but without followers like me or other learning influencers, it would not have had the impact it has.

So, returning to the philosophical discussion I had with my daughters about 'In the end, we are all just a drop in the ocean', we arrived at what we want this statement to stand for. You are just a drop in a big sea, but ultimately, many drops in the ocean create a wave of change that can transform the world.

The ecosystem is thus becoming quasi-infinite

Everyone can contribute to the SDGs, with projects that sometimes start very small and suddenly take the world by storm. This is also how I started the non-profit organization sCooledu with my, at the time, very young daughters in 2017.[4] Initially I did this because I disagreed with their schools' lack of digital vision. Soon, however, this became a project that allowed me to host more than 15,000 pupils and 1,800 teachers in workshops on digital citizenship and being human in an increasingly digital and virtual world. To this day, wherever I have to be for keynotes, I also try to visit schools to imagine with the children their future in an increasingly fast-moving world.

It's not much, but it makes me happy, and I still hope to help a child now and then, like the little girl who turned out to be a Roblox creator. Her dream to change her destiny should no longer be a dream but instead become a reality.

Fortunately, more and more organizations recognize the need and benefit of contributing to sustainability. For some organizations, it has become crucial in their survival, because otherwise they cannot attract or retain talent. More and more employees are looking for purposeful work and want to be associated with organizations that positively contribute to society. However, not just employees will make demands on your organization. Increasingly, contributing to sustainability will affect your chances of survival, as customers are becoming more selective. In the B2B market, there are also increasing demands on organizations regarding their contribution to the SDGs, such as their carbon emissions. In some cases, it is even necessary to contribute to sustainability targets to avoid fines or risk contracts being terminated.

Focusing on the SDGs can also benefit organizations by stimulating the learning mindset of employees, thus promoting innovation. Addressing sustainable development challenges requires thinking outside the box, challenging the status quo, which can lead to the creation of innovative products, services and business models. This innovation is essential to remain competitive in rapidly evolving markets.

Embracing the SDGs goes beyond mere morality; it's now a crucial strategic choice for businesses impacting a globally interconnected world. The influence of ecosystems is expanding exponentially, emphasizing the need for SDG support. Finally, I would like to share the story of Bisila Bokoko, a multi-award-winning entrepreneur, speaker on global leadership and author of *We All Have a Story to Tell* (*Todos Tenemos Una Historia Que Contar*; 2023). If one word could sum up everything Bisila Bokoko conveys, it would be 'inspiration'. Her personal story is one of a racialized woman who has learned to grow despite setbacks; her business, her wisdom, her love of books and her philanthropic spirit are an example to many.

With her contribution, she briefly shares how to make your dreams come true, how to learn from failures, how to be happy despite the obstacles and fears that can get in the way of our learning mindset. This award-winning United Nations author, founder of the Bisila Bokoko African Literacy Project and owner of a life full of anecdotes and valuable lessons reveals a vital trajectory that will help us take that step we all need to move forward in the story of our lives. A story in which you choose whether you want to be that little ripple that has an impact on the infinite learning ecosystem. For me, Bisila Bokoko is already an inspiration when it comes to a learning mindset, leadership and the importance of an ecosystem approach that builds a better future for all.

BISILA BOKOKO, UNITED NATIONS HONOREE AND EXECUTIVE CHAIR, GLOBAL LEADERSHIP SPEAKER, ENTREPRENEUR, AUTHOR: USE YOUR SMILE TO CHANGE THE WORLD, DON'T LET THE WORLD CHANGE YOUR SMILE

We can choose to be hindered by our past or use it as a source of strength that allows us to rise above our expectations. I learnt these lessons from my great-grandmother, who escaped domestic violence by embracing learning as her key to leading her own life. She proudly wore her nickname, Señorita Escuela, after not only taking control of her own life but also passing on her love of learning to others by starting a school. I think I inherited my dedication to learning from her, even though her approach, which suited the zeitgeist of the time, was very disciplinary, and also gave me anxiety and self-doubt. Although I was initially driven by fear of failure, I gradually learned that failure was just a step on the way to becoming better. Therefore, I am now convinced that learning can be fun and that learning is a way of life that we should share as much as possible.

We are all born with a learning mindset; it is part of the human being, but we need to keep that lightbulb actively lit to enable us to improve constantly. Regardless of the diversity we are born with, every human being has the ability to light that lamp within themselves. But it is the responsibility of everyone in the ecosystem to contribute to it – and not just through the education system that today is not democratic and does not offer us equal ways to discover our learning mindset. Indeed, education alone does not provide the opportunities to nurture our learning mindset for the rest of our lives.

When I realized that I could light that lamp myself, I changed my belief system. Because I too sometimes felt that I did not fit into the system. However, I discovered that we need to find learning within ourselves and take ownership of our learning. For this, we need to let go of fear, and smiling can help. For example, I learned to smile at myself every morning to remind myself of the relationship I have with myself. Don't let anyone else have power over you by telling you what you can do, what you need to learn or that you are not good enough, because then your smile will be taken away from you. Let go of that fear and let go of letting other people have power over your life. How people see you is their question, but you need to ask yourself how you see yourself. You need to give yourself love and positivity, not criticism and judgement. If you can do that with yourself, you can do the same with others. So it all starts with yourself, but are you able to accept yourself?

Through self-acceptance, you overcome self-doubt and even imposter syndrome. Stop comparing yourself to others. Trust that what you think you admire in others is also in you and that it is your promise to yourself to find it and allow it to blossom. Stop being too easily satisfied and telling yourself that you cannot achieve your dreams. Don't look only at what is not perfect in you, because, by focusing on that, you are creating that truth through a self-fulfilling prophecy. So change the story about yourself that you think is true and look at what you want to achieve and make that your story.

In today's world, technology can be an equalizer. Not just for yourself, but for learning and growing with others. I think especially of the many people in the world who cannot adapt to a system where they have to sit in classrooms to learn because they don't have the resources. This is why the United Nations SDGs are so important, especially SDG 4, which is my mission, because everyone has the right to access education and knowledge at all times. Because education can also be a weapon in positive terms for equal rights. Just think of the many girls in Africa and other regions who do not have the opportunity to go to school when they are menstruating. Technology can help them to not miss out on too much education, but it is still not widespread, so we all need to do something about that.

Leaders can do much more than just put values on websites or claim to support the SDGs. They should take action, because education, health and the economy are everyone's responsibility. Unfortunately, in many cases, education is at the bottom of leaders' priority lists, both for their own employees and for others outside their organizations. To my regret, not only business leaders but also government leaders do not seem to understand that learning should be a top priority and that new technologies and a connected learning ecosystem have added value to offer here. Unless we have an educated population that embraces the mindset of learning, we will turn ourselves around instead of developing as a society. It is leaders everywhere who must lead by example and show young people and all generations that learning can be a powerful and positive weapon, and a catalyst to achieve many more of the SDGs.

In other words, investing in learning has benefits in multiple directions. For example, I had the opportunity to work with a Texas oil company that had facilitators in Africa to help local people climb the ladder of success – not just to learn for the company, but to improve their lives. In this way, as a company leader, you can do something good for yourself and others, creating a ripple effect that spreads beyond the ecosystem. Moreover, you will find that when you do well as an organization, you attract other talent who want to work for companies that do well.

I saw the same thing at another company that had made it its mission to help others and invest in learning for everyone in the ecosystem. They offered employees the opportunity to spend time outside work helping and working in our library and school in Africa. This created a great incentive for people to be not only good employees but also good people!

As a leader, your mission should be to make people better, not for the company but for everyone's future. This supports everyone's learning mindset in the infinite learning ecosystem and gives people the wings to fly ever higher. This is what makes learning leaders unique: they can be happy when other people flourish and see that as the ultimate form of success.

Endnotes

1 S Cain. Why a generation is choosing to be child-free, *The Guardian*, 25 July 2020, www.theguardian.com/books/2020/jul/25/why-a-generation-is-choosing-to-be-child-free (archived at https://perma.cc/X9BD-7PD3)
2 United Nations. The 17 Sustainable Development Goals, sdgs.un.org/goals (archived at https://perma.cc/Z2YX-9C3F)
3 D Sivers. First follower: Leadership lessons from dancing guy, YouTube, 2010, www.youtube, 2010,com/watch?v=fW8amMCVAJQ (archived at https://perma.cc/R3VQ-LLGR)
4 sCooledu. Home, www.scooledu.org/ (archived at https://perma.cc/43UD-JS9B)

Let there be no conclusion

Embracing a learning mindset means making your own conclusion about what is relevant to you. Therefore, it is not up to me to do this for you. But I do want to ask you to start thinking about the following questions: What is my next step? What can I do with what I have read? Do I know myself? Can I inspire others? Am I already a learning leader, or do I dare to take on the challenge of building a learning ecosystem with my team and helping others in this infinite ecosystem where we are all connected?

When you think about your next step, you have started one of the most essential aspects to strengthen your learning mindset. You are reflecting on what is relevant to you. In doing so, you might use the retrieval practice technique, where you reflect on all you read. By doing this, you also strengthen your neural pathways and, therefore, your learning capacity. This is the first step. However, I recommend you challenge yourself by consciously thinking about what keeps you from learning or embracing innovative technologies. By doing this very consciously, you can identify what your drivers are. Only once you have recognized all the obstacles can you effectively turn them into positives and, who knows, maybe even use them as superpowers. No more stigmas or negative emotions, but a view of the future that is in your own hands. Only then can you grow from your learning mindset and inspire others. For this, you use even more of those competencies, such as empathy and openness, but use your imagination and curiosity together. When you use all the described competencies together with your team or even your friends, you can also apply consistency from different backgrounds and expertise. While doing so, don't forget to see the world through the eyes of children, as I like to do with my daughters and children all over the world who inspire me and, of course, often amaze me!

Collaborative and social learning stimulates the learning influencer, which can create a ripple effect for the learning mindset. I found one of the most crucial learning moments in my own development to be looking at what makes people unique. But the best thing about opening up to what makes people unique is that you learn even more about yourself by observing the world from their perspective. If you take this step in your development, you can also become a learning leader who can bring together human competencies and technology to support others in their growth.

If you want to encourage social and collaborative learning in your organization, deepen the competences you need to thrive in this rapidly changing world. Embrace (neuro)diversity in your team and encourage others to challenge the status quo. Failure is then no longer a loss, but a learning moment. It is also together with a group of extraordinary learners that you can dare to look to the future beyond your own circle of influence, to the infinite learning ecosystem where everything is connected. As I said, I don't want to determine what is relevant to you, but I do hope that I have been able to inspire you to adopt a learning mindset that starts with yourself and with what. Because only then will no one have to merely survive and we can all thrive together.

What's next?

The learning mindset and genuine human connections are the prerequisites for finding added value in the symbiosis of humans and technology. Perhaps that is why I should have written this book earlier than *Learning Ecosystems*. Because, as I have often said, you can't force anyone to change if they don't see the need for it themselves. You can't make anyone learn or unlearn if they believe they don't have the capabilities to do so. I also received many questions from executives, after publishing *Learning Ecosystems*, about implementing a learning culture and whether technology can help. Of course, it can, but everything starts with the learning mindset of the individual, with you!

As a learning expert, I realize that with this book, I can only plant a seed in you. You have the responsibility to continue to develop the learning mindset that makes the neurons in your head work so that learning becomes a joy. As you experiment and innovate, there will be many *Aha!* moments accompanied by alpha waves that will balance you mentally. Finally, the ultimate goal is for you to embrace the habit of actively engaging in continuous learning that will allow you to take responsibility for your future.

To establish this habit, you will benefit from regularly returning to this book and reflecting on what is important to you at the various stages of developing the learning mindset. However, I want to give you an additional tool to help you decide what your next step might be. To this end, I have developed a Profiler with tips to support your learning journey. This journey starts with determining where you are now, after which you will gain insight into your development goals and tips for continuous improvement.

Take the test at: TheLearningMindset.org

Love learning, share this love and inspire the world for the future of our children!

INDEX

Note: Page numbers in *italics* refer to tables or figures.

5G 40, 41
6G 41

abuse 63
accountability 63
adaptive and flexible learning 17
ADD (Attention Deficit Disorder) 86, 87
ADHD (Attention Deficit Hyperactivity
    Disorder) 86, 87, 194
Adobe 73
Africa 234–35
AI Safety Summit (Bletchley Park) 43, 63
AI winter 48
Airbnb 178
AlphaGO 48–49
'AlterEgo' 59, 105
Amazon 73, 123, 168
Antwerp-Bruges port 51
API 218
Apple 60
artificial empathy (AE) 106–07
artificial general intelligence (AGI) 49–50,
    54
artificial intelligence (AI) 1, 167, 213
    artificial empathy (AE) 106–07
    birth of 42–43
    ethical impact and risk 61–62
    evolution of 48–55
    human-brain-based AI 42–48
    imagination 104
    learning influencers 173–82
    learning mindset, adoption 168–73
    pattern recognition 20
    policies and frameworks 62–64
    team development 162–63
    text-to-speech and voice cloning 37
artificial narrow intelligence (ANI) 48–49
artificial super intelligence 55
Asimov, Isaac 55, 61–62
augmented reality (AR) 60
autism 86
Autonomous swarm intelligence 51

Bandura, Albert 151
Becker, Howard 85
belief 7–8
BeReal 42

Berger, Hans 56
Biden, Joe 64
biological intelligence operating system
    (biOS) 61
Biophilia (Wilson) 114
Bletchley Declaration 64
blockchain 80
Boelpaep, An De 146–47, 159–61
Bokoko, Bisila 169, 229–32, 233–35
BookTok 123
Borst, Monique 179–81
brain–computer interfaces (BCIs) 55–56, 86,
    105, 112, 179, 222
Branson, Richard 92, 138, 186
Brown, Noam 50

Captain Kirk's Universal Translator 37,
    57–59
CCPA (California Consumer Privacy
    Act) 62
cells that wire together fire together 120–21,
    151
Charles University 205
chatbots 54, 111
ChatGPT 45, 52, 63, 72, 131, 147, 149,
    168, 215
ChatGPT4 47, 53
chess 48
chief data officer (CDO) 170
children's digital literacy 80
China 63
Christakis, Nicholas A. 121
Churchill, Winston 200
cognitive skills 88
Collins, Stella 10
community of practice (COP) 156
competences, embracing 100–10
    curiosity 8, 100–03
    empathy 106–07
    imagination 8, 93, 103–05
    openness 102, 105–06, 137
    optimism 108
    resilience 107–08
computer science 2
    convergence of neuroscience and 43–45
confidence-based learning (CBL) 133–35,
    134

consilience 111–15
    learning mindset intersection
        and 112–15
    unity of knowledge 111–12
Consilience: The unity of knowledge
    (Wilson) 111, 114
continuous and lifelong learning 17
Cortical Labs 61
Covey, Stephen M. R. 193
cryptocurrency 80
Culture, The 58
curiosity 8, 100–03
cybernetics 43–44

Dall-E 104
Dam, Nick van 77, 157
Dartmouth Conference (1956) 42, 43, 46,
    48
Dartmouth Summer Research Project on
    Artificial Intelligence 178
data privacy 62–64
Deep Blue 48
Deepmind Challenge 48–49
dementia 19
Demuynck, Helena 90–91
DishBrain 61
Disney Plus 102
Don't Bother Me Mom – I'm Learning!
    (Presnky) 89
dopamine 11
Dweck, Carol 6
dyslexia 92, 93–95, 196–97

Ebbinghaus Forgetting Curve 207
Edelman Trust Barometer 192–93
Edgar Dale's Cone of Experience 32
Edmondson, Ami 189
Egypt 171, 172
electroencephalography (EEG) 56
Eliza 52
Emile (Rousseau) 29
emotions 12, 13–14, 18–19
empathy 106–07
enterprise social networks (ESNs) 122, 154,
    155, 156
Epic Games 149
Etihad 134
European Commission 62
    Directorate-General (DG)
        Translation 128
explainability 63
exponential growth 41–42
extended reality (XR) 37, 220

Facebook 39, 199
feedback mechanism 44, 145–46
feedback, constructive and
    consequent 130–32, 135–37
*First follower: Leadership lessons from
    dancing guy* (Sivers) (video) 231
Fortnite 88
Fowler, James H. 121
Frederick the Great 74
functional magnetic resonance imaging
    (fMRI) scans 37, 59–60, 92
future of work 72–80
    education and 76–78, 77
    learning hubs 78–80
    school and 74–76

games and learning 88–89
Gamification 168
Garcia, Constanza 125–27, 135
GDPR (Europe's General Data Protection
    Regulations) 62
Gen Z 73
generative adversarial networks (GANs) 52
generative AI 52–55, 162–63
Germany 168
Gerstner, Louis V. 170
Gilder's law 40–41
Go (game) 48
Godin, Seth 138
Goffman, Erving 86
Google 140, 179, 186, 189
Google Glasses 60
Grok (chatbot) 63
Growth and Learning Mindset
    workshop 136–37
growth mindset 6–7

habituation 19
Hack Future Lab 185
hand–eye co-ordination 88
happiness and learning 10–11
Hebb, Donald 120–21
high-functioning autism (HFA) 87
Hilton Marsa Alam 172–73
Hodak, Max 57–58
Holmes, Elizabeth 200
Homo digitalis 78
Hoy, Cathy 187, 190–92
human-2-human (H2H) knowledge
    sharing 124
human-centric society 63–64
human-to-human (H2H) level 221, 223–24
hyper-diversity 122

IBM 170
imagination 8, 93, 103–05
imposter syndrome 89–91, 199, 200
Index of Trust in Leadership (2023) 193
informal and diverse learning 17
innovation 37–64
    attention mechanisms 46
    distributed representations 46
    fear of 38–42
    Moore's law and 39–40
    policies and frameworks 62–64
    speed of 38–39
    see also artificial intelligence (AI)
Instagram 42, 122, 124
Instructional Design and Technology
        Micromasters 206
intelligence-to-intelligence (I2I) 223–24
interdisciplinary learning 113–15
Inventor: Out for blood in Silicon Valley,
        The (film) 200
iPhone 177

Jacobson, Lenore 82
James, William 32
Jana Gutierrez Kardum 205, 206–08
Japanese Confucian 168–69
Jobs of Tomorrow reports 72
Jobs, Steve 92, 177
Journey to the Center of the Earth (film) 185

Kaizen method 136, 203, 216
    problem solving 205–08
Kaizen: The key to Japan's competitive
        success (Masaaki Imai) 136
Kapur, Arnav 59
Kasparov, Garry 48, 49
Kennedy, Phil 56
knowledge experience platforms
        (KXPs) 147, 155
knowledge gap, bridging 157
Kodak 169–70
Kolb's Learning Style Inventory 29
Kotter, John 187–8
Kurzweil, Ray 224

L&D (learning and development) 31, 124,
        125–27, 143, 144, 145, 150–51, 153,
        157, 174
labels and learning styles 29–30
lab-grown brains 61
Labour Deal 216
large language models (LLMs) 45, 47, 53,
        54, 60, 170, 178, 220
    impact on jobs 72
Layer 7 Cortical Interface 58

League of Extraordinary Gentlemen, The
        (film) 185
League of Extraordinary Learners 189–200
    LearnScapes, learning leader
        becomes 214–18
    problems and opportunities 200–05
Lean In (Sandberg) 199
lean learning 22–24, 143–51
    defects 150
    elimination of waste 144–51, *144*
    inventory 148–49
    movement 150–51
    overprocessing 145–46
    overproduction 145
    skills 147–48
    social learning amplifies 158
    time, wasting 146–47
    transport 149
lean startups 23
Learning & Development in the Digital Age
        (Dam) 77
learning disability and labelling 84–89
Learning Ecosystems 13, 134, 143, 150
learning hubs 78–80
learning influencers 119–30, 173–82
    competencies and communication skills,
        use of 127–37
    learning influencer × learning
        channels 124–27
    non-verbal communication 125–27
    rebels 137–40
    sparking innovation 119–27
    thought leader vs. 123
learning leaders
    learning influencers 173–82
    learning maturity model 219–25, *219*
    learning mindset, adoption 168–73
    psychologically safe
        environment 189–200, *196*
learning management systems (LMSs) 122
learning maturity model *144*, 144–51,
        219–25, *219*
learning mindset
    defining 5
    drivers of 6–9
learning pyramids 31–32
learning, definition 9–10
LearnScapes 167, 213
    learning leader becomes 214–18
    learning maturity model 219–25, *219*
Leunig, Tim 75, 109
Leyen, Ursula von ders 62
LGPD (Brazil's Lei Geral de Proteção de
        Dados) 62
Libratus 45, 49–50, 163

lifelong learning 73–74
    school and 74–76
limbic system on learning 13–14
Linchpin: Are you indispensable?
    (Godin) 138
LMS systems 218
low self-esteem 89–91
Lucy (sci-fi movie) 32, 33, 55s
Ludd, Ned 38
Luddism 38
Luddites 38, 72, 163

machine learning (ML) 46, 49
Machine that Changed the World, The 23
Mager, Michael 58
Mahmoud, Mossab 171, 172–73
Mans, Maarten 186, 216
marketing 157
Masaaki Imai 136
Mauri, Terence 169, 185, 193
McArthur, Scott 113–15, 178
McCarthy, John 43
Melcalfe's law 41–42
memorization 21, 76
mentor/expert approach 155
mentoring 146
Merton, Robert K. 82
Meta 60
Meta Quest 3 149
Meta Ray-Bans 60
metaverse 185
Microsoft 60
Microsoft Vista 145
Millenials 73
Mindset: The New Psychology of Success
    (Dweck) 6
mistakes, sharing 135–37
MOOCs (massive open online courses) 206
Moore's law 39–40
motivation 11
multi-agent reinforcement learning
    (MARL) 51
multitasking 45
Musk, Elon 56–58, 63, 178–79, 197
Musschenga, Bert 196
myths (learning and teaching) 27–33
    10% of the brain myth 32–33
    labels and learning styles 29–30
    learning and age 27–28
    learning pyramids 31–32

Nagle, Matt 56
narcissism 199–200
National Institute of Standards and
    Technology 64

natural language processing (NLP) 53
Nature 56
negative experiences 81–95, *81*
    label or diagnosis 84–89
Netex 154
Netex Learning Cloud Share 124
Netflix 50
neural decoding 57
neural networks (NNs) 43–44, 50–51, 53
neural reward system 89
Neuralink 56, 57–58, 179
neurochemicals 10–12
neuro-linguistic programming (NLP) 53
neurons 20, 47, 71
neuroscience and computer science 43–45
Neuroscience for Learning and Development
    (Collins) 10
neuroscience of learning 2, 5, 10–14
New York 185
Nielsen's 1-9-90 rule 155–56
non-invasive brain interfaces 59–60
non-verbal communication 125–27
noradrenaline 11–12

observation 20
OpenAI 47, 52, 131
openness 102, 105–06, 137
    feedback, constructive and
        consequent 130–32, 135–37
optimism 108
'organoid intelligence' 61
*Our Iceberg is Melting: Changing and
    succeeding under any conditions*
    (Kotter and Rathgeber) 187
overexcitability (OE) 87

parallel processing 45
pathological narcissism 199–200
pattern recognition 20
Paula, Marcelo Alvisi De 12, 13–14
peer coaching 154–55
perseverance and resilience 88
Phaedrus (Plato) 38
Piaget, Jean 8
policies and frameworks 62–64
POPI (South Africa's Protection of Personal
    Information) 62
Positive Disintegration (Dąbrowski) 87
Presnky, Marc 89
priming 19
problem-solving skills 88, 93
Project Aristotle 189
psychological safety
    Kaizen method and problem
        solving 205–08

problems and opportunities 200–05
psychologically safe
    environment 189–200, *196*
puzzle-solving skills 94

Rapoport, Benjamin 57–58
Rathgeber, Holger 187–8
realism 109–10, *110*
rebels 137–40
    in cross-functional innovative
        teams 139–40
Red Hat 206
reference models (SCORMs) 218
reinforcement learning 44–45
relearning 24, 26
resilience 88, 107–08
retrieval practice, power of 21–22
reward 11
Rizzi, Matteo 138
Robinson, Ken 74, 75, 104
Roblox 42, 79, 80, 122, 232
Robux 80
Rosenthal, Robert 82
Rousseau, Jean-Jacques 29
'Runaround' (short story, Asimov) 61–62

sales training 15
Sandberg, Sheryl 199
Schneps, Matthew 94
sCooledu 231
Sedol, Lee 48, 49
self-awareness 81
self-directed learning 16–17
self-fulfilling prophecies 81–84,
    85, 87
self-limiting beliefs 81–84
sensing people and situations 94–95
serotonin 11
Shatz, Carla 120
Sinek, Simon 128–29
Sivers, Derek 231
skills and competences, difference
    between 99–100
Skinner, B. F. 15, 151
Smelyansky, Igor 176
Snap 60
Snapchat 39, 42, 106
Snow Crash (novel) (Stephenson) 185
social conscience 111
social learning 151–61
    amplifies lean learning 158
    drivers of 152–61, *153*
    technical security 158–59

Social Theory and Social Structure
    (Merton) 82
Socrates 38
SpaceX 179, 197
spatial understanding 88
*Speed of Trust: The one thing that changes
    everything, The* (Covey) 193
spike-timing-dependent plasticity
    (STDP) 119–21
Star Trek 59, 128, 178, 185
Start with Why (Sinek) 128–29
Stephenson, Neal 185
stories 14
stress hormone 12
sustainability
    global responsibility 227–30
    humanity, future of 230–35
Sustainable Development Agenda 228
Sustainable Development Goals (SDGs) 72,
    168, 205, 216, 228–30, 233–35
    SDG4 229–30, 234
    SDG8 230
Synchron 58–59

*Talents & Rebels: Dealing with corporate
    misfits* (Rizzi) 138
Tarabasz, Anna 24–27, 129
Tarzan (fictional character) 152
teamwork 154–55
Tesla 197
Theranos 200
TikTok 29, 39, 42, 50–51, 105, 106, 123,
    124, 126, 154, 223
Toyota 23
training
    defects in 150
    vs. learning 14–17
Turing, Alan 43, 63
Turing Test 43

unconscious learning 45
United Nations Honoree and Executive 229
United Nations Sustainable Development
    Goals (SDGs) 72, 168, 205, 216,
    228–30, 233–35
unlearning 24–27, 143
unsupervised learning 45
*Upside of Disruption: Leading and thriving
    in the unknown, The* (Mauri) 169
urgency of learning 72–80
    education and 76–78, 77
    learning hubs 78–80
    school and 74–76

VAK theory (visual-auditory-kinetic) 29–30
van Hooydonk, Stefaan 101–03
Verhasselt, Christine 22
Vernes, Jules 55, 185
Verstraelen, Erwin 170
Vidal, Jacques 56
virtual reality (VR) 60
visual memory 93–94
visual spatial reasoning 94

Weiner, Norbert 43–44
Weizenbaum, Joseph 52
WhatsApp 145
Who Says Elephants Can't Dance? Leading
    a great enterprise through dramatic
    change (memoirs) 170
why, power of 128–29

Wilson, Edward O. 111, 114
Workplace Curiosity Manifesto, The (van
    Hooydonk) 101
Workplace Intelligence 73
World Economic Forum (WEF), Future of
    Jobs Survey 72–74

X (formerly Twitter) 131
xAI 63
xAPI 218

YouTube 29

Zajonc, Robert 19–20
Zoe (film) 55
Zuckerberg, Marc
    149, 185

Looking for another book?

Explore our award-winning
books from global business
experts in Human Resources,
Learning and Development

Scan the code to browse

www.koganpage.com/hr-learning-
development

Also from Kogan Page

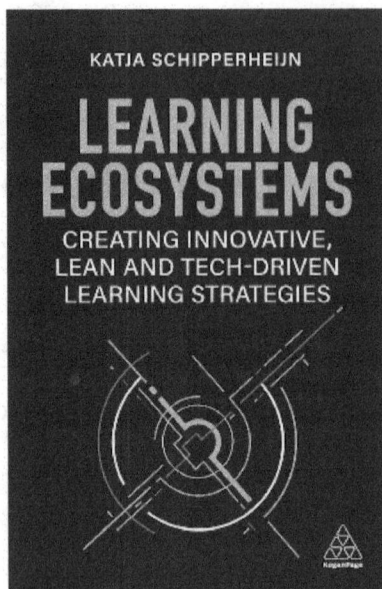

KATJA SCHIPPERHEIJN

LEARNING ECOSYSTEMS

CREATING INNOVATIVE, LEAN AND TECH-DRIVEN LEARNING STRATEGIES

ISBN: 9781398607408

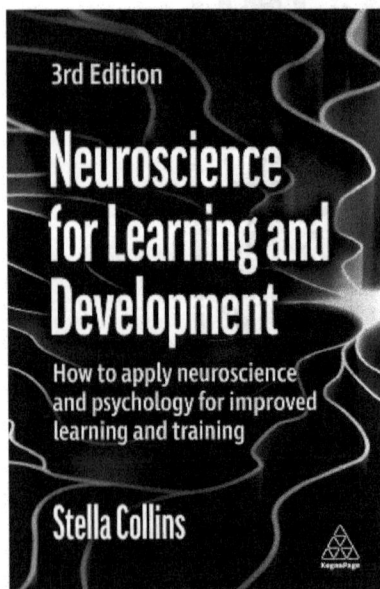

3rd Edition

Neuroscience for Learning and Development

How to apply neuroscience and psychology for improved learning and training

Stella Collins

ISBN: 9781398608337

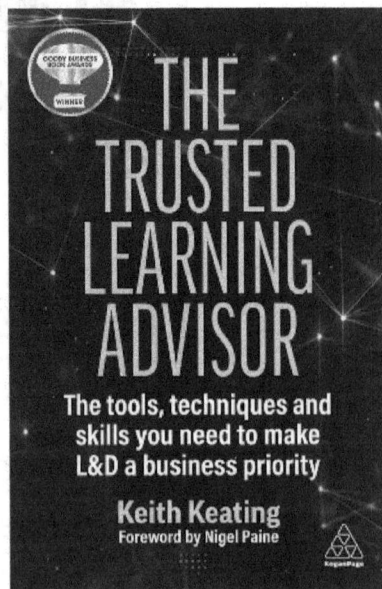

THE TRUSTED LEARNING ADVISOR

The tools, techniques and skills you need to make L&D a business priority

Keith Keating
Foreword by Nigel Paine

ISBN: 9781398612457

www.koganpage.com

From 4 December 2025 the EU Responsible Person (GPSR) is:
eucomply oÜ, Pärnu mnt. 139b – 14, 11317 Tallinn, Estonia
www.eucompliancepartner.com